THE DIRECTOR
AT WORK

ROBERT L. BENEDETTI

California Institute of the Arts

With a Foreword by
JOHN HOUSEMAN

Prentice-Hall, Inc., Englewood Cliffs, New Jersey 07632

Library of Congress Cataloging in Publication Data

BENEDETTI, ROBERT L.
  The director at work.

  Includes index.
  1. Theater—Production and direction.
  2. Shakespeare, William, 1564-1616. Hamlet.
  3. Shakespeare, William, 1564-1616—Stage history—
Oregon. I. Title.
PN2053.B37 1985   792'.0233   84-15047
ISBN 0-13-214909-5

Editorial/production supervision and
  interior design: Joyce Turner
Cover design: Wanda Lubelski Design
Manufacturing buyer: Barbara Kittle

Printed in the United States of America

10 9 8 7 6 5 4 3 2 1

ISBN 0-13-214909-5 01

Prentice-Hall International, Inc., *London*
Prentice-Hall of Australia Pty. Limited, *Sydney*
Editora Prentice-Hall do Brasil, Ltda., *Rio de Janeiro*
Prentice-Hall Canada Inc., *Toronto*
Prentice-Hall of India Private Limited, *New Delhi*
Prentice-Hall of Japan, Inc., *Tokyo*
Prentice-Hall of Southeast Asia Pte. Ltd., *Singapore*
Whitehall Books Limited, *Wellington, New Zealand*

CONTENTS

FOREWORD by JOHN HOUSEMAN   ix

PREFACE   xi

ACKNOWLEDGMENTS   xiii

Part One: The Director

ONE   THE DIRECTOR'S MIND   3

TWO   WHAT A DIRECTOR DOES   9

*The Process of Discovery   10, The Director's Motivation   11,
The Conservative Position: Fidelity   13, The Liberal Position:
Relevance   14, The Radical Position: Director as Creator   15,
The Variable Position   16*

THREE   THE DIRECTOR AS TRANSLATOR   17

The Life of the Play 18, The System of Norms 20, Style 22, The Director as Executive 23, Summary 24

Part Two: Getting Ready

FOUR   THE FIRST ENCOUNTER   27

Research 29, The Hamlet Log 33

FIVE   UNDERSTANDING THE ACTION   36

Action and Plot 36, Action and Character 37, Action and the Given Circumstances 38, Understanding the Story: Plot 40, A Sample Breakdown of Hamlet 42

SIX   THE SHAPE OF DRAMA   44

The Sense of Crisis 44, Focusing on a Theme 47

SEVEN   UNDERSTANDING CHARACTER   52

Character and Action 52, The Network of Relationships 54, The Individual Character 56, Character and Language 58, Character Specifications 59

EIGHT   FORMING A PRODUCTION CONCEPT   61

Preparing the Preliminary Production Script 62, The Scene/Character/Time/Place Breakdown 64, The Landscape of the Play 66, Preparing the Ground Plan 68, Setting to Work 70

Part Three: The Director at Work

Introduction 71, Alignment 72, The Hamlet Log 73

NINE   THE DESIGN PROCESS   75

The Design Process: First Discussions   76, Sketching: Working in a Dynamic Mode   77, The Central Metaphor   77, The Model   79, Changes During Rehearsal   80, Costumes, Props, and Lights   81

TEN   CASTING   86

The Criteria for Casting   87, The Casting Process   87, Preliminary Auditions   88, Judging the Audition   89, Callbacks   90, Casting Against Type   91, Final Casting   92

ELEVEN   FIRST REHEARSALS   109

Preparing the Work Climate   110, First Cast Meetings   111, First Reading   113, Your Frame of Mind in Rehearsals   115

TWELVE   EXPLORING THE ACTION   125

Choice and the Flow of Action   126, The Shape of the Action   127, The Strategy of Exploration   127, Guiding the Exploration   128, Communicating with Actors: Discussion   130, Side-coaching   131, Notes   132, Cumulative Exploration   134

THIRTEEN   EARLY STAGING   145

Generating the Blocking   146, Specifying the Mis en Scene   148, Planning the Technical Elements   149, The Stage Manager   150

FOURTEEN   SHAPING, PACING, AND FOCUSING   164

Shaping the Score of the Production   165, The Tempo-rhythm of the Production   166, Shaping the Performance for the Audience   168, Pacing the Production   169, Focusing the Production   170, Special Rehearsals   171

FIFTEEN   FINAL SYNTHESIS   183

Audibility   184, Editing the Blocking   185, Visual Metaphors   185,
Technical and Dress Rehearsals   186, Previews, Opening and
After   188, Weaning the Production   190

AFTERWORD: A CAREER IN DIRECTING   212

APPENDIXES

1. Master Scene/Place/Time/Character Chart   215
2. Prompt Script for Scene 14   219
3. Opening Remarks to the Cast of Hamlet   227
4. Sample Notes to Hamlet   231
5. Deadlines and Urgencies in Hamlet   235

FOOTNOTES   237

INDEX   238

THE HAMLET LOG

Part 1 First Contacts   33
Part 2 Early Preparations   49
Part 3 Preparation for Casting and Design Meetings   60
Part 4 First Design Conference   82
Part 5 Principal Casting   93
Part 6 Second Design Conference   96
Part 7 Costume and Sound Meetings   103
Part 8 Final Casting and First Rehearsals   116
Part 9 Roughing Out the Scenic Action   135
Part 10 First Run-throughs   151
Part 11 Working Through for Connections   172
Part 12 Pacing   177
Part 13 Final Synthesis   191
Part 14 Opening and After   200

EXERCISES

1. Your Personal Profile   8
2. The First Encounter   28
3. Researching the Play   32
4. The Given Circumstances   39
5. Telling the Story   41
6. The Shape of the Action   47
7. Mapping Relationships   56
8. Living Language   58
9. Character Specifications   59
10. Cutting a Script   64
11. The Scene/Character/Time/Place Chart   65
12. The Landscape of the Play   67
13. Generating a Ground Plan   70

FIGURES

3-1. Modes of Existence of a Play   19
6-1. Traditional Play Structure   46
7-1. Mapping Relationships in Hamlet   56
9-1. Everyman at the Tyrone Guthrie Theatre   78
9-2. The Hamlet Model in Rehearsal   80
10-1. Working on the Model   97
10-2. The Hamlet Model   97
12-1. An Early Rehearsal   136
12-2. Blocking a Group Scene   137
15-1. A Hamlet Portfolio   201

FOREWORD

by John Houseman

I have known Robert Benedetti for many years during which I have admired him as a dynamic and resourceful director and teacher of theatre. I suspect that when he invited me to write a foreword to this, his latest book—*The Director at Work*—he was unaware of my own ambivalence on this particular subject. For years, as head of the Drama Division of the Juilliard School, I refused to include a course in Directing in our curriculum. I argued that it was our function to form actors and not to encourage undergraduates in their premature and presumptuous desire to command others in a craft which they themselves had barely begun to master. Add to this my strong conviction, born of painful personal experience, that no one is qualified to direct actors who has not himself or herself, at one time or another, in one form or another, been one.

The term of *director,* in the sense in which most people, including Benedetti, employ it today, is a fairly new addition to the theatrical vocabulary. It follows the comparatively recent development of an historical sense in the theatre and coincides with the eclectic programming adopted by the best of European theatres during the latter half of the nineteenth century. Its first and most celebrated exponents included the Duke of Saxe-Meiningen, Stanislavsky, Craig, Antoine, Rheinhardt, and in this country, in very different ways, such effective theatrical figures as Belasco, Kaufman, and Elia Kazan. Before that, as long as theatrical performance followed traditional or naturalistic conventions, there had been little need for such a dominant figure backstage. It is believed that Aeschylus produced his own dramas, and we may assume that Shakespeare had a positive say in the performance of his plays by the acting company of which he was a leading member. Garrick must have controlled the behavior of his supporting casts, and we know that Irving ruled over his archeologically elaborate productions with total authority. Yet, most of the time, the attitude was that of a leading British actor-manager who, on being approached by a tremulous understudy about to play Horatio to the great man's Hamlet, instructed the youth to "stay six feet away and do your damnedest!"

It is only recently that theatrical conditions and the nature of theatrical performance have called forth the figure of the dictator-director and created a function that involves not only total (hopefully benevolent) domination of the company but also, in some cases, virtual co-authorship of the play under production.

Is this function likely to continue indefinitely? I'm not sure that it is. In his fascinating diary of his first eight years with Britain's National Theatre, Peter Hall reports a conversation with that other leading exponent of the director-dictator theory of theatre, Peter Brook:

> We both feel that the concept of the director is moving away from the autocratic interpreter, the conductor who presents his view of the work, to someone who is much more like the trainer of a football team. The director trains and develops the group, but it is the group that must play the match.

Elsewhere he wonders if

> the desperate turning over the past that all directors do is only a search for accidental resonances which would surprise the original author and would mean nothing to his original audience. In a sense we are all making new art objects out of old plays, almost as if we were writers. A dangerous activity.*

In *The Director at Work,* Benedetti seems to accept the director's authoritative function as a creative necessity. His detailed account of his own "personalized" Shakespearean production, put together under typical festival conditions (with a company of actors assembled for the occasion and allowed only limited rehearsal time), is of value, not only as a subjective record of how he himself used his dictatorial position but also as an example of some of the problems of classical production prevalent under present American theatrical conditions. Such a detailed and subjective analysis of Shakespeare's most challenging play in the various phases of its conception and production—from auditions to opening night—should be of great interest not only to the aspiring "director" but also to the general reader who is concerned with theatre but does not himself harbor directorial ambitions.

Benedetti's extended and detailed "*Hamlet* Log" is preceded by an analysis of the director's function and an appraisal of the qualities required to exert it successfully. For definitions of the directing process, Benedetti quotes a number of competent and eloquent sources, ranging from some of our country's most successful young directors to Stanislavsky, Aristotle's *Poetics,* Michel Saint-Denis's superb *Rediscovery of Style,* and for good measure, *Zen in the Art of Archery!*

With all this, he has not entirely dispelled my own doubts as to the degree to which all this can or should be *taught.* Directing is a delicate and demanding activity; it calls for scholarship, experience, taste, infinite patience, great physical stamina, and a capacity for leadership. It demands from its practitioners, besides the knowledge and skills that can be acquired, the instinctive and delicate balance between sensitivity and megalomania of which this book is a fascinating example.

*From *The Peter Hall Diaries,* New York, 1984.

PREFACE

Becoming a director is not so much a matter of learning a formula or particular techniques but rather of coming to understand the principles and strategies which motivate and guide a director's actions in any specific instance. What is offered here, therefore, is designed to help you learn to *think* like a director so that you can develop your techniques to suit the specific situations you will encounter in your work.

This book is addressed to those interested in learning to direct for the live theatre, whether it be commercial or experimental, professional or amateur. It focuses on that most common type of production in which a preexistent text is being "interpreted" through the efforts of a production team under a director's guidance, though much of what is discussed here will also apply to other directing situations, such as the development of new material through ensemble creation.

Directing is essentially the guidance of a process, so I have divided the study into three parts: the first discusses the nature of the director's job and the qualities of mind which it requires; the second covers the director's preparation prior to the beginning of rehearsals; the third traces the evolution of a production through the rehearsal process.

Each chapter in Part Two will contain exercises designed to help you to practice the ideas being discussed.

To illustrate how these principles and strategies might be applied in a real situation, a single actual production will be used as an ongoing example. I have chosen Shakespeare's *Hamlet* for this purpose because it is a never-ending challenge to directors and invites a variety of approaches. Throughout Parts Two and Three you will find entries from the log of my 1983 production of *Hamlet* at the Oregon Shakespearean Festival.

RECOMMENDED READING

Directing being the eclectic task it is, there is really nothing about the theatre that a director might not need to know; anything you can do to ground yourself in a general understanding of the theatre will be to your benefit. At the same time, it will be particularly useful if you prepare for your study of this book by reading three short works, each of which contains ideas which contribute to our premises here:

1. *The Poetics* of Aristotle (Gateway Editions)
2. *The Rediscovery of Style* by Michel Saint-Denis (Theatre Arts Books)
3. *Zen in the Art of Archery* by Eugen Herrigel (Vintage Books)

Aristotle's *Poetics* is perhaps the most important single work in the history of Western drama. His aim was to describe the "ideal" qualities of drama at its best; he examined the best of the plays known to him and produced a detailed description of those properties they had in common. This short essay has the density of a set of lecture notes (which some scholars think it to be), and you will have to read it slowly, allowing the logic of its argument to develop step by step; the first twenty or so sections will be sufficient to our purpose. Try to grasp Aristotle's underlying principles or "way of seeing" the drama, and don't take too literally the specific examples he uses. Some 1,800 years after it was written, the Renaissance rediscovered *The Poetics* and turned it into a virtual rulebook for playwrights; its influence lasted for centuries. Remember, however, that Aristotle did not intend to make rules; *The Poetics* is a *description,* not a *prescription.* Seen in this way, Aristotle's ideas can help us to understand even those plays which were written in reaction against the Aristotelian form.

The second book, *The Rediscovery of Style* by Michel Saint-Denis, is centered around the attempt to find the specific reality created by a play through the qualities and values embodied in its language and structure. It often seems especially difficult for us to achieve this sense of a play's reality when it is based upon principles different from those observable in everyday life, when it is what we loosely call "stylized." We need Saint-Denis's sense of the "reality within style" as a healthy counter-influence to our pervasive American Naturalism, enforced more than ever through the mass media. Saint-Denis's book will also be interesting to you as a fascinating look into one important director's formidable mind.

The third book, *Zen in the Art of Archery,* is a delightful account of one man's experiences while learning the ancient discipline of archery in Japan. It has become enormously popular in America because it communicates so well the spirit of *process* whereby creativity, education, and all aspects of human growth are best facilitated. It will be important to us because it stresses the difficulty of developing the unteachable qualities of the intuitive self and the patience and discipline required by any creative process.

All three books are available in paperback editions and each can be read in a single sitting. I hope you will do so before continuing with your study of *The Director at Work.*

Robert Benedetti

ACKNOWLEDGMENTS

During the preparation of this book, a number of directors completed a questionnaire about their work or discussed their techniques with me; they are listed here alphabetically. My great thanks to all of them.

Lee Breuer, Mabou Mines
Robert Brustein, The American Repertory Theatre
Joseph Chaikin, The Open Theatre
David Chambers, New York
Alan Cooke, Los Angeles
John Dillon, The Milwaukee Repertory Theatre
Gil Dennis, Los Angeles
David Emmes, The South Coast Repertory Theatre
Zelda Fichandler, The Arena Stage
Lou Florimonte, The California Institute of the Arts
Richard Foreman, The Ontological-Hysterical Theatre
Gerald Freedman, New York
Tom Haas, The Indiana Repertory Theatre
John Houseman, The Acting Company
Nagle Jackson, The McCarter Theatre Center
Mark Lamos, The Hartford Theatre Company
Michael Leibert, San Francisco
Ruth Maleczech, Mabou Mines
Tom Markus, The Virginia Museum Theatre
Donovan Marley, The Denver Center Theatre Company
Charles Marowitz, Los Angeles
Jack O'Brien, The Old Globe Playhouse
Martin Platt, The Alabama Shakespeare Festival
W. Duncan Ross, The University of Southern California
Alan Schneider, The University of California, San Diego
Dan Sullivan, The Seattle Repertory Theatre

My special thanks to the students in my 1982 and 1983 MFA Directing Seminars at the California Institute of the Arts, who reviewed the drafts of this book and contributed many helpful criticisms and ideas: Elaine Devlin, Andrew Shea, Sean Fenton, Paige Newmark, Douglas Rushkoff and Bernard Lenhoff.

Thanks also to Eugene Schlusser and Roger Hodgman of The Victorian College of the Arts in Melbourne, Australia, where the final draft was completed.

R.B.

PART ONE
THE DIRECTOR

ONE
THE DIRECTOR'S MIND

The old saying that nothing is certain but uncertainty is especially true of directing. Every show, every cast, theatre and audience presents a different set of problems; solutions to these problems may work in one instance but not in another. The effective director, therefore, works continuously in a problem-solving mode, dealing with each situation according to its own specific nature. Though most directors develop a method of their own, the actual process of directing requires on-the-spot improvisation. Once you have developed a sense of the principles and strategies of directing you will be able to invent your own techniques to suit the specific situations you encounter. Our aim in this book, then, is to help you learn *to think like a director*.

While preparing to write this book, I sent a questionnaire to some thirty American directors whose work I admire, asking questions about their methods and theatrical values. They represent a wide cross section of American theatre, from large resident theatres doing the classical repertory to small experimental groups committed to avant-garde performance. As you would expect, their answers are as different as their theatres and their personalities, but I began to notice some striking similarities as well. Not only are there surprising agreements about some aspects of the directing process, but I began also to notice the recurrence of certain attitudes and feelings. As different as these successful directors are as people and as artists, there are also certain fundamental qualities of mind which they tend to share. A kind of "portrait of the director" began to emerge.

The most striking similarity among the responses I received is the repeated use of certain active words and phrases, such as "sharing," "collaboration," "commitment," "creative energy," and "flow." These recurrent images express a kind of energy that is uninhibited and unselfish, flowing outward from the self to others—to fellow workers, to the audience, and finally, to the world at large. Effective directors, I concluded, tend to be people who are vitally interested in their world and open to life experience; they are, in a word, *curious* about the human condition.

This active curiosity and openness to life leads most directors to be people with eclectic tastes and a wide range of interests. Many of my respondents urge those training for directing to gain experience outside the theatre both before and during their careers; many place special emphasis on experience in art forms other than theatre. Mark Lamos says:

> the director must incorporate all the arts into his work: ballet, dance, history, literature, painting, sculpture, architecture.

Gerald Freedman is specific on the same issue:

> My advice to prospective directors is to get as broad an education as possible. Read the great works and study art history. Do some acting, and experience concerts, ballets, and sporting events . . .

Charles Marowitz recommends going even further:

> Go for a very long journey around the world to countries you have never seen and whose languages you cannot speak. Take along just enough money to survive and eschew all offers of help and assistance. Court death and disaster. Learn the meaning of the word *risk* in existential terms—then try to translate it into esthetic terms.

This spirit of adventure, of being in quest of the truth of the human condition, seems to be one of the things that attracts people to directing in the first place. It is important that you keep this spirit alive during the course of your training and career. As David Chambers puts it, "Keep in mind that there is no way to reflect life unless you have one. In short, live!"

The director's curiosity about life naturally attracts him or her to the drama, which at its best is capable of penetrating life's mysteries. As Zelda Fichandler says, "a theatre (or a training institution) is, in fact, a laboratory, and what we are studying there is human life." She goes on to point out that, like the scientist, the director must be able to discriminate what is observed:

> We must develop our eye for differences; resist reducing matters to our own personal styles, repeating what we have done before, thinking that if it "feels right" to us then it necessarily *is* right. An observation from Heraclitus, the Roman philosopher, attracts me; I have it tacked up on my bulletin board: "The more knowledge inherent in a thing, the greater the love. He who imagines that

all fruits ripen at the same time as the strawberry knows nothing about grapes."
Curiosity is the nose by which we want to be led. . . . It is a call for continuous
stretching of our capacities of observation, empathy with the is-ness of what we
are giving physical life to, going out to meet the needs of The Other—whether it
be a play or a person—rather than reducing those needs to what feels comfortable
for us. It urges us to open up the object of our curiosity, and not to contract it
by preconception or simple laziness. Habit is the enemy of originality and should
be banned from the work place. Freshness of perception is everything.

You can feel in this statement the dynamism that marks all of the
responses to my questionnaire; the director is continually growing, continually
learning through his or her art. It is not only the content of the plays we direct
which teaches us, but the very act of directing itself, of helping to generate and
to shape a human event that is distilled, through art, to its truthful essence.
Seen in this way, directing is not only an art, it is a life process.

Indeed, all of the directors who answered my survey express a total
involvement of their life experiences in their work as directors. Alan Schneider
says it best when he explains why he could *not* answer my questions about
"the essence of directing," "your relationship to the text," and "your frame of
mind in rehearsal":

> What is the essence of living?
> What is your relationship to other people?
> How would you describe your frame of mind when you are at your 'best' in the
> morning?

It is impossible for most directors to separate their art from their lives
because of the nature of theatre itself. Our time in the theatre should be a time
of tremendous aliveness, a time when we recognize ourselves and celebrate our
membership in the human community. Since the director is the point of
synthesis through which all the energies of the performance pass, the director's
own aliveness is inevitably and directly involved in the production.

This is not to say that the director's energy is primary in a production;
rather, the director is responsible for facilitating the contributions of the entire
production team. In a sense, the director has been most succesful when the
audience feels most in touch with the energies of the actors. I am always
suspicious when people say of a production, "What brilliant direction—too
bad the actors weren't better." It is the most common failing of directors that
they impede rather than liberate the energies of their fellow artists.

This was recognized by the directors who answered my survey; over and
over my respondents stress the importance of collaboration. The element of
collaboration can be one of the greatest joys of directing. As Zelda Fichandler
puts it:

> It is a collaborative form. There's too much for any one person to bite off, and
> the most illustrious directors in history have always had people they share their

work with. . . . "Collaborator" is a really wonderful word; it means "to labor with."

This spirit of collaboration is endemic to directing: in shaping that little time of heightened aliveness which is the living play, the director joins his or her life on a profound level with that of the material and with the community of artists and spectators. For good or ill, the director is never alone in the work, as Nagle Jackson points out:

> Most of a director's life is dealing with people. If you're not a social animal, forget it.

Even though a director may not necessarily be gregarious by nature, his or her skills of communication and relationship are essential to the work; beyond this, most directors seem to *enjoy* collaboration.

The collaborative nature of directing requires also that the effective director be a good executive, able to communicate knowledgeably with other theatre artists. An understanding of many aspects of theatre is invaluable, and it is no accident that most directors emerge after working in other areas of theatre. Many of those answering my questionnaire echo John Houseman in advising young directors to "become an actor first"; Alan Cooke suggests also learning to write, in order to become "a bridge so meaning can move from the page to the gesture, the image"; Donovan Marley specifies that you "spend five years learning everything possible about the jobs of all the collaborative artists in the theatre."

Another quality of the good executive which shines from the answers to my questionnaire is what I call "quiet authority," a special blend of openness and firmness. As Michael Leibert says of any production's chance for success:

> The single most important element is the collaborative effort, but it must have a firm beginning if it is to have a successful end.

The director guides the work of his or her fellow artists, but creates the "room" which allows them to solve their own creative problems. The qualities which most contribute to this ability are centeredness and patience: the centeredness of "knowing who you are" so that the demands of your ego can be kept from intruding on the work of your fellows, and the patience to remember that it is sometimes more important for actors or designers to solve a problem for themselves than that the problem be solved quickly. Michael Leibert's main advice to young directors is

> Learn to keep quiet. Actors need to make mistakes on their own, or their understanding will never be truthful.

In order for the director to "learn to keep quiet," he or she must be able to cope with the enormous pressure, frustration, and anxiety which accompanies any creative endeavor and which may tempt us to short-circuit the creative process for ourselves and for others. The anxiety of the creative endeavor is rooted in its mysteriousness, as psychiatrist Rollo May points out in his book *The Courage to Create*:

> Creative people, as I see them, are distinguished by the fact that they can live with anxiety, even though a high price may be paid in terms of insecurity, sensitivity, and defenselessness for the gift of the "divine madness," to borrow the term used by the classical Greeks. They do not run away from non-being, but by encountering and wrestling with it, force it to produce being. They knock on silence for an answering music; they pursue meaninglessness until they can force it to mean.[1]

While all creative effort involves the anxiety of this "encounter with the unknown," those which require the collaboration of a group of artists are fraught with additional sources of potential anxiety. The director faces the meaninglessness of the empty stage and wrestles it into meaning entirely by *indirect* means—through the creativity of the playwright, the designers, the actors, and eventually the audience. This lack of direct control may create a background of low-level frustration against which the director will work for weeks at a time; at its worst, it can be maddening. Many of my director friends need to refresh themselves after rehearsal with manual labor such as gardening, cooking, even something as simple as shining shoes . . . anything that they can "do all by myself and be done with!"

The ability to cope with anxiety is especially important to the director because the work of the entire theatrical ensemble will often reflect his or her own emotional condition. Even when creative problems seem to defy solution, the director must not succumb to hysteria or despair; nor may the director be a Pollyanna and refuse to recognize problems; rather, the work must continue with honesty and openness.

A portrait of the effective director begins to emerge from all this. It is a portrait with many faces, to be sure, but one in which certain qualities of mind are clear. The effective director tends to be

1. Well grounded in the theatrical tradition, but also
2. Eclectic, with a wide range of interests including the other arts;
3. Open and involved with life, curious and observant;
4. Adventurous, with an appetite for risk-taking;
5. Skillful at collaboration (if not by nature gregarious) and an able executive with good communication skills;
6. Capable of quiet authority and yet vulnerable; that difficult blending of child and adult necessary to all artists;
7. Patient and centered, able to function under pressure and to live with anxiety.

Although this formidable list makes the director sound impossibly saintly, it does at least present the ideals toward which many directors aspire through their personal discipline, each in his' or her own way. You too can begin to identify these qualities in yourself through the following exercise. As you continue in your study of directing, you can be guided by a specific sense of your particular needs and strengths.

Exercise 1: Your Personal Profile

The chart below gives you an opportunity to assess your relative strengths and weaknesses in terms of the qualities of mind which may be useful to a director. The scale ranges from a +3 to a −3 according to these definitions:

+3. This quality is "natural" to me almost all the time;

+2. I am this way much of the time;

+1. I am this way at times; awareness will help me to develop this further;

 0. This is neither a strength nor a weakness; I am neutral on this issue;

−1. I have the capacity for this, but it takes real effort to bring it out;

−2. This is a real weakness of mine; I will have to work hard on this;

−3. I have no capacity for this at all.

Create a profile of yourself by indicating your self-assessment in each of the areas we have discussed. In areas of greatest weakness, think of ways you can begin to maintain awareness of these issues, since simple awareness is often sufficient to improve performance. It would be interesting to review your self-assessment at various times in your future development.

−3 −2 −1 0 +1 +2 +3

1. A broad understanding of the theatre
2. An eclectic interest in other arts
3. Openmindedness and curiosity
4. Insightful observation
5. Appetite for risk-taking
6. Collaborative spirit
7. Communication skills
8. Patience and centeredness
9. Quiet authority
10. Ability to live with anxiety

Can you think of other qualities a director ought to possess?

TWO
WHAT A DIRECTOR DOES

If you watched a director over the course of an entire production process, you would see that he or she shares in the wearing of many hats: literary scholar, acting coach, production manager, designer, critic, and surrogate audience; of all the many specialists in the theatrical ensemble, the director is the one generalist. Moreover, the various skills required of the director are rarely organized or applied in exactly the same way from production to production; different projects in different circumstances demand different priorities. In a one-set realistic play, for instance, the director's work as acting coach may be crucial, while in a large-scale musical his or her organizational skills may be more important.

Whatever particular skills are demanded by a given production, however, there is a central function which the director must fulfill in any circumstance. I asked my thirty directors how they would describe this essential aspect of directing, and most of them said something like the famous remark by Tyrone Guthrie, quoted by Duncan Ross, that a director must "be an ideal audience of one." This involves either directly substituting oneself for the audience or, as Joseph Chaikin puts it, "imagining the audience while focusing on the process" of rehearsal.

The director's purpose in being an "ideal audience of one" is specified by several respondents, including Nagle Jackson:

Above all, the director is the audience's advocate. It is his responsibility to see that the story is told with clarity, with force and interest, and without extraneous clutter. Everything else is gravy.

The idea of story-telling is the central concern of many other directors; here it is described by Jack O'Brien:

> We are story-tellers, first, through the skill of the text to the actors themselves, and subsequently, to the audience. I think the essence of moving the audience is giving the company the same story to tell, to a man, to the lift of a finger. Everyone is telling the same tale, and the truth, then, can be inescapable.

Most of the answers I received were some variation on these related ideas: that the director is centrally responsible (1) for understanding the story the author wishes to tell, (2) for mobilizing all the various capacities of the theatre to tell it, (3) for insuring that it is well told by serving as a surrogate audience member. All the various skills required of a director are organized so as to fulfill this central function.

THE PROCESS OF DISCOVERY

When Stanislavski was asked what a director needs to know, he answered that in addition to everything an actor needs to know, a director also needs three more special skills:

> First, he must know how to work on the play with the author, or without him if the author is dead; and he must know how to make a complete and profound analysis of the play. Second, he must know how to work with the actor . . . Third, he must know how to work with the scenic designer, the composer, the costumer, and all the rest of the production crew. The director must work on himself as much as an actor does, and he must do ten times more. He must be ten times as thorough and ten times as disciplined, because he must teach not only himself but the actors.[2]

These principles are echoed by most of my respondents, the most eloquent statement coming from Zelda Fichandler:

> The play is a locked universe and each director has her own key to it. And then leads the other contributing artists—designers, composers, actors—to find their own keys, harmonious with her own, in order to open up the universe still further, and in order to make it specific in terms of their own special domains: light, sound, environment, behavior, and so on. We seek this: a unique perception (the director's) of a particular world (the play) expressively embodied by the means of the theatre so that others (the audience) can share it, know it, see it. We must strive to perfect a process for discovery, for without such a process, the universe of the play stays closed to us and our own world as opaque as it was before.

The idea of a "process of discovery" is at the heart of this book. As both Stanislavski and Fichandler described it, this process has three phases: First, the director makes a "profound analysis" in order to develop a "unique perception" of the "particular world" of the play; next, the director joins with the actors and the other members of the production team to discover ways to "embody" that world; finally, the production is brought before the audience as a unified and accessible experience which invites them to discover the world of the play for themselves.

We can summarize this three-phase process of discovery:

1. *Analysis*: the penetration of the text in order to fully grasp the story of the play and the manner of its telling;
2. *Translation*: the discovery of theatrical means to re-create the text as a living event;
3. *Synthesis*: the editing of the experience to make it accessible to the audience and to give it its own integrity as a work of art.

In Part Two we will trace this process in detail, but first we will examine the fundamental relationship of the director and the play from which comes the motivation that drives the process of discovery.

THE DIRECTOR'S MOTIVATION

It may seem obvious to say that the process of discovery begins with the choice of a play, but the crucial importance of this choice is often overlooked. Directing is a long, arduous process and you need a strong personal commitment to the material to support you throughout this process. Michel Saint-Denis put it this way:

> The first problem for a director is to select a play. The choice is important and should have an idea behind it . . . without initial impulse the production may be tepid and lack conviction. It seems to me that the success of a production depends first of all on the shock the play gives you when you read it through. Nothing can replace this initial impact, this first revelation. It may be confused or mysterious, but you will always have to come back to it for guidance. It works on you both as an excitement and as a brake.[3]

All the directors who answered my questionnaire speak of their need for a deeply personal relationship with the plays they direct. Some go as far as Dan Sullivan, who says:

> I can only *do* a play well when there is a strong connection between the play's life and my own.

Others echo the idea that if the director has a strong and specific involvement with the play, there is a better chance that the audience will too.

This is eloquently expressed by Jack O'Brien when he describes what he means by "understanding the play":

> For me, it is a kind of visceral commitment. I must have a response to the text, not only in terms of my comprehension, but in the necessity to move that material through me and, with the help of the company, out to others. If my reaction (to the play) is intellectual and objective, that will be the nature of the experience for others. But if I have some real connection to the material, some deep conviction about it, I think the sense of danger and consequence are more readily communicated. Odd, in a way, to reduce it to purely personal reactions, but that's what it comes down to—belief!

The director, like any artist, works best from a personal creative source which involves belief, commitment, or even an obsessive need to give public form to the experience embodied in a particular play. This involves more than a purely private, idiosyncratic connection with the material, of course; it requires also an ethical commitment to the potential value of the experience for the audience. As Stanislavski put it to his disciple, Gorchakov:

> A director cannot limit his role to being a medium between author and audience. He cannot be just a midwife, merely assisting at the birth of the performance. The director must be independent in his thinking and must arouse with his work the ideas necessary to contemporary society.[4]

Such a sense of purpose, whether it be political, philosophical, or esthetic, is an irreplacable source of energy which can sustain you through the often exhausting process of producing a play.

In the best of circumstances, then, your material will touch some deeply personal feelings while simultaneously evoking an ethical desire to be of service to your audience, thus coordinating your private responsibility to your own creativity and your public responsibility to your text and audience. In order to find plays with which you can have such a connection, you must develop the habit of reading as many plays as possible to develop a backlog of scripts which excite you. Unfortunately most directors do not read enough, and as a result, they are often dependent on others for the selection of the plays they do.

But what about the "professional" situation in which you are hired to direct a play which you have not selected for yourself, or which you have selected to fit certain requirements, or where the material is by definition of limited value (as, say, in most episodic television)? Michel Saint-Denis describes this situation:

> A director is rung up and asked to direct a play. He reads it, he doesn't like it, or not much, and he says yes, finding in his indifference a sort of professional virtue because it's good to do what you don't like (as if the absence of love could lead to an increase in lucidity).[5]

Could you, in such a situation, say no? Should you?

There is an ethical consideration here, of course, which each of us would have to resolve in the specific situation. The answer is never simple and rarely reached without anguish. Countering our desire for "nobility" is our eagerness to work and our knowledge that good work is sometimes done for bad reasons. It was that paragon of high idealism, Henrik Ibsen, who said to The Norwegian Theatre in 1859:

> In theatre one learns to be practical, to admit the power of circumstance, and, when absolutely necessary, to abandon one's higher ideals, for the time being.[6]

It may be that purely financial or career considerations will be sufficient motivation to support your work. But be aware that directing is hard work and there are not many rewards to sustain you during the lengthy process except a real concern for the material. If a play is suggested to you, you must see if the possibility of such a relationship exists; if not, you will have to decide in each case if the rewards of payment or career advancement are sufficient to make it "absolutely necessary to abandon one's higher ideals, for the time being."

Remember at such times, however, that the director's relationship to the text becomes the source of all the other aspects of the production process, and that the audience's eventual experience of the play will tend to reflect the director's attitude toward the material. For instance, a director who fundamentally mistrusts a play may force extraneous production gimmicks on it, or push the actors to a frenetic pace, in an effort to conceal or correct its "deficiencies." When this happens, the production is often cut off from the play's true energy and the result may be a glib but hollow production. On the other hand, a director who is in awe of the material may adopt a timid approach and produce a museum-like production which is mere theatrical taxidermy.

You must, in short, strive to respect the text, but also to respect your own creativity as well as the integrity of the production and its independent life. This requires an attitude toward the text which lies somewhere between the extremes of arrogant disregard and slavish obedience.

Within this range of attitudes there are many ways in which a director may relate to a text; this relationship varies greatly between directors, and even between different productions by the same director. In describing these various attitudes toward the text, we can use a political metaphor and say that directors may be either conservative, liberal, or radical so far as their treatment of the text is concerned. Let us briefly examine each of these points of view.

THE CONSERVATIVE POSITION: FIDELITY

One major distinction among the conservative, liberal, and radical points of view centers on the degree of transparency of the director's work. The conservative would insist that the production of a play be as transparent as possible, its function being to transmit the text directly, completely, faithfully—and therefore anonymously—with a minimum of "distortion" caused by the director's personal point of view. In this effort to "conserve" the play, the conservative director adheres strictly to the text as written, accepting it as the best form through which the "timeless" beauty of the play may be communicated.

Ultra-conservative directors may even insist upon a re-creation of the original theatrical conditions for which the play was written. An example would be the work of a director like England's Ronald Watkins in re-creating Shakespeare's plays on an Elizabethan stage, using boy actors in the women's roles, without cutting or intermissions, and with what is deduced to be Shakespeare's original blocking and costuming.

There is much of value in the conservative approach to certain texts, especially those which sprang from special linguistic, social, or theatrical circumstances which have since changed or ceased to exist. For instance, I doubt that anything short of a total reconstruction could communicate the full impact of the medieval morality plays, and two of the richest theatre experiences of my life were the Pro Musica re-creations of *The Play of Daniel* and *The Play of Herrod*. Something special can happen when the innate energy of a play is reunited with the essential conditions from which it sprang: Shakespeare, for instance, is to my mind more satisfying out-of-doors than indoors, except for those late plays he wrote for the Blackfriars Theatre.

This is not to say, however, that the original form and context of a play, however ideal for the play itself, will necessarily best serve the needs of the contemporary audience; the main shortcoming of the conservative position, in fact, is that such directors sometimes consider their responsibility to the text above their responsibility to the audience.

THE LIBERAL POSITION: RELEVANCE

By contrast, the liberal point of view holds that the value of a play lies in the way it lives relative to the present moment, and that a successful production results when the essential spirit of the play, transmitted by but not entirely bound in the text, is happily married to the specifics of a given cast, theatre, and audience, even if this requires some adjustment in the play's form such as changes in period, language, or even structure. As Robert Brustein puts it:

> A play must be seen in reference to understandable experience, and that means finding the immediate equivalence in our experience.

For Brustein, this equivalence is often manifested as a "central stage metaphor" which translates the essential action of the play into a context rich in association for the contemporary audience. Productions like Orson Welles's Nazi *Julius Caesar* or Peter Brooks's circus-like *Midsummer Night's Dream* are good examples; indeed, most contemporary professional directors fall somewhere into the "middle ground" of the liberal position. While there is much which is "creative" about this way of working, it also requires a dominant sense of responsibility to the original, which both inspires and limits the director's purely personal creative impulses.

THE RADICAL POSITION: DIRECTOR AS CREATOR

The radical esthetic eschews the forms of the past altogether and returns to the *radix* or *source* of a play in order to generate new forms inspired by the original; thus the text may, for the radical director, be only a source of inspiration for a new, intuitive creative process. A production like Jerzy Grotowski's *The Constant Prince* (based upon Calderon's *Life is a Dream*) is an example of how the auteur director goes beyond interpretation into the realm of primary creation.

You may decide, at some time, to go beyond the interpretive mode and function as the primary creator, either by using a text as the basis for a new creation in this way, or by adapting a piece of nondramatic literature for the stage, or by generating your own text as playwright or as the leader of a group process. You might even dispense with a text altogether and create directly in the performance idiom, either in the narrative tradition of conventional drama or by doing without a story altogether and working in the more abstract form which is now often called *Performance Art*.

A wide variety of forms and methodology have been developed by avant-garde directors. One of the most common strategies of the radical approach is to begin with an established text, then go beyond the limits of interpretation by allowing the original to inspire a new creation. For Richard Foreman, this is mainly a process of selection and enhancement of meanings already implicit in the original:

> Each text (if it's good) has multiple meanings, many of which escaped its author. A director *chooses* his meanings, again *vis a vis* the characteristics of his performers. But since I am an author and have my own "message," I try to find where the author has said something out of his *various* meanings which *I* find relevant to my own concerns! I am true to him in that he "allows" me to be true to myself!!

Charles Marowitz goes further and speaks of the creation of an entirely new work which is inspired by the original:

> "Understanding the play," as I see it, means being able to convert the playwright's experience into some parallel experience of your own (not necessarily synonymous with the author's). If an author's text manages to stimulate a dialogue between what he says and what you take him to mean, there is a basis for theatrical

collaboration. Reiterating the author's text by *faithfully* interpreting it through actors and production seems to me merely the equivalent of semaphore. Any play worth its salt must conjure up a parallel play in the director's imagination with which he infects his actors, thereby producing endless variations on the original theme.

Another radical director, Lee Breuer of Mabou Mines, has worked in this way, most notably in his recent retelling of a Greek classic as a Black church service in *The Gospel at Collonus*. Breuer has also often entered the realm of primary creation by serving as his own author; even then, however, he reports that the process of directing his own work is not radically different from interpreting someone else's. The creative interaction between "author" and "director" continues to function, even when both hats are on the same head.

A wide variety of forms and strategies have been developed by radical directors, but the best of them seem to have one thing in common: They are generated not merely by formal or technical experimentation, but rather out of a pressing need to manifest a specific vision; in short, the best experimental work seems to come from having something important to say which requires finding a new way to say it.

As Lee Breuer points out, any such process uses many of the same principles described in this book; the difference lies more in the director's objectives than in the process itself. The difference between most (not all) experimental work and traditional theatre is more a matter of *what* than of *how*. In all, then, while this book will not treat directly the problems of the author/director, much of what is said here will be of use to you should you decide at some point to pursue this sort of work.

THE VARIABLE POSITION

We have surveyed the range of positions you may take concerning your responsibility to the text, from the conservative, to the liberal, to the radical. In theatre, as in politics, there may be some antipathy between these positions: Conservatives tend to view liberals as "self-centered and superficial," while liberals see conservatives as "academic and dull." The radicals are often set apart (and set themselves apart) as being in "a different business" altogether.

Happily, you need not adopt any one of these positions in a fixed way: Different projects may require different attitudes toward the source material. Trevor Nunn's *Nicholas Nickelby*, for instance, was essentially conservative in approach, while his *Cats*, produced a few months later, was a more radical undertaking, and his next, a Chekhovian *All's Well that Ends Well*, was a liberal treatment of Shakespeare. Remember that each text invites a particular attitude: Some, by their specific detail, insist upon a literal approach, while others invite a looser, more creative approach. Your artistic life will be richer if you are capable of functioning from various positions.

THREE
THE DIRECTOR
AS TRANSLATOR

While the drama as literature may be "for the ages," the theatre as a living experience is "in the here and now." The director is the artist responsible for the translation of the timeless values of the drama into the immediate moment of the theatrical performance. In this sense, the director *translates* the play from its literary form into its new manifestation as a living theatrical event. Like any translator, the director is responsible for both an accurate interpretation of the original and an effective translation which makes its essential meaning and style available to a particular audience within particular theatrical circumstances.

In doing this, the director is not only translating from one medium to another (from literature to theatre) but also may be translating the essential meaning of the play from one time or place to another, or from one set of cultural or theatrical assumptions to another. For instance, Shakespeare's *Merchant of Venice* is not the same play in a world which has known the Nazi Holocaust as it was in anti-Semitic Elizabethan England; nor is it the same play in a modern theatre with its darkened auditorium, fixed seating, and rigid social conventions, as it was in the open-air Globe with its highly social atmosphere. Thus the director must translate not only from literature into theatre, but also from the cultural and theatrical values that infused the play at its birth to the values and conditions through which it will be experienced by the present audience. In the same way that one would select an English word to translate a French one, a director might choose one historical period as an effective translation of another, or one character type as a translation of another.

For instance, I remember vividly a production of Shakespeare's *Timon of Athens* directed by Michael Langham at Stratford, Canada. In place of Athenians walking about in togas, the production gave us the early sixties "jet set" as a translation for the elite society which Timon so lavishly entertains: military men in suave uniforms, fashionable women in alluring Jackie Kennedy gowns, beat poets looking like Alan Ginsberg, Timon in patent leather slippers and raw Italian silk jackets, with music by Duke Ellington. Into this world came rebels in Castro fatigues, and observing all was a cynical reporter in the mold of H. L. Mencken.

These translations of class and type did much to awaken associations that brought an otherwise remote play's meaning home to the contemporary audience. They were based upon a specific and thorough understanding of the elements of the original and an accurate identification of the analagous elements in our own society.

The point here is not that all older plays should be "modernized" or set in different periods: I doubt very much, for instance, that moving *The Taming of the Shrew* from sixteenth century Padua to the American Frontier reveals much about either the play or life in the Old West. The aim is not merely to make the play easier or more entertaining for the modern audience, but rather to manifest as much of the play's power as possible. When the play's original language, or its cultural and psychological associations, have, through changing values or conventions, become impediments to our understanding, then there may be a need for some degree of overt translation.

Even when the specifics of the play remain unaltered, however, the director is still translating its essential energies as the performance develops using the nature, values and perceptions of the immediate cast and audience.

THE LIFE OF THE PLAY

As the production develops, we can see the play passing through a number of manifestations, from a piece of pure literature existing within a literary tradition, to an incipient score being explored by actors and designers, to a sequence of actions within an environment, to the event of the living performance, to an image living in the awareness of the audience, until at last the production takes its place in the theatrical tradition.

If we are concerned with the "essential life of the play," we must ask where, along this continuum from literature to theatre, the essential play can truly be said to exist? Consider Figure 3-1, which places the "literary" life of the play at the left and the "theatrical" life of the production to the right: Where would you say the "play" exists? Stop a moment and consider each possibility.

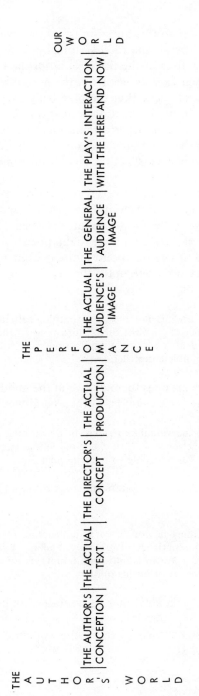

Figure 3-1. Modes of Existence of a Play.

Notice that the answer to this question is another way of distinguishing among the conservative, liberal, and radical points of view. The conservative would argue that the play lives at the literary end of the line, in the author's concept or in the text itself as it comes from the author's hands. The liberal respects the text, but would argue that the play truly lives somewhere in the middle of the line, either in the interaction of text and interpreter (as Stanislavski held) or in the interaction of performance and audience (as Meyerhold believed). The radical, on the other hand, creates directly in the medium of the theatre and holds that the play exists at the right, in the immediate experience of the audience.

There is yet another answer, however, one which embraces elements of all these positions. It is one developed by Rene Wellek and Austin Warren in their book, *Theory of Literature*. In the chapter entitled "The Mode of Existence of a Literary Work of Art," they state that a poem (or, for our purposes, a play) cannot be located at any one point along the line in Figure 3-1. First, they point out that it is not at the left, in the timeless, changeless object idealized by the conservative position:

> The literary work of art has not the same ontological status as the idea of a triangle, or of a number . . . Unlike such "subsistences," the literary work of art is, first of all, created at a certain point in time and, secondly, is subject to change and even to complete destruction . . .[7]

Nor, they make it clear, does the play live in the middle of the line, in its interaction with interpreter or spectator, as the liberal would hold:

> A poem . . . is not an individual experience or a sum of experiences, but only a potential cause of experiences . . . In every individual experience only a small part can be considered as adequate to the true poem.[8]

Rather, the work of art as a "potential cause of experiences" has a life of its own:

> Thus, the real poem must be conceived as a structure of norms, realized only partially in the actual experience of its many readers. Every single experience (reading, reciting, and so forth) is only an attempt—more or less successful and complete—to grasp this set of norms or standards.[9]

The essential energy of a play, then, is contained in its system of norms, and this energy can be manifested in various ways every time the play is read or produced. We must ask next what exactly this system of norms is and how it is communicated by a text.

THE SYSTEM OF NORMS

The idea of a system of norms may be difficult to grasp at first since it involves a global sense of how all the elements of a play work together to produce a single, unified effect. Think of it this way: The system of norms or standards that lives in the play may be likened to the genetic code of a seed, which carries the propensity of that seed to grow in certain ways. Imagine, for instance, two tulip bulbs planted in two different places: The soil and climate in each location will produce plants of different size, color, and so on; but as different as they may be, we will still recognize each as possessing the underlying pattern of "tulipness." Just so, different productions of *Hamlet* by different directors in different times and places may differ in many important ways, but each may also express that underlying system of norms which we recognize as "Hamletness," so long as each respects rather than distorts those norms. As Wellek and Warren point out,

> We can distinguish between right and wrong readings of a poem, or between a recognition or a distortion of the norms implicit in a work of art, by acts of comparison . . . Our consciousness of earlier concretizations (readings, criticisms, misinterpretations) will effect our own experience: earlier readings may educate us to a deeper understanding or may cause a violent reaction against the prevalent interpretations of the past.[10]

Each production is a single attempt to embody the seed of *Hamlet*, then, and while each must inevitably be incomplete, the "real" *Hamlet* lives only in the body of all such attempts and the system of norms that guides them.

Specifically, Wellek and Warren describe the system of norms as existing on several levels or "strata." The first is the purely sensory impact of the rhythms and sounds of the language; next is the informational function of the words as units of meaning; next, the qualities and feelings with which the message is endowed by the connotative aspects of language, and by the arrangement of language as image and metaphor; finally, the "world" created by the narrative power of the language, with values and symbolic implications which we call "myth."

This list was developed to apply to all literary works of art, and it describes well the workings of dramatic language up to a point. For our purposes, however, we must extend the last two items (the creation of a world and the telling of a story within that world) to include those devices used especially by drama. Primary among these is the creation of an event happening, as Aristotle put it, "as if before our eyes," which we call *dramatic action*; next is the creation of a world which not only contains but influences the action, which we call *given circumstance*; and last is the creation of *characters* who may seem to act of their own will.

All these elements are organized so as to interact with one another in an organic synergy, like the genetic elements carried by a seed, from which springs the unique and individual nature of the play. The actors, the designers, the physical theatre, and finally, the audience are the soil and climate in which the play must live; the director functions as the "gardener" who cultivates the seed of the play in this specific climate and soil. As the Zen tradition holds, the job of the gardener is "to extend nature in the direction nature is already going."

Nature, for the director, is the intrinsic life of the play embodied in its system of norms. You must begin, then, by penetrating to the heart of the play, opening yourself to it, and allowing its system of norms to live in you as you will eventually want it to live in your audience. It is by embodying the play in this way that you truly serve as "an ideal audience of one."

STYLE

The text of a play communicates on two levels: It gives us specific information, and it gives us information about that information—what in communication theory is called "metacommunication." Take this example from everyday life: If during a rehearsal I say to you, "I think your idea about this scene is worth trying," the *manner* of my delivery will tell you whether I am genuinely excited about the idea or am merely humoring your crackpot notion. This "meta-communication" is transmitted by my tone of voice and inflection, my volume, my rhythm, the expression on my face, my posture, and so on. In short, it is communicated by my *style* of delivery.

Just so, everything you know about a play is carried by its language, and the nature of that language endows every element of the play with certain feelings and qualities. Just as the elements of personal style are inflection, facial expression, posture, and gesture, so the elements of written style are diction and syntax (choice of words and their arrangement), rhythm, tonality, imagery, and figurative devices such as metaphor and antithesis.*

The play as a whole takes on specific stylistic qualities which are generated by these aspects of its language. The words of the text may be experienced as the residue of an entire world, and that world may be re-created through them. Part of your concern in working with the designers, for instance, will be to generate a stage environment that accurately reflects the qualities of the text in matters of texture, composition, coloration, imagery, and such. Your work in shaping the flow of the production's energy will likewise be aimed at reflecting the rhythmic qualities of the language. Most important, your work with the actors will use a sensitivity to the style of the play's language to assist them in finding the specific reality of their characters.

We can say, then, that *style is the pathway from intention to execution.* Since style is the "medium" through which the "message" of action is conveyed, it endows that action with its specific quality and meaning. To say that a play has a style, therefore, does not imply that it is "stylized" or "artificial"; *all* plays have style, and the style specifies the action, thereby giving the play its precise and unique reality.

This idea of "reality of style" was the cornerstone of the teaching and practice of Michel Saint-Denis:

*You will find a detailed discussion of these elements in Part Two of Robert Benedetti, *The Actor at Work, Third Edition*, New York, 1981.

Reality of style is composed of what elements?

Of construction and composition. Composition in musical terms. Construction considered in all its different parts and the way in which they are connected.

Of rhythm.   Relationship between the different rhythms first taken in big chunks.

Of the tone and color of the language, and how the text goes from one tone to another.

There is no meaning or psychological construction in a play which can be separated from its style. The one contains the other. Style has its own meaning. It is through, not apart from, text and style that meaning and psychology should be analysed.[11]

Our aim in production, then, is to manifest the particular reality of the play not only by telling the story (embodying the action as a living event) but also by capturing the precise tone, texture, and meaning of the action as communicated by the play's style. Only then will we have produced an authentic manifestation of the system of norms which can transmit the essential life of the play.

THE DIRECTOR AS EXECUTIVE

The development of a specific production is the business of a fairly complex organization. The director serves as the "captain of the ship," coordinating the efforts of this organization toward the specific goal of the production. The director may actually *do* very little, but he or she is responsible for the delegation and alignment of the efforts of many people of differing temperaments, each of whom is concerned with a particular aspect of the whole. In addition, the director decides, on a day-to-day basis, on the best uses of the available resources of talent, time, space, and money. In this executive capacity, the director often stands at the difficult point between management and labor, and between the demands of art and of commerce, helping to shape and guide the project on a day-to-day basis.

In all these ways, the effective director must be an able executive. The executive aspect of the director's job has four main components:

1.   *Structuring*: The director is responsible for the formation of the acting ensemble, except in a resident company in which major casting is done by the artistic director (usually with the participation of the director).

2.   *Focusing*: Given the production team, the director must establish a sense of direction for the organization in terms of the project at hand. This may be done through a more or less detailed "production concept" or through a set of priorities, mutual goals, and methods of exploration by which the creative ensemble will generate the final form of the production out of its own encounter with the energies of the play, the director serving to facilitate and regulate that encounter.

3.   *Alignment*: The director then assists each member of the team to contribute to the group purpose in a way which supports and enhances the efforts of all other group members. It is a crucial part of the director's job to establish a working situation which will allow each element of the production to be created so as to take its place in the unity of the whole. When this alignment of effort is achieved, each member of the creative unit receives more energy from the project than he or she gives to it, and the undertaking becomes self-motivating. In order for this to happen, the director must engage in some degree of "social engineering," so that the dynamics of the group is kept in a productive state despite the inevitable tensions of the creative effort.

4. *Editing*: As the efforts of all the various people at work on the production begin to coalesce, the director edits and adjusts these individual efforts so as to produce a single whole with its own integrity. A good production must be more than the sum of its parts, and the director is the central intelligence responsible for bringing all the parts into a creative synergy. This editing function is, on a day-to-day basis, one of the most important and demanding aspects of directing, requiring great tact, discrimination, and authority.

SUMMARY

We have said that the director's main responsibility is to understand the story the author wishes to tell, to mobilize the capacity of the theatre to tell it so as to retain its essential style, and at the same time to assure that it is well told by being "an ideal audience of one." The specific process has three phases: analysis of the play, translation into theatrical form, and eventual synthesis in the completed production.

This progression is by no means a matter of simple formula; at each step, the director must find his or her way through a "process of discovery." As in any art, the outcome is never certain. Dan Sullivan expresses it vividly in his questionnaire response:

> Everytime I direct a play I get frightened . . . I know you have a completed thing—a playscript—and you have to find your way with it to another completed thing—a production. In order to get the second thing you have to disassemble the first, and that's what scares me: Maybe, once you've taken it apart, it won't go back together.

Part Two of our study will be concerned with the "taking apart" which precedes the onset of rehearsals and design meetings; Part Three will then be concerned with the "putting together" which, hopefully, is the business of the rehearsal process.

PART TWO
GETTING READY

FOUR
THE FIRST ENCOUNTER

Let us assume that you have been fortunate: You have been given a chance to direct *Hamlet* and you feel both a strong personal relationship with the play and a sense of purpose about undertaking the production at this particular moment in your life. You are now settling down to get to know this play in earnest.

The wise director meets a play as he or she might meet a potential friend: with eager anticipation and alertness, openness and humility, and without prejudice. As Michel Saint-Denis put it in *The Rediscovery of Style*, the director

> . . . must be submissive and creative at the same time. In other words if he is to succeed in being both faithful to the work and efficient in his treatment of it, the director has to substitute himself for the . . . dramatist and recreate the play.[12]

The director, in other words, strives to create a process of production which is analagous to the process whereby the play was originally created. This involves beginning at the beginning instead of at the end of the process; it means reading the play at first not as a potential production (that will come later) but on its own terms as literature.

While your encounter begins in a literary way, however, your approach is different from that of a literary scholar: You are both concerned with meaning, structure, and style, of course, but each has a particular focus. The scholar tends to concentrate on the verbal and conceptual aspects of a play, while the director strives to experience the play more viscerally, with greater attention to the explicit, literal level of the action. In short, the scholar is interested primarily in what the play *says*, while the director is primarily interested in *what happens*. These approaches overlap and have much to contribute to one another, but their different objectives ought not to be confused.

The specific techniques of the first readings are given here by Michel Saint-Denis:

> Let the play come to you. Read it again and again, and not in a fragmentary way. Try to read the play for the first time at a single sitting so as to get the feeling of the whole. Then go on reading it until the play speaks to you, until you can remember easily the sequence of events, the main movements of the text and the connecting passages, until you know clearly where the play is weakest and strongest. Delay for as long as you can thinking about the production itself.[13]

Let's put Saint-Denis's recommendation to work on *Hamlet*.

Exercise 2: The First Encounter

Even though you may have read it before, empty your mind and approach *Hamlet* "as if for the first time." Remember Saint-Denis's advice to read it "at a single sitting so as to get the feeling of the whole," and to avoid "thinking about the production itself." Assume nothing, least of all that you understand the play or know what it's about. If ideas about staging or other technical considerations occur to you, simply notice them, empty your mind, and return to a naive and pleasurable involvement with the play.

After you have read it at least once for pleasure in an esthetic rather than a practical frame of mind, begin to think about what excited you in it. Avoid thinking about what ought to have excited you ("what a profound statement on the contemporary experience!") or in glittering generalities ("what a great play!"). Be specific and honest about your feelings. Is it the play's *ideas* that excite you? The *story* it tells? A particular *character or relationship*? Some *association* with your own life?

The ability to read in a naive, literal way will be of enormous value to you. At every stage of the directing process you will return to the text, and you must train yourself to see what is really there, not merely the reflection of your own preconceptions or interpretations.

Patience is required. As you will see in my *Hamlet* log, it took months of careful reading by myself, the designers, and the actors before the text had yielded many of its specific clues. Even so, in rehearsal after rehearsal, new recognitions arose; each time it was as if I was hearing a line for the first time, and I would think, "Now why didn't I understand that before? It's obvious!"

This is what my friend Gil Dennis calls *discovering the text through the actors,* and as thorough as your prerehearsal study may be, remember that it is intended only to prepare you for this process.

Remember too that a great play is a life-long study. A single production will be only a step in the journey of your understanding of such a play; and, if you are lucky enough to come back to it later in life, you will find a whole new understanding awaiting you.

Our American propensity for quick results often short-circuits this process. In his autobiography, Laurence Olivier speaks of feeling rushed with only a few months to prepare to direct a play; John Houseman answered my question about studying the play thus:

> I read it at least once a day for a month or more. If it is a classic, I read it in several different annotated editions and do a certain amount of research—historical and theatrical.

While the best research is the repeated reading of the play, some outside information may be useful in helping you to enter into the world of any play. Let's consider the various forms such directorial research may take.

RESEARCH

The aim of your directorial research is not to find a fixed understanding of the play, in the way a literary critic might develop an interpretion, but rather to assemble supportive information and ideas which will help to prepare you to *recognize* the truth when it arises in the course of your work. As Gil Dennis insists, your true discovery of the text will occur only through your actors; research does not supplant this process, but rather prepares you for it. Research may even suggest specific rehearsal strategies to help your actors and designers discover the play for themselves, since it is their understanding which is in many ways more important than yours.

In the larger resident theatres research receives special attention; most of them have a *dramaturge* or *literary manager* who has the responsibility to assess new plays and to accumulate research materials on plays under production. Elsewhere, however, directors are left to their own devices. Like the literary scholar, you will use the traditional mechanisms of research: the library's card catalogue, bibliographies, indexes, annotated editions of the play, and so on. The public libraries in large cities and the libraries of most universities will have theatre collections, and reference librarians who can help you to locate material that may not be accessible through the card catalog.

A director's research has three principal thrusts: interpretations of the play, information on the play's theatrical life, and material on the culture from which the play sprang. Let's consider each.

1. THE PLAY

All but the very newest plays carry something of a body of criticism, either in the popular press or in more august tribunals. A play like *Hamlet* is an extreme example; the whole of a respectably sized library could be devoted to it. The director should make a survey of this material; not only essays by scholars, but also program notes from other productions, and reviews (especially in magazines with a commitment to serious criticism). With older plays or translations, information about the original forms of the text may be useful. When they exist, statements by playwrights themselves are important. If the playwright is living, correspondence can be attempted—it is surprising how many playwrights are willing to answer specific questions about their work, and even to give some useful suggestions about staging.

One note of caution here, however: While the playwright is the primary authority on the play, his or her view of the play is not necessarily the only valid one. The creative process involves the accidental as well as the intentional, and there is no guarantee that the playwright will see—or even accept—what he or she may have actually created. There have been times when directors and actors have fulfilled a play beyond the original expectations of the playwright, as Strindberg and others have acknowledged. So even with the help of the ultimate authority on your play, you will still have to make up your own mind. The gathering of all these other critical opinions—including the writer's own—will only increase your range of interpretive choice.

Another aspect of interpretive research is examining those traditions and conventions which were influential on the author during the writing of the play. This involves considering a number of things:

A.   Sources from which elements of the play were taken;
B.   Conventions of language, such as prosody in verse plays;
C.   Conventions of construction, such as the kind of plots common to Jacobean revenge plays or Restoration comedies, or the principles of "the well-made play" as they might influence a Sardou or an Ibsen.

These considerations can be lumped together under the heading of *genre*—those qualities shared by a particular type of play during a particular period in history. Obviously, all classical tragedies share some qualities (massively simple units of action concentrated on the fate of a single hero, for example), just as most nineteenth century melodramas have much in common.

Reading other plays within the same genre and period can be very useful for understanding the literary parameters within which the author was working. The great danger of such study, however, is that it may cause the director (or actors) to think in a generalized way about the particular play, blinding them to its unique reality. Be careful, then, to use a study of genre and period only to illuminate the specific and intrinsic qualities of your text.

2. THE THEATRE

This deals with the natural habitat of the play; your aim here is to re-create the experience of attending a performance of the play as first produced. You might seek out information on some or all of the following:

A. The original language of the play.
B. The architecture of the theatre for which it was written.
C. The staging and scenic conventions of the time.
D. The acting style of the time.
E. The social environment in the theatre.

Once you begin to have a sense of the play as it was first performed, you may want also to consider the production history of the play. How have other directors treated it? What have past designers done with it? There may be useful inspiration in the work of the past, though again, you must translate this understanding into your own time and theatrical and social circumstances.

3. THE WORLD

Here you will use the play as an artifact to reconstruct a sense of the world from which the play sprang. Any information we can see in it or get from other sources about its world will help us to understand it as a living element in its own culture. This is especially important to the theatre. Whereas the novelist can use description and narration to paint explicitly the landscape of the novel, the dramatist must imply a great deal through association, must trigger in the audience a fuller understanding based upon shared values, beliefs, and experiences. If we are truly to understand the play and to help our actors live in its world, we must have the full sense of those associations on which the author drew. Here is a partial list of these materials:

A. *Metaphysics:* How was the universe understood to work and what was humanity's place in it?
B. *Religion:* What was the sense of God?
C. *Ethics:* What was a "good" person?
D. *Psychology:* How was the mind understood to function?
E. *Politics:* What was the relationship of citizen and state? How did the law reflect this? What was the relationship among various levels of society?
F. *Economics:* How did people support themselves on various levels of society?
G. *Esthetics:* What was considered beautiful?
H. *Fashion:* What was the taste of the time? How did clothing influence movement and reflect values?
I. *Architecture, Transportation, Plumbing, and so on:* What was the physical environment like?
J. *Manners:* How did people behave on an everyday basis? What was considered polite?
K. *Specific events, people, or customs* referred to in the play.

All this can re-create the world view that was shared by playwright and audience when the play was written. Even if your production happens eventually to be set in a different period, it is necessary to have a full understanding of the original.

These "archeological" materials can be particularly useful in rehearsals. Using those aspects of the world view that are operative or influential in the specifics of the play (avoid burdening your actors with useless detail), you can find ways to generate direct experiences of the play's world for the actors. Music, painting, dancing, the wearing of clothing, eating—all can be useful in this way. We want not merely to understand the world, we want to *live* in it.

In summary, remember that in all three types of research your aim is not information per se, but guidance for the creative process. Your research should best prepare you to recognize the truth when it arises, so that you can be like the Master in *Zen in the Art of Archery*, who, after years of patient watching, sees the moment when the true shot finally happens, and bows in acknowledgment.

Exercise 3: Researching the Play

Research materials on *Hamlet* are so plentiful that you may be overwhelmed into paralysis; try to limit the task by getting advice (from critics, annotated editions, and so on) about the most useful sources. I will suggest here a few of the works I found especially helpful in each of the areas of research we have discussed.

A.   THE PLAY

The excerpted commentaries at the back of the Signet Classic edition of the play are useful; some of these are available in full length (plus others) in an excellent little paperback anthology, *Twentieth-Century Interpretations of "Hamlet"* edited by David Bevington. Englewood Cliffs, N.J.: Prentice-Hall, 1968.

Reading other plays by Shakespeare would also be valuable.

B.   THE THEATRE

Shakespeare at the Globe. 1599-1609 by Bernard Beckerman. New York: The Macmillan Company, 1962.

C.   THE WORLD

Shakespeare's Eden: The Commonwealth of England 1558-1629. New York: Barnes & Noble, Inc., 1971.
The Elizabethan World Picture by E. M. W. Tillyard. New York: The Macmillan Company, 1944.
I also recommend listening to Elizabethan music and looking at examples of Elizabethan painting, architecture and fashion.

D.   A DAY IN THE LIFE

After you have read some of these works, try this exercise: Create a fictitious character of an average theatre-goer of Shakespeare's time; write a complete diary entry for this person for the day on which he or she saw the first production of *Hamlet*. Start with waking up in the morning and end with going to sleep at night; follow your character through the entire day, trying to capture the feeling of ordinary life. Include the specifics of visiting the theatre: How did the person learn of the performance? How did he or she get into the theatre? What was the building like, outside and in? What was the atmosphere inside? Describe the performance in some detail as to its staging, the manner of the acting, and the audience's response.

THE HAMLET LOG

As explained in the Preface, each of the chapters which follow will be accompanied by an excerpt from the detailed production log of my 1983 production of *Hamlet* at the Oregon Shakespearean Festival. This production of *Hamlet* was chosen as the subject for the log because of the complexity of the play and the enormous scope of the production circumstances. Understand, however, that the type of large-scale resident repertory production the log chronicles is not held up as superior to some other kind of theatre. (Indeed, it has many shortcomings, which the log will make obvious.)

Nor is this particular production held up as a model; the techniques and concepts presented by this book are not successfully applied throughout and you will observe me making plenty of mistakes. The log simply records the way things really happened throughout one production in one particular circumstance, "warts and all."

I hope you will enjoy comparing the choices you would make in directing this play with those chronicled in the log and in my examples.

HAMLET LOG, PART ONE: FIRST CONTACTS—JUNE 15-AUGUST 15

I am in Colorado working on a production of *The Time of Your Life* when Jerry Turner, the producing director of the Oregon Shakespearean Festival, calls. He asks if I'd be interested in directing *Hamlet* in his spring season. He knows that I've done *Hamlet* once before (at Chicago's Court Theatre three years earlier) and understands that I may not want to work on the play again, but I explain that, unlike some directors, I very much enjoy working on a show more than once (assuming the material is worthwhile) and that *Hamlet* in particular remains a challenge. My first production opened up a number of possibilities which I am eager to explore. I offer to jot down my thoughts about the show in a letter, which I do; the letter is sent a few days later.

Before writing, I reread the play. I am struck by how different it seems after only a few years. In particular, I feel the urgency of Hamlet's situation as a life crisis, no doubt because of the changes occuring in my own life. I review some of the research I had done for the first production and find seeds of this idea in several essays, especially in Maynard Mack's excellent "The World of *Hamlet*," in which he traces Hamlet's progress toward a spiritual enlightenment:

> The crucial evidence of Hamlet's new frame of mind . . . is in the graveyard scene. Here, in its ultimate symbol, he confronts, recognizes, and accepts the condition of being man. It is not simply that he now accepts death, . . . It is instead the haunting mystery of life itself that Hamlet's speeches point to, holding in its inscrutable folds those other mysteries that he has wrestled with so long. These he now knows for what they are, and lays them by. The mystery of evil is present here . . . The mystery of reality is here too . . . And last of all, but most pervasive of all, there is the mystery of human limitation.

Some quick calculation reveals that Shakespeare was probably 37 or 38 when he wrote the play. I am persuaded that what we call the "mid-life crisis" is at work in the play; in any case, it is at the heart of my response to the play at this moment in time.

In my letter, I describe my understanding of the main action of the play, which is the working out of the conflict between impulse and reason within Hamlet. This central tension is made manifest on the level of plot by the "battle of wits" between Hamlet and Claudius and each of the other plotlines (those involving Polonius, Ophelia, Laertes, and Gertrude) can be seen as directly connected to this central struggle.

This view of the play's structure opens the possibility of an active Hamlet who, far from being paralysed by indecision or melancholy, attempts to deal with his situation as best he can, given the circumstances and his own moral reservations about them. I will therefore prefer a straightforward production focused on this inner action, with an exceptionally strong Claudius to drive the outer action of the plot.

I also review the cutting of the play developed for my first production. Length is always a consideration with this play of nearly 3,900 lines; I had cut about 500 lines (about 15 percent), but I can already see a number of passages I want to restore, having a better understanding of their purpose. Nevertheless, I know I'd like the production to run no more than three and one-half hours, including two intermissions. I feel that television has made it nearly impossible for our audiences to maintain an attention span much greater than ninety minutes; my cutting of the play is designed to meet this limit, with a first act that runs about seventy minutes, and a second act of sixty minutes, and a third of fifty. With two intermissions, the total length would be about three and one-half hours.

This three-act division heightens the intrinsic shaping of the play's action, since there is a natural break after Hamlet has set up the play–within-the-play, and again after he leaves for England. I especially like the fact that each intermission would occur after a major soliloquy in which Hamlet makes a crucial choice: the first after "The play's the thing wherein I'll catch the conscience of the King," and the second after "Henceforth my thought's be bloody or be nothing worth." This second intermission will also emphasize the passage of time during Hamlet's absence from Denmark and help to point up the fact that he returns a changed man.

I am stressing these parameters in my early thoughts about the play because I want there to be no misunderstandings about the kind of production I intend.

A month later, having read my letter, Jerry calls to say he wants to pursue the idea further. He wants me to come to Ashland soon to cast the title role: he must be sure that the director is happy with the available casting, and that the actor selected can be put under contract for the lengthy run of the show (nearly nine months and one hundred performances).

FIVE
UNDERSTANDING
THE ACTION

Through your first readings and research you have been developing a sense of the intrinsic unity of the play; now you are ready to begin taking the play apart to find out how it achieves its unity, what "makes it tick."

As we said in Chapter 3, a play comprises several elements, each of which is a norm within its system of norms. During your detailed analysis of the play you will examine many of these elements individually, striving to understand how each contributes to the whole, beginning with the most important of these elements, the action.

ACTION AND PLOT

Aristotle defined drama as "an imitation of men in action." The term *action* as used here might seem to refer simply to what happens in the play; indeed, we sometimes use the term *plot* as if it were synonymous with action. The action in Aristotle's sense, however, is not the same thing as the plot, and it is important that you understand the difference.

When speaking of action, Aristotle used the word *praxis*, which really means "a force which tries to *do* something" (in the sense of *prac*tical, which comes from the same root); perhaps the phrase *motivating force* would be the best translation. The action, then, is really the underlying dynamic energy that drives the plot.

The plot, on the other hand, is the way in which the specific events generated by the action are organized so as to provide a dramatically satisfying experience, usually based on the working out of a central conflict through a crisis and a climax. The plot, then, is not the same thing as the action, but it is the main way in which we come to understand the action.

The action of great plays is usually a reflection of universal patterns of human striving, such as the search for significance in our lives (*Death of a Salesman*), our attempts to surpass our mortal limits (*The Bacchae*), or our pursuit of ambition at the cost of goodness (*Macbeth*). In this way, action is closely related to *theme*: we could say that it is the active form of the theme; so that by its very nature, a dramatic action shows us something about our lives. It might, for instance, make us realize that however imperfect the choices offered by life may be, we are nevertheless forced to choose (as in *Hamlet*) or that even when we are offered no choices at all, we must go on anyway (as in *Waiting for Godot*).

The action of a play, then, is the main reason for the play's existence; even if the play is deficient in every other element, a strong action can give us something of the experience of drama; but if the action is weak or trivial, the most intricate plot, the most interesting characters, the wittiest dialogue can never compensate. The action is the center, the heart of the play.

ACTION AND CHARACTER

A dramatic action cannot occur unless there are people through whom it can work; for this reason, Aristotle called the characters of a play the "agents of the action." Since the skillful dramatist can make characters seem so alive that they seem to have a will of their own, characters may appear to cause the action by the choices they make. Actually, they have been created by the playwright in order to tell the story, so that it would be more correct to say that the characters are caused by the action!

As a director, you will guide the actors in the creation of their characters according to this sense of the character's function as an agent of the action. Each character must be created so as to do what the play requires of her or him (this is what Stanislavksi called the actor's "superobjective"). The true function of character, then, is to serve as a conduit for the action.

It follows that the more we know about the characters, the more vivid and engaging the action can be. An effective characterization helps bring the action close to us by allowing us to feel as if we were involved in it ourselves (to empathize) through what Aristotle called our fellow-feeling (*sympathaeia*) for the characters.

Just so, our sense of character personality, of who they really are, is communicated not so much by how they look or sound as by what they *do,* and by our sense of the kind of thinking that generates the reactions and feelings through which they participate in the action. We come to understand the way a character thinks also by what he or she says, so that the dialogue itself is also a conduit for the action.

Every element of the drama, in fact, can be seen as springing from and contributing to the action that lies at the heart of the play: The plot has a certain form because it expresses the action; the characters have certain forms because of the way they function within the plot; the characters think and therefore speak in certain ways so as to fulfill this function; and so on.

This is the unity inherent in all well-made drama: Each element is inextricably bound with all the other elements so as to create an organic whole, and no one element can be changed without changing the whole. It is this inherent unity of the play which you will strive to grasp so that you can re-create it in the unity of your production: *you want to put your production together in the same way that the play was put together so as to re-create a unified expression of its dramatic action.*

An action requires three things: first, a place, time, and situation in which to happen, which we call the *given circumstances*; second, it needs *characters* for it to happen through; last, it requires something that needs to be worked out, a *conflict*. Once you have characters in conflict in given circumstances, events are generated which form a plot. We will consider each of these elements separately, beginning with the given circumstances.

ACTION AND THE GIVEN CIRCUMSTANCES

It is impossible to consider a dramatic action separately from its circumstances; the playwright has conceived of the action within its circumstances, and has created those circumstances so as to produce an action possessing certain qualities. You must identify the operative aspects of the given circumstances and ensure that they are translated into the stage environment through the physical staging and through your actors' awareness. Then, as the action unfolds, these circumstances will effect it in a natural way.

The given circumstances of a play fall into four broad categories summarized by these questions: what is happening, to whom is it happening, and where and when is it happening?

   I.   WHAT is happening?
       A.   What has happened prior to the moment the play starts which has led to the immediate situation?
       B.   What about the immediate situation requires action—in other words, what is the *conflict* within the situation?

II.   WHO is involved?
      A.   What is the *general* relationship of the characters as a group (*eg.* the Danish
           Court); what are the social, political, and/or philosophical aspects of this
           "group identity"? How do they influence the action?
      B.   What are the most important *specific* relationships within the group and
           how do they effect the action?
III. WHERE is it happening?
      A.   What is the physical climate?
      B.   What is the socio-political climate?
      C.   What is the ethical climate (that is, how do people "behave" here)?
      D.   How is the sense of place used during the play?
IV.   WHEN is it happening?
      A.   What is the historical time?
      B.   What is the time of year?
      C.   How is the flow of time organized during the play?

The answers to these questions come primarily from a close reading of
the text for specific intrinsic evidence, though your research has also prepared
you to recognize those implications which the author has drawn from the
audiences' shared assumptions.

When we examine the given circumstances as laid out in the first two
scenes of *Hamlet*, we see, first, an armed castle ready for possible invasion in
the midst of a bitter winter. We know that this is a medieval court (the evidence
suggests that the date is about 1054) which operates on feudal values (essentially, that "might makes right"). A ghost has been seen on the battlements
and appears to be that of the old king, Hamlet's father, who has recently died.
We learn that the old king's brother, Claudius, has been elected to the throne
with the consent of the court, despite Hamlet's superior claim. Moreover,
Claudius has married his widowed sister-in-law and is now Hamlet's step-father.
Hamlet has returned from school at Wittenberg too late for his father's funeral
but in time for his mother's wedding and Claudius's coronation.

Though these are only the main points (we will include much more about
the relationships in the next chapter), we can see at once that there is much
guidance here about the quality of the stage environment, specifically regarding
sets, lights, costumes, props, and the overall style of the production. A careful
examination of the given circumstances, then, can provide the director with
the beginnings of a production concept.

Exercise 4: The Given
Circumstances

After re-examining *Hamlet*, answer the questions in the detailed
list of given circumstances above. Notice that you must consider
the evidence available in the entire play, not just in the first few
scenes. For example, we do not learn for certain that Hamlet is
actually thirty years old until Act V, when the Gravedigger states

that he became a gravemaker on "the very day that young Hamlet was born," and has been "sexton here, man and boy, thirty year."

Having understood the givens, you are ready to trace the flow of the action as it moves through the beginning, middle, and end of the play.

UNDERSTANDING THE STORY: PLOT

In the last chapter, Michel Saint-Denis suggested reading the play

> until you can remember easily the sequence of events, the main movements of the text and the connecting passages . . .

In most drama, the sequence of events is based on ordinary causation: One thing happens, which causes another thing to happen, and so on. The individual events that form the sequence of the plot must, as Aristotle suggested, connect in a way that is at least *possible*; it is better if the connections are *probable*, and best if they seem *necessary* without, however, being presented in a predictable way and thereby losing their power to surprise us.

The dramatic value of the plot comes from complications that increase the tension and suspense. This tension is generated by a *seed of conflict* existing within the given circumstances which needs only to be unleashed by an *inciting incident*.

In *Hamlet*, for example, the first two scenes lay out the situation, as we have seen. Despite his strong feelings about what is happening, Hamlet is powerless to do anything; he must "hold his tongue." The situation is rife with tension, but if nothing more were to happen, this tension would simply persist. Something does happen, however, which sets a whole sequence of events into motion: The Ghost tells Hamlet that he was, in fact, murdered by Claudius; Claudius, moreover, had seduced his loving Queen; Hamlet must avenge this double shame by murdering Claudius. The Ghost's revelation and command is the inciting incident which truly sets the play's action into irreversible motion.

This inciting incident also establishes the seed of conflict in the play. Conflict occurs when two forces are in opposition (force and counterforce), or when a force encounters an obstacle. In some plays, the force and counterforce are embodied in a *protagonist* and an *antagonist*, (popularly called the hero and the villain) as in *The Bacchae* or *Othello*; in other plays, the counterforce is an obstacle presented by the situation itself (as in *Romeo and Juliet*, *Mother Courage*, or *Waiting for Godot*); in still other plays the obstacle exists within the main character (as in *Death of a Salesman*).

Hamlet possesses both an external conflict (between Hamlet as hero and Claudius as villain) and an internal conflict (within Hamlet himself—between understanding and will, thinking and doing). The external conflict reflects the internal, as it does in many of Shakespeare's plays (most notably in *King Lear*). The external conflict of *Hamlet* was borrowed by Shakespeare from his source plays, but the internal conflict is his own invention; it makes Hamlet one of the very first truly modern characters in the history of drama.

The force driving Hamlet is the quest for revenge and this force pits him not only against Claudius, but also against his mother, Ophelia, Polonius—even against himself. Thus the central conflict permeates all the relationships and generates all the complications of the plot. Because Hamlet has been ordered by the Ghost to avenge his murder, he decides to "put on an antic disposition"; because he is acting oddly, Claudius sends for Rosencrantz and Guildenstern to spy on him, and Polonius suggests that Ophelia be used in a similar way; and so on, each event growing out of the one before and causing the one after, complications growing until the tension reaches a breaking point and the outcome becomes inevitable.

Of course, not every play is organized in precisely this way. We see some plays, especially in the last hundred years, in which the sequence of events is not bound by ordinary cause and effect. In some, the plot may be fragmentary or highly episodic, as in Brecht's *Mother Courage* or David Rabe's *The Basic Training of Pavlo Hummel*. In these plays the sequence of events is centered around an idea or a central character, with the events arranged so as to develop the idea or to reveal the character. In other plays, such as Strindberg's *Ghost Sonata* or Ionesco's *The Bald Soprano*, the events defy ordinary causality and instead reflect the causality of dreams (what Artaud called "the logic of the irrational") or some other logic invented by the playwright.

Regardless of the way in which the events may be organized, however, a good play has the quality of being a single event. You must recognize the nature of the connections which bind all of its parts into one unified whole, for it is this whole which is the story your production must tell.

Exercise 5: Telling the Story

One good way to grasp the story of the play is by making a *breakdown* of the plot. Trace through the play scene by scene, asking yourself: What happens here; how does it come from what has just happened; and how does it lead to what will happen next? What has changed when this scene is over?

Keep your breakdown as brief as possible; your aim is to develop a simple but precise understanding of the story, with awareness of the way in which each event is a link in the unbroken chain of the plot. (See the sample synopsis of the opening scenes of *Hamlet* below.)

When you have completed your breakdown, try to identify the inciting incident and the central conflict.

A SAMPLE BREAKDOWN OF HAMLET, SCENES 1, i, AND 1, ii

(Each Paragraph below is a major section of a scene; each sentence is a single unit of action, usually called a beat; the major turning point of the scene—called the *crisis*—is marked with three asterisks. These terms will be explained in greater detail later.)

Act I, Scene i   It is a winter midnight on the battlements, which are in a state of alert; a ghost which is like the recently dead King in appearance has twice appeared to the watch. The soldiers have brought a visiting scholar, Horatio, to try to speak to it tonight, which he does when it appears; but the ghost stalks away. Confirming that the ghost is indeed like the dead King, Horatio declares, "This bodes some strange eruption to our state."

Horatio explains the reasons for the "warlike preparations" currently being made: The dead King (Old Hamlet) was challenged in combat by Old Fortinbras of Norway over some lands, and killed him; his son, Young Fortinbras, has raised an army of mercenaries to recapture the lost lands. This explanation is interrupted by the reappearance of the Ghost, who is again challenged by Horatio. Just as the Ghost seems about to speak, a cock crows and it stops; they attack it, but it vanishes. Horatio suggests that they inform Hamlet, to whom the Ghost may speak; *** they agree and leave to find the Prince.

Act I, Scene ii   It is the next morning; the coronation of Claudius has just been concluded and the court greets its new King, who honors the mourning for the old King and justifies the discretion of his recent marriage to Hamlet's mother, Gertrude, an action supported by all. In his first official audience, Claudius conducts several pieces of business: The current threat from Young Fortinbras is answered boldly, and the aid of his uncle, the King of Norway, is enlisted against him by an ambassadorial delegation. The petition of Laertes to return to France is granted. Finally, the disturbing behavior of the Prince, who persists in his mourning, is dealt with: First his mother tries to persuade him to "cast thy nighted color off," but he refuses; Claudius commends his grief but insists that it is time to be "manly" and to accept what has happened; he urges Hamlet to "think of us as of a father" and announces to the delighted court that Hamlet is henceforth "most immediate to our throne." Both Claudius and Gertrude command Hamlet to leave his schooling and remain at home;*** Hamlet agrees to "obey *you*, madam," thus offhandedly insulting Claudius. Making the best of Hamlet's answer, Claudius declares a period of celebration.

Left alone, Hamlet gives vent to his suppressed disgust about the marriage, angry that he must hold his tongue. He reiterates that "It is nor cannot come to good." Horatio and the soldiers enter, glad to find Hamlet alone; Hamlet greets Horatio with great warmth, relieved to be able to share his feelings with his friend. Horatio, with the support of the soldiers, describes the appearance of the Ghost; Hamlet is troubled at the news, stressing that the Ghost appeared armed and angry. *** Hamlet decides to watch tonight and to speak to the Ghost; he swears them all to secrecy; alone, he speaks his fears again: "All is not well . . . I doubt some foul play . . . foul deeds will rise."

SIX
THE SHAPE OF DRAMA

The essence of the dramatic experience is change, specifically when a conflict produces a flow of action moving us toward its resolution. It is the momentum of this journey from conflict toward resolution which will give your production of the play its *dynamism*, and it is the shape of that journey which will give your production its *rhythm*. You must therefore grasp both the drive of the play's action and the way in which it rises and falls so as to produce a satisfying dramatic experience.

THE SENSE OF CRISIS

As the action of the play, driven by the central conflict, moves from the inciting incident through the various complications of the plot, a point is reached when the elements of the conflict are poised: Something has got to give. Aristotle describes this moment as the *crisis* or "turning point," when the mounting tension (the ravelling) has reached its peak. Something now occurs which breaks the impasse and turns the energy of the play toward resolution (the unravelling or *denouement*). From the moment of crisis on, the play moves inexorably toward its climax.

You can identify the crisis of a play, then, by working backward from the ending and looking for the moment when the outcome becomes inevitable, given the world of the play; that is, the point when the play offers no more options to the eventual ending. In *Romeo and Juliet*, for instance, the play could have had a happy ending if, and only if, Friar Lawrence's trick involving the sleeping potion had worked: Romeo could have returned to rescue the sleeping Juliet from her tomb and they could have escaped to live "happily ever after." Once Romeo enters the tomb thinking that Juliet is really dead, however, everything must come out as it does. The crisis, therefore, is that moment when Friar Lawrence's letter explaining the trick fails to reach Romeo—a moment which Shakespeare only describes but which Zefferelli chose to exploit to great effect in his movie version.

In *Hamlet*, the central conflict cannot be resolved as long as Hamlet refuses to take action. Several times he is given the opportunity to take his revenge, but he hesitates; it is his hesitation which is the primary obstacle to a resolution of the conflict. The crisis would occur, then, at the moment when Hamlet becomes ready to act. Tracing backward from the ending, this moment seems to occur at the outset of the sea voyage, as Hamlet watches the army of Fortinbras and decides at last to stop thinking and to start doing: "Henceforth my thoughts be bloody or nothing worth!" And indeed, he returns only a few days later a changed man, ready at last: Despite a clear premonition of death as he agrees to fight Laertes, he is ready. As he says to Horatio, "The readiness is all." (More on this in the *Hamlet* production log.)

As you can see, identifying the exact moment of crisis is really a way of defining the action. In order to specify the crisis, we must become clear about what we see as the central forces at work in the play. In some plays there are several plot-lines or several thematic lines, each of which may have a crisis of its own. In order to produce a unified production, you must decide which will be the principle focus and which crisis will therefore be the basis for the overall rhythm of the production.

The precise nature of a play's crisis will reveal much about the underlying system of causality which binds the play into a unified whole. In *Romeo and Juliet*, for instance, it is a mere accident which causes the crisis, and this is appropriate for a play about destiny. But the crisis in *Hamlet* is expressed in psychological terms and grows directly out of the conflict within Hamlet; moreover, it is a moral choice and so focuses the play on moral issues.

In some modern plays, there is no climactic resolution; instead we are left at the moment of crisis with an unanswered question, as in Pinter's *The Dumbwaiter* in which the curtain falls on a moment of choice (will Gus shoot Ben?) or in Beckett's *Waiting for Godot* in which the possibility of resolution is denied ("Let's go. *They do not move.*") Even in these cases, however, the basic shape of rising action leading to a crisis is the underlying rhythm of the experience.

Notice that the movement of the action toward the crisis is not usually a straight line; each individual episode (or scene) that leads to the crisis has a rhythmic shape of its own, with its own crisis (but without a resolution, so that we are moved on into the next scene). In each scene there are yet smaller units of action which have mini-crises of their own; these are traditionally called *beats*. The beats are linked by cause and effect to form the scenes, the scenes are linked by cause and effect to form the play; notice especially that on all three levels the crises are usually caused by choices made by the characters.

The rhythmic texture of the whole is produced by the way the action flows through each of these levels so as to produce a single, compound effect. The rise and fall of dramatic tension as the play's action unfolds, moving sometimes quickly and sometimes slowly, sometimes with great force and sometimes more quietly, creates a rhythmic experience as rich and as specific as that of any symphony. Unlike a symphony, however, in which the composer can provide specific instructions about tempo and changes in dynamics, the rhythm of a play is more a matter of implied proportion.

As you traced the action of *Hamlet*, for instance, you could sense when the action wanted to move slowly, and when more quickly; when dramatic tension could be relaxed through humor or reflection, and when it should be at fever pitch. Within these proportional guidelines, you will have to guide the specific rhythmic qualities of each element in your production as it emerges in rehearsal. You will want, therefore, to heighten your sensitivity to these elements during your initial study of the play.

This, then, is the basic shape of traditional dramatic action: A central conflict is established by an inciting incident; it causes a sequence of complications to unfold as tension mounts; and at last a moment of crisis occurs which resolves the central conflict and unleashes the climax. This traditional shape can be described by the graph in Figure 6-1.

This graph traces the rise and fall of the energy of the play as it moves forward in time. In a well-unified production we experience this rise and flow

FIGURE 6-1.   Traditional Play Structure.

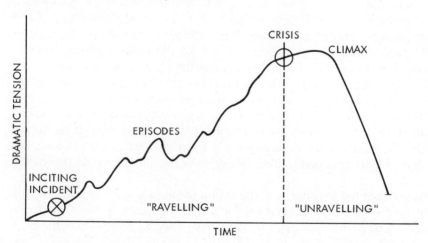

as a single rhythm. This particular rhythm is fundamental to the performing arts; it is the shape of a symphony, for instance, and of most dances. In fact, it is the fundamental rhythm of breath, of life itself.

Of course, no single play has this perfectly ideal shape. In some, the inciting incident may be delayed, giving you the problem of a prolonged exposition which may be difficult to pace (as in *The Tempest*); in others, the crisis and climax may occur early, leaving you with a prolonged denouement which is anticlimactic and difficult to sustain (as in *Romeo and Juliet*).

Whatever the shape of the specific play, you must recognize the milestones of inciting incident, crisis, and climax in order to guide the rhythm of the production so as to fulfill this element of the play's system of norms. Many of the directors I queried agree that one of the most important aspects of directing is the musical, or purely rhythmic, shaping of the performance which establishes the priorities for the weighting and tempo of each individual moment.

Exercise 6: The Shape of the Action

Review your breakdown of *Hamlet*, noting the shaping of the action:
1. Specify the inciting incident.
2. Determine for yourself the main crisis of the play; be specific.
3. Outline the minor crises which lead to this main crisis (they may or may not coincide with the divisions of the scenes) and mark each (in my sample breakdown, each scene crisis is marked ***).
4. Specify the climax.
5. Now plot these points on a graph like Figure 6-1; make the shape of your action line as specific to the rise and fall of the tension, scene by scene, as you can.
6. Vary the heaviness of the action line to indicate the dynamic of the action, heavy for intense action, lighter for more quiet times.

FOCUSING ON A THEME

Most good plays contain a variety of thematic elements interwoven in the action. Each is a specific perspective from which the action can be viewed, or a possible meaning which can be drawn from it. For instance, *Hamlet* contains several recurrent themes, some of which could be summarized thus:

   1. The complex relationship which binds sons and mothers (the so-called Oedipal theme);

2. The way in which unchecked evil breeds ever more evil (as we see in the poison which flows from Claudius, both literally and figuratively, until it infects the entire court);

3. The conflict between the absolute ethic of the feudal world and the relative ethic of the humanist world, which tears Hamlet between his sense of duty to the Ghost's demand for vengeance and his "university" sense that "two wrongs do not necessarily make a right";

4. The need for the balancing of Will and Understanding ("Thus conscience doth make cowards of us all.")

Each of these thematic lines moves through the play, and the action brings each into focus at various times. A good production should allow all the significant themes of a play to be expressed, but it is also useful to establish your sense of priority among the possible themes by selecting one as your dominant concern.

In a sense, you are trying to answer the question, "Why was this play written?" You are substituting yourself for the dramatist (as Saint-Denis suggested) and identifying again the motivating energy which drives the play. If you can experience this energy (and we often experience it without being able to verbalize it), then you will be able to see how it is expressed in the very fabric of the play's action.

Your charting of the play's action has enabled you to recognize the specific episodic crises leading up to the main crisis and eventual climax of the play; these are the moments at which the action of the play is crystallized. While these milestones of the action may or may not be the same moments at which thematic meaning is also crystallized, you can look at them from the perspective of your thematic priority and begin to understand the specific relationship of action and meaning which unifies the play.

In *Hamlet*, for instance, I selected the theme of "the balancing of Understanding and Will" as my highest priority. From this perspective I could look at each of the crucial choices which move the action and see in each the development of this central theme and how it moved toward its fulfillment in the central crisis and eventual climax of the play. The most important choices in the scenario of the play, as I saw it, were:

1. Hamlet's reaction to the Ghost's command, and his swearing to obey.

2. Time passes, and even though he has thwarted Claudius's attempts to use Polonius, Rosencrantz, and Guildenstern, and even his beloved Ophelia, to spy into his true purpose, Hamlet is frustrated by his own lack of more definite action. He chooses next to use a play to "catch the conscience of the King."

3. The play-within-the-play indeed catches Claudius's conscience, and Hamlet is then faced with the choice of killing him at prayer; he chooses to wait for "a fitter place."

4. A few minutes later, Hamlet thinks he has Claudius in "a fitter place," his mother's closet. If he were to pause and reflect a moment, he would realize that the figure behind the arras could not be Claudius, whom he has just left at prayer; but he is swept away by his passion (he has "tainted his mind") and mistakenly kills Polonius.

5.   His passionate error puts him into Claudius's power, and he is exiled. As he is about to leave for what he suspects will be "knavery in England," he watches the army of Fortinbras and realizes how remiss he has been in acting with understanding, and vows that "henceforth" his thoughts (Understanding) will "be bloody" (Will).

6.   This crucial choice having been made, fate sweeps him toward the climax via his choices on the ship and his choice to fight Laertes despite a clear premonition of his own death, until, his fate already sealed, he makes his last choice, to kill Claudius.

With this specific perception of the unity of theme and action, you will be better prepared to assist your fellow workers in aligning their efforts with the intrinsic energies of the play, and better prepared to make the influential design and casting choices you must soon make.

THE HAMLET LOG, PART 2: EARLY PREPARATIONS—AUGUST 16-30

During the weeks that preceed my trip to Ashland for auditions, I read the play many times over. Despite my previous production (or rather, *because* of it) I try to read the play as if for the first time, forgetting that first (or any) production as best I can, reading for "mere pleasure." Of course, I retain certain key questions which arose from my earlier work, seeking answers to them with fresh eyes.

The most important question is the exact location of the crisis, since answering this question will force me to specify my understanding of the action of the play. I have found that identifying the crisis helps me to clarify the nature and configuration of the main action of the play, and to understand how each plot line, each character and relationship, contributes to the whole—in short, I can begin to understand the superobjective of each element of the play.

As I look for the crisis, I begin working backward from the end of the play to see at what point the outcome is finally determined. In the last scene things happen so quickly, and with such a sense of inevitability, that I cannot see a point at which the play offers any real alternatives to the course of the action. True, there are a number of things that might have happened differently—what if Gertrude hadn't drunk the poison, what if the swords hadn't been accidently switched, and so on. But these possibilities lie outside the world of the play; I am searching for alternatives offered by the play itself, and in the climactic duelling scene none seem to exist. In fact, it is interesting that everything in the latter part of the play (from Hamlet's sea voyage on) happens not by anyone's plan but by accident—that is, by the action of "a divinity that shapes our ends/Rough-hew them how we will."

I look next to the brief scene with Hamlet, Horatio, and Osric which preceeds the dueling scene, and here there is a choice of great importance made by Hamlet—to accept the challenge offered by Claudius and Laertes through Osric. This choice is given special emphasis by Shakespeare because Hamlet seems to have a dire premonition concerning it ("But thou wouldst not think how ill all's here about my heart"). He senses foul play and has a premonition of his own death, but he dismisses his fear as cowardly ("as would perhaps trouble a woman"), and in any case irrelevant, since there is nothing we can do to forestall our fated end ("If it be now, 'tis not to come; if it be not to come, it will be now; if it be not now, yet it will come"). He chooses instead to "defy augury," to face the unknown without "deep plots," and to simply be *ready*, for he now knows that "Readiness is all."

This choice, it seems to me, sums up what Hamlet has learned in the course of the play. He is neither scheming to kill Claudius nor retreating from his responsibility; he is simply ready to act in the moment according to a deep sense of purpose, trusting to the "providence that shapes our end" to bring whatever it may, including death. In a real sense he is finally ready to live because he is also ready to die.

As important as this choice is, however, I do not think it is the crucial choice of the play; given Hamlet's frame of mind, there seems to be no real alternative. The crisis, then, I think, will occur at that moment when Hamlet *becomes ready* to make this choice. As I trace back through the play, I see that he seems ready when he comes back from the sea voyage; the story he tells Horatio about the finding and forging of Claudius's treacherous letter is a peon to readiness. How amazing it is, he says, how heaven itself conspires with us when we are ready. He happened to find the letter in the dark, he happened to have the penmanship he needed to forge it, he happened to have his father's signet ring to reseal it: in all these things "was heaven ordinant." Indeed, providence is all-powerful once we stop resisting her, and Hamlet will not resist her after his return from the sea. His ponderings on mortality with the gravedigger are the thoughts of someone who has developed intimacy with his own mortality; his actions at the funeral of Ophelia are spontaneous and unrestrained.

The crucial choice for Hamlet, then, and for the play, is his choice to be ready for whatever may come. No longer will he resist the opportunities offered by providence by undue reflection; nor will he try to dictate to providence by scheming or pressing the issue beyond what is reasonable. This choice, I believe, is made in the last of the great soliloquies (Act IV, scene iv) just before he embarks for England. As he watches the army of Fortinbras marching to fight over a plot of worthless earth, he realizes that his own dilemma counts for little in the vast scheme of things, and that his prolonged moral deliberation has exceeded reasonable limits. He asks himself first whether God, endowing man with the capacity for "godlike reason," intended him to live in "bestial oblivion" (in his case, the forgetfulness of his Father's commandment: "Remember me" is the last cry of the Ghost). Hamlet then shifts to the opposite extreme:

Now, whether it be
Bestial oblivion, or some craven scruple
Of thinking too precisely on th' event—
A thought which, quartered, hath but one part wisdom
And ever three parts coward—I do not know
Why yet I live to say, "This thing's to do,"
Sith I have cause, and will, and strength, and means
To do't.

This is not a new thought for him, but his determination at last to get on with it comes in the face of a larger perspective and a sense that his self-esteem is on the line:

Rightly to be great
Is not to stir without great argument,
But greatly to find quarrel in a straw
When honor's at the stake.

At last Hamlet is in the position E. M. W. Tillyard describes in *The Elizabethan World Picture* as the true Elizabethan sense of "goodness," having both the Understanding of that which needs to be done and the Will to do it. Just as Lear has Will without Understanding, Hamlet has Understanding without Will—and the main action of both of their plays is the painful process whereby the deficiency is made up and balance (and goodness) achieved.

This central perception of the play's underlying action will provide the foundation on which the many judgments required to initiate the production can be based. Casting, the early design discussions, my further work on the text, and my planning for the rehearsal process will proceed from this sense of the central thematic values and arrangement of the play's action.

Of course, we are not always blessed with what seems to be a strong sense of the "soul" of the play—(I did not have it during my first production, which was in many ways was a "sketchbook" for this second production) so that sometimes our early rehearsals serve as a mutual exploration of the play in order to discover just such a production focus.

I have no doubt, of course, that the specific form in which this recognition will manifest itself in this production will spring from the creative interaction among myself, the designers, and mainly the actors, and that my present view of the play really amounts to little more than a working convenience. I feel fortunate though, given the complexity of the undertaking, to have it, since the set, the costuming, and the casting will perforce be decided months in advance of rehearsals.

SEVEN
UNDERSTANDING
CHARACTER

Now that you have developed a grasp of the essential action of the play, you will begin to examine the means through which that action is made tangible: the characters, their thoughts and behaviors. Your study of these elements will further illuminate your sense of the action, giving it greater specificity. At the same time, your sense of the action will guide you in the recognition of the most important aspects of character, language, and the other elements of the drama.

CHARACTER AND ACTION

When we discussed the unity of plot, we saw that each event in the plot sequence was linked by the principle of cause and effect: Something happens which causes a reaction, the reaction being a new event which in turn causes another reaction, and so on. Most often these reactions occur through a character who, in response to one event, decides to do something, which in turn causes someone else to decide to do something, and so on.

This is an important (and often neglected) fact in understanding the chain of causation which unifies the plot: *The point at which one link of the chain connects with another is usually a choice, conscious or unconscious, made by one of the characters.* It is through making these choices that the characters serve as what Aristotle called the "agents" of the action.

Because Hamlet fears that the Ghost may be a devil in disguise, he decides that he must have clear proof of Claudius's guilt. The arrival of the Players gives him the idea for the "Mousetrap"; Claudius's reaction to the play-within-the-play—momentary remorse and prayer—in turn leads to Hamlet's choice of whether to kill the praying Claudius or not. He chooses to postpone the killing "to a fitter time," and this leads to the killing of Polonius, which brings about Hamlet's exile, which in turn leads to the events on the ship, which finally prove to Hamlet that Heaven is "on his side," so that he returns ready to act at last.

Of course, events do not always result directly from choices made by characters: sometimes this is an indirect process: In drama, as in life, the ramification of a choice is not always predictable or direct. Coincidences and accidents do happen; Hamlet just happens to come upon the praying Claudius, and he doesn't mean to kill Polonius. Nevertheless, the importance of such coincidences and mistakes is the way in which they generate and influence the actions of the characters, which remains our main concern. Drama is, as Aristotle pointed out, an imitation of *human* action.

At each step in the sequence of the plot, then, we see how the choices made by the characters move the action. These choices both express and, in a sense, determine the nature of those characters: Claudius is a schemer who manipulates people with no regard for their fate (Polonius is similar in this), Rosencrantz and Guildenstern are ambitious and "make love to this employment," Hamlet is obsessed with ethical and moral concerns on the one hand ("conscience doth make cowards of us all") and driven by duty and his own emotions on the other.

This is why understanding the flow of the action is also the basis for understanding the characters: The playwright created each character so that he or she would make the particular choices required to advance each step in the action. Understanding the specific way in which each character contributes to the flow of the action, moment by moment, is what Stanislavski called the *superobjective.* It is this understanding which you, as director, most owe to your actors. This is what Jack O'Brien means when he says:

> I think the essence of moving the audience is giving the company the same story to tell, to a man, to the lift of a finger. Everyone is telling the same tale, and the truth, then, can be inescapable.

When dealing with a traditional plot based upon ordinary causation, then, it is useful to think of the sequence of events as growing out of a central conflict established by an inciting incident and being linked by pivotal choices made by the characters. You could even create a synopsis of the play by tracing these pivotal choices. This would provide an extremely useful sense of the play's structure for a director, since it generates an understanding of the function of each character within the whole, and prepares us to assist the actors in focusing on those choices (and hence the qualities of character influencing those choices). When the director has grasped the overall structure of the play in the way we are describing here, he or she will be prepared to assist the actor in finding this superobjective.

THE NETWORK OF RELATIONSHIPS

As we have seen, the action of most plays moves by the causal linking of events, one event causing another through the reactions (choices) of the characters. One character chooses to do something, and in reaction another character chooses to do something else, and so on. The way in which the characters influence one another is determined by the nature of their relationships—or, one might say that the relationships have been created by the playwright so as to allow the characters to influence one another in specific ways required by the action. In a real sense, then, we can say that *character relationships are the conduit through which dramatic action flows.*

Of all the given circumstances, the relationships among characters deserve the most careful examination. The director must see clearly the entire network of the relationships within the play, for it is through this network that the action must flow. No single character can be understood outside of this network, and these relationships must in turn be understood as serving the main action of the play. This is not only important to an understanding of the play's unity; it will also serve as the basis for casting of the play, as we will discuss in Chapter Ten. For now, let's examine some of the ways in which relationships serve action and meaning.

In traditional plays, there will be a central relationship through which the main conflict flows: it is usually this central relationship which contains the seed of conflict. The characters involved in this central relationship are mutually interdependent; you can't say much about Othello, for instance, without taking Iago into account, and vice versa. Even in a play without an antagonist and protagonist in conflict, there will be a central relationship of mutually defined characters who act together to bring about the action: Didi and Gogo in *Waiting for Godot*, for instance. Whatever the structure, the important thing is to realize that the action flows through relationship because the characters do things to each other, and that the characters therefore define each other.

Besides serving as the conduit for the action, relationships may also serve to express the thematic concerns of the play. Most commonly, this is achieved through contrasted pairings of characters, the contrast serving to make the point; so-called "sub-plots" usually function in this way. In *Hamlet*, for instance, Hamlet is compared to Laertes and, to a lesser degree, to Fortinbras. All three are sons bent on avenging the deaths of their fathers, and the play compares the effect of the task on each. Laertes falls prey to his own passion and loses his honor through the deceitful plot of the poisoned sword; Hamlet, by contrast, heeds the Ghost's advice, "But howsoever thou pursues this act, Taint not thy mind . . ." and maintains his sense of morality throughout, though he is *so* morally cautious that he fails to "pursue this act" at all. It is Fortinbras, whose father has been killed by Hamlet's father, who gives Hamlet his final example of how one should behave in this situation. As Hamlet stands watching the army of Fortinbras, he says,

> Examples gross as earth exhort me.
> Witness this army of such mass and charge,
> Led by a delicate and tender prince,
> Whose spirit, with divine ambition puffed,
> Makes mouths at the invisible event,
> Exposing what is mortal and unsure
> To all that fortune, death, and danger dare,
> Even for an eggshell. Rightly to be great
> Is not to stir without great argument,
> But greatly to find quarrel in a straw
> When honor's at the stake.

It is no accident that Fortinbras inherits Hamlet's rightful throne at the end of the play.

While Shakespeare was especially fond of the device of contrasted character pairings, even modern playwrights use them in similar ways, often as exemplars who embody aspects of a choice facing the protagonist. In *Death of a Salesman*, for instance, Willy's brother Ben and his next door neighbor, Charlie, embody the opposing aspects of the choice he faces: to live with quiet acceptance of his own self-worth as Charlie does, or to win fortune and status through daring enterprise as did Brother Ben. (Compare the way in which Shakespeare uses Falstaff and Hotspur to embody the choice between youthful diversion and kingly duty facing Prince Hal in *Henry IV, i*).

The pairing of characters is not always based on an adversarial relationship (as in hero and villain) nor on a thematic contrast. Sometimes characters are paired as a complementary team, and such pairings usually reveal some psychological or emotional truth. In Beckett's *Endgame* for instance, Hamm and Clov embody the comic and tragic postures toward life; like Lear and Gloucester in *King Lear*, they also embody the physical and the spiritual modes of human torment. When characters are thus used to embody various aspects of the human condition, we often feel as if they would, taken together, form a single personality. The great teams of our tradition all reflect this.

Other characters may fit into the network of a play in various ways, some as simple as the delivery of information (the Greek messengers), or to represent a particular point of view (the "raissoneur" in a French farce). Whatever the function, each character must be seen as an active and essential element in the entire network through which the play's action and meaning flows.

Exercise 7: Mapping Relationships

One good way of clarifying your understanding of your play's network of relationships is to make a schematic expression of the relationships, like an organizational flow chart or a map of the network of relationships. Place what you consider the central relationships at center, then work out from them, trying to account for all the characters in the play (including "group" characters like the Rabble in Hamlet). Use heavy lines to indicate the main routes of interaction, light or dotted lines for minor ones. Invent any other mapping devices you may need, such as intersections, by passes, or indirect routes of influence. Use arrows to indicate the direction of the major influence when it is unilateral, or double-headed arrows to indicate a reciprocal relationship. Below is an example from *Hamlet*.

THE INDIVIDUAL CHARACTER

Your work on your play so far has helped you to develop a clear idea of the function of each of the characters within the scheme of the overall action, what Stanislavski called the superobjective of each character. Consider: the greatest difference between a character in a play and a person in real life is that the character has a given reason for being. As a created element within a created whole, the character has a specific task to fulfill in relation to that

FIGURE 7-1.   Mapping Relationships in *Hamlet*.

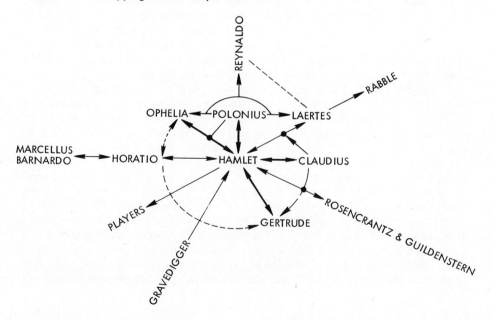

whole; the entire "life" or "reality" of that character is derived from this function.

Your understanding of a character will differ from that of most actors in this regard. You are seeing the character from the outside, concerned primarily with the way he or she functions within the network of relationships through which the action flows; the actor is necessarily on the inside looking out, concerned primarily with the invisible world of needs, choices, and objectives, and seeing the world of the play through that character's eyes. One of your most important tasks as a director is to assist the actors in doing this, and your study of individual characters prepares you for this coaching in the same way that a good orchestra conductor knows something about the bowing of a violin.

The business of coaching, of course, differs from actor to actor: Some need a good deal of assistance; others need to be left entirely alone (even, perhaps, when they think they are in trouble). All your actors, however, need to receive a clear initial sense of the direction in which they are to work, with regular feedback on their progress. The basis for this sense of direction, and for your evaluation of their progress, is your understanding of the function of their character within the scheme of the whole.

Beyond this, your study of character is also intended to prepare you to cast the play so that the actors have a reasonable chance to fulfill the requirements of their parts; this requires that you examine the specifications provided within the text for each character.

The text provides information about each character in three ways: through *explicit* information (Hamlet is 30 years old, a university student with a penchant for philosophical reflection); through *hearsay* descriptions by other characters (Ophelia says he has an "unmatched form and feature"); and through material *implied by the action* (Hamlet is deeply religious and physically adept). Each of these may be valuable, but keep in mind that they are not equally dependable as evidence. The first (explicit information) must be taken at face value, even when some translation may be necessary; the second (hearsay evidence) has to be judged according to the reliability of the speaker (Hamlet may not be as handsome as Ophelia thinks he is); the last (implications from the action) may be tied to interpretive choices of your own. For instance, we know that although Gertrude used to "hang upon" her dead husband, she was seduced by Claudius and now enjoys an active sexual life with him; we can infer from this that she is a very voluptuous and physical woman who is ruled by her passion, and/or that the old king was a stern and somewhat overprotective father and husband who left his wife unsatisfied, and/or that Claudius is an attractive and sexy guy who is a pretty smooth operator.

When we make such *inferential choices*, we must test them by working them through in our mind, imagining them in actual scenes, and discovering whether they are supported or resisted by the specifics of the text, for finally it is the requirements of the action that must reveal the rightness of our understanding of character. The action is the world in which the character lives, and no personality can be judged out of its context.

CHARACTER AND LANGUAGE

There remains one enormously important source of information about character: The way in which personality is encoded in speech itself. In fact, well-written dialogue can do much to generate the sense of character directly in a sensitive actor.

For instance, the character's choice of words (diction) can express educational and social background; the structuring of that language (syntax) can reveal the quality of the character's thought processes; the emotional weight of certain words (connotation) can express values and feelings. Powerful images and sensory associations can not only reflect the character's mind, but trigger the actor's own memory as well.

More subtly, the act of articulating well-written dialogue can directly influence the actor's organism. A playwright, unlike a novelist, writes for the living voice; he or she understands that the text will be performed by an actor, and the shaping and qualities of speeches are created with their effect on the speaker in mind. Thus, the psychophysical impact of the language on the speaker is one of our main concerns: The rhythmic and tonal qualities of the speech and the effect on the speaker's consciousness through the muscular act of articulation makes the character's speech a mechanism whereby the playwright can reach directly into the consciousness of the actor.

One of your first rehearsal tasks will be to assist the actors in immersing themselves in the language of the play and allowing the experience of it to resonate in them in both physical and psychological ways. It will be useful, therefore, if you do it for yourself too.

Exercise 8: Living Language

Select one important speech by any character in *Hamlet* for the following experiments:

1. Paraphrase: To begin appreciating the author's choice of specific words that carry not only literal meaning, but also emotional and musical values as well, try making a translation from his words into your own; try to capture as much of the value of the original as you can. Be aware of what is lost in translation.

2. Song and dance: As a way of experiencing the rhythmic and tonal qualities of the author's language, try turning this same scene into a musical number involving song and dance: What sounds are dominant in the original; what are its rhythmic

qualities? Try to reflect these specific qualities directly in your musical version; don't generalize by using operatic or musical comedy style indiscriminately.

3. Collage: To heighten your response to the imagery and sensory associations of the text, try expressing your speech as a collage: What materials, what textures, what colors and composition, will capture the life of the speech in a visual form?

CHARACTER SPECIFICATIONS

Whether it is explicit, implicit, hearsay, or deduced from the character's speech, the information we get from the text about character falls into four broad categories: physical qualities, social qualities, psychological qualities, and moral qualities (for a full discussion of each, see *The Actor at Work*, Lesson 16). One or another of these may be dominant depending on the nature of the play and the role; moral qualities, for example, tend to be more important in tragedy than in comedy, and more important in major characters than in minor ones. Obviously, however, all four types of qualities work in tandem to express the essential personality of a character; in our example of the "voluptuous" Gertrude, for instance, we were using a physical quality to express a psychological quality.

Let's look at some of the character specifications in *Hamlet*.

Exercise 9: Character Specifications

Using the following list, make a personality sketch for each of the major characters in *Hamlet*. For now, use only the information that is explicit in the text, or which is supplied by reliable witnesses; you want to be sure of the hard evidence before you begin to make implications.

1. Physical traits—Age, physique, condition, body type, vocal characteristics, any unusual marks or handicaps.
2. Social traits—Manner of relating to other people, range and intensity of various relationships.
3. Psychological Traits—Is the character's thinking simple or complex, fast or slow, insightful or shallow?
4. Moral traits—What does this character consider good or evil? What is his or her code of ethical conduct?

You have now completed your preparatory analysis of the play; you are ready to begin forming specific ideas about the production to translate your understanding into a living stage event.

THE HAMLET LOG, PART 3:
PREPARATION FOR CASTING
AND DESIGN MEETINGS—AUGUST 16-31

Over the next two weeks I continue to review the script and some criticism. Since I know that some cutting will be necessary, I am eager to provide the actors with an initial version; it is far easier to restore a cut than to make one after lines have been learned. I have made a chart of all the characters and the scenes in which they appear, and am consolidating some of the smaller roles into a few ongoing characters, both to cut down on the size of the cast and to assist the audience in keeping track of who's who.

I have also made a chart of the relationships, since this will be the main consideration in the casting. I am especially concerned about the relative ages of the central characters, and about the familial and political units they form.

I've reviewed the language a bit, and have enjoyed reading aloud to myself for the feel of it; the prosody is quite irregular, but for each variation there is a compelling emotional or dramatic reason. You can actually feel the drive of the story through the language; Shakespeare clearly had both a strong need to write this play and the mastery of language and stage that he needed to do it.

I find also that a sense of the physical environment is gradually becoming clear, though the images are those of colors, textures, and shapes rather than of a specific setting.

EIGHT
FORMING A
PRODUCTION CONCEPT

You have now "taken the play apart" through your analysis of its action, structure, character, and language; you are now ready to begin "putting it back together." The first step is to decide how you will use the resources of the stage to manifest the life of the play, and to prepare to communicate your approach to your fellow workers. This is the formation of your *production concept.*

In the European tradition, where resident companies and longer rehearsal periods are more common than in America, the production concept is often allowed to evolve gradually, in the flow of rehearsals. I remember watching a rehearsal at the National Theatre of Strasbourg: A temporary working set of stock flats had been erected in the rehearsal hall, with some rudimentary lighting. The director was working with two actors on a scene in which an argument between them resulted in one of them walking out in a huff; they were evidently having trouble shaping the action to this point. After a few attempts, the director called to a young man and woman seated nearby; they turned out to be the scenic and lighting designers. After some animated talk, they started pushing walls and step units around, altering the configuration of the space. The actors joined in and ran bits of the scene as the space took a new shape; finally one of the actors rushed up a step unit, and the lighting designer positioned a backlight at its top; delighted with the effect, everyone took a break.

As I watched, I thought of descriptions of similar scenes in Nikolai Gorchakov's *Stanislavski Directs.* For Stanislavski, the action of a scene was inextricable from the environment in which that action occured; when an adjustment in the interpretation of a scene was made, the rehearsal was often interrupted "while the desks were being removed from the stage and the correct square table was being found." Once the correct design of action and environment was found, the evolved ground plan was rendered into a complete set, often long before the production opened, so that a good many rehearsals were conducted with set, costumes, and lights.

In today's theatre, especially in America, it is rare to find opportunities to work in this evolutionary way. Since the time needed to construct sets and costumes usually exceeds the rehearsal time available to us, we are often forced to determine much about the physical staging of the play well in advance of the actual rehearsals. In such cases, you must develop your production concept, especially as it determines scenery and costuming, in the same spirit as Stanislavski's search for the correct table: You and your designers will work together to discover the unity of action and environment that will make the physical staging of the play an expressive embodiment of the world of the play.

It is important, therefore, that you think of your production concept not as a description of the final form of the production, but rather as the starting point for the evolutionary process by which that form will be generated through your interaction with your producer and designers. The production concept is really a way of communicating to your fellow artists in a way which assists them in aligning their efforts with yours. To this end, it should clearly communicate at least four things:

1. Your values and priorities regarding the play's action, its structure and meaning;
2. Your ideas about the characters and their relationships;
3. Your ideas about the play's physical environment;
4. The strategy by which the evolutionary process of design and rehearsal will proceed.

In this chapter we will discuss each of these elements of the production concept, and the final preparations you must make for those critical first meetings with the designers.

PREPARING THE PRELIMINARY PRODUCTION SCRIPT

The basis for your initial discussions with designers will, it is hoped, be a careful reading of the play by all concerned. At some early point, then, you should specify the preliminary form of the script. Several considerations may be important here.

Some plays appear in several versions: An older play may have more than one edition (*Hamlet* has several which differ in important details); a foreign play may have several translations, some of which are quite different from one another; even a recent play may have been published in two or more forms (for example, the original edition of *The Glass Menagerie* and its later "acting version"). In all these cases, you must review the alternatives and select the one you prefer; if no one is entirely satisfactory, you may even consider preparing your own version.

The matter of adjustments to the text is another consideration. While conservative directors are against textual alterations in principle, most directors take a somewhat more liberal stance and will consider moderate adjustments of a script for several reasons. And while such adjustments are best made in the actual flow of rehearsal, there are some which may be made in advance for reasons of clarity and efficiency. Let's consider some of the reasons for cutting a script:

1. *Cutting for length*
Some plays, both old and new, need trimming. An uncut production of *Hamlet* in today's theatre, for instance, would probably approach or exceed four hours running time; a European audience might be capable of maintaining concentration for such a period, but the rhythm of American life tends to make three hours a limit that is exceeded only at great peril.

The length of segments between intermissions is also a concern, though this must be seen within the context of the whole evening and in relationship to the flow of the action. There is a natural sag in audience energy about an hour into an act, so it is important that the shape of the action provide the necessary momentum to compensate for this. In some situations, then, the number and placement of intermissions may be an important choice (as the *Hamlet* Log demonstrates).

2. *Changes to simplify staging*
It is sometimes necessary or preferable to simplify the production demands of a play by reducing the number of locales or the number of characters. Scenes requiring a shift in locale may be cut, combined, or relocated (the short scene in which Horatio receives Hamlet's letter from the sailors is sometimes cut; its essential information can be eliminated or moved into another scene). Smaller roles may be written out or combined into ongoing composite roles to reduce the size of the cast (several gentlemen, servants, and messengers in *Hamlet* were combined into Cornelius and Voltemand). Sometimes the need to double the available actors into several roles may necessitate some script adjustments.

3. *Adjustments for shape and focus*
More problematical are adjustments designed to enhance the director's view of the essential shape of the action or the thematic focus of the play. Such a course of action must be clearly justified by a deficiency in the play or by the impossibility of realizing the author's intention without such changes; even then great care and discretion are required. Nevertheless, not all plays are perfect in their construction, nor is a script generated in one theatrical circumstance necessarily right in every detail for another, so we should not rule out the possibility of such adjustments as the need arises.

4. *Indications of possible major cues*
Your preliminary production script may also contain an indication of what you envision about the dynamics of the production, especially as they might effect the set, costumes, or lights. Where, for instance, do you think important shifts in time or place occur? The passage of time in *Hamlet*, for example, is an important element in the action, and the preliminary script specified it scene by scene ("early morning, three weeks later").

Even more important may be the location of major shifts in emotional tone. In *Hamlet* I feel that the prolonged celebration of Claudius's coronation becomes increasingly licentious, peaking in the mousetrap scene, which should have an animalistic and nightmarish quality (which we manifested physically by torchlight and animal masks). The tone then shifts radically to the introspective, solitary quality of the praying scene that follows.

Important changes in characters should be noted as well. For instance, the change in Hamlet when he returns from his sea voyage needs to be reflected in his clothing, and Gertrude's dress in the last scene helps to express the moral change caused in her by her confrontation with Hamlet in the Closet scene.

Such indications as these are not meant to determine actual light or sound cues, or specific costume changes, but they will help the designers to begin thinking about the play dynamically, with something of your sense of its shape and progression. Since change is the essence of drama, this sense of the play's dynamic is an important aspect of your early communications.

Remember, of course, that your preliminary production script is subject to change. You will finally discover the text only through the rehearsal process, and it is here that the final adjustments to the text (if any) will be made. Any preliminary adjustments should be communicated to the actors and designers in this spirit.

Exercise 10: Cutting a Script

Select a sequence of at least three scenes from *Hamlet* and try cutting it. For purposes of this exercise, imagine that you must reduce its length in any way possible, and reduce the number of actors and locales required as well. See what you need to do to maintain the essential action and meaning. An example from the prompt book of *Hamlet* will be found in the Appendix.

THE SCENE/CHARACTER/TIME/PLACE BREAKDOWN

Preparing a Scene/Character/Time/Place Breakdown will help you go even further in understanding the potential dynamic of your production as a reflection of the dynamic of the play.

This chart begins simply as an outline of which characters appear in which scenes; as such, it is enormously useful in your communication with your costume designer, and in your preparation for casting. If you add to your chart the time and place of each scene, you will find that it also opens up a new perception of the way time and place are organized in the play, which will be invaluable in your discussions with your scenic and lighting designers.

As you trace the entrances and exits of the characters, and the groupings they form, you will see that the play breaks into units I call "rehearsal scenes," segments that would make efficient use of groups of characters for rehearsal purposes. These segments may be shorter than the scene divisions specified by the author; I use a shorthand method of naming such scenes, for example, 22A, 22B (Act II, scene ii, rehearsal sections A and B). With these breakdowns, the chart will be very useful in planning later rehearsal strategy. You may see a value, for instance, in one day rehearsing all the court scenes as a group, not so much for the sake of efficiency as to focus on the developments and changes of relationship which occur within that group of characters.

In a play as complex as *Hamlet*, such a chart obviously helps to keep details straight; but even in a logistically uncomplicated play like *Waiting for Godot*, you will begin to see that the chart expresses much more than mere mechanical details: It can be a graphic expression of much that you have come to recognize about the play's unity; it can help to crystallize the flow and function of each character in relation to the whole, and of the author's manipulation of time and place as they effect action and meaning.

I find the preparation of this chart an invaluable culmination of my study of the play and an essential step into the specifics of the production concept.

Exercise 11: The Scene/Character/Time/Place Chart

On a legal-size sheet of lined paper, draw ten vertical columns to the right of the margin line, each about one-half inch wide. At the top of the page, block out three horizontal bands about one inch high. In the left-hand margin, label these "Scene," "Time," and "Place." Continuing down the left-hand margin, write the names of all the characters in *Hamlet* on the remaining horizontal lines.

Start working through the first two acts of *Hamlet*, filling in the chart scene by scene. Note the important details of time and place in each scene, and place a mark on the line of each character who appears in it. When you come to a long scene, such as 22, decide if you want to break it into rehearsal scenes labelled A, B, C, and so on.

In the empty space at the bottom of the page, make whatever notes seem important about each scene. I also like to record the length of the scene, in pages and fractions of pages, for reference in planning rehearsals.

As you work, see what perceptions begin to crystallize about the play's structure, its use of time and place, and the functions of the characters.

(The actual chart used in the Oregon *Hamlet* appears in the Appendix.)

THE LANDSCAPE OF THE PLAY

Your study of the play has begun to generate in you a sense of the play's world. Like any world, it has certain underlying natural principles which give it a logic of its own. When we enter the play's world, we have a sense of a specific place; there is a consistency between its physical properties and the behavior and values of its inhabitants.

Beside the qualities of the place, the time of the play is also influential. In your research and study of the given circumstances you have seen how the historical moment in which the play occurs carries with it certain values which are operative in the action and in the lives of the characters. Our concern for the period is driven not so much by an historical interest as by our desire to better understand the *life* it contains. As Stanislavski put it to one of his student directors in *Stanislavski Directs*:

> Do you want the audience seeing your production to be interested in the lives of human beings or in an excellent likeness to the prints of that period? . . . One should always strive for a combination (of historical accuracy and inner life).[14]

Our aim, then, is to reveal the quality of life within the world of the play, not only the way in which it is like our own lives, but the way in which it is different. By journeying into this other world we may learn, by comparison, about our own.

This sense of a play as a journey into a time and place was beautifully expressed by Zelda Fichandler in an interview :

> Sometimes I say that doing a play is like going on an "anthropological dig" where you're collecting data about a culture, be it the ancient Greeks or today's America. You're laying open the roots of that culture: how certain people felt, thought, ate, worshipped their gods, made love, had children, raised them; you uncover the whole culture. You go on a *dig*, which is a fine word because it means you're getting down to the bottom of things. And these little marks on the page, these little animal tracks that we call words, are just the surface; they're like tracks in the topsoil that we have to dig beneath, to discover the bones and the shards and the things that will tell us what kind of animal made those marks. We have to put all the pieces together and make a world out of it, a civilization.

This sense of journey and exploration is at the heart of our concern for the physical landscape of the play. We want to reflect the play's landscape in our physical production, but not in mere external detail; we want to understand it as the condition of the life of the characters and of the events which occur between them. The set, lights, props and costumes must themselves become characters in the play, expressing the life of the action in its human as well as its historical dimensions.

Through your study of the play's action, its given circumstances, the life of its characters, and the stylistic properties of its language, you have been digging into the play's landscape for some time now, and you will continue to dig throughout your rehearsal process; but already you have found enough evidence to generate many of the physical specifics of your production. Soon you will have to communicate your sense of this landscape to others. This can be done through verbal description: Through analogies, metaphors, and imagery; or, perhaps best of all, by taking your designers on a trip into the play's landscape, talking through the action, looking at the scenery as you go, stopping to enjoy certain key passages in which meaning is crystallized, meeting the characters.

Exercise 12: The Landscape of the Play

A. The Physical Climate—From your understanding of the given circumstances, action, characters, and language of *Hamlet* (Exercises 4 through 9) begin to imagine ways of expressing the physical world of the play in concrete terms such as,

1. Texture (rough, smooth, hard, soft)
2. Color
3. Value (bright, dark)
4. Kinesthetic Quality (nervous, joyful, depressed)
5. Specific Imagery (a fortress, a disco, and so on)

Prepare a collage which expresses this landscape, using drawings, bits of fabric, wood, metal, paper, or pictures cut from magazines. Your aim is not to design a set but to create a concrete expression of the physical qualities of the play's landscape.

B. The psychological climate—Consider also the effect of the play's physical world on the values of the characters, and vice versa: What is expensive or desirable? What is cheap or common? How does the ethical behavior of the characters reflect this? How does the physical and social climate of Denmark, for instance, allow Claudius to do what he does? How does it effect Hamlet's choices?

Your first collage was an expression of the "outer" world of the play; alter it, or make a new one, which expresses this "inner" psychological landscape.

C. The historical moment—What is important about the moment in history when the play occurs? How does it effect the values and behavior of the characters? What associations do we have toward this period today? Should you keep to the playwright's time and place or is there a better time and place in which to set the play for your audience? Adjust your collage to express the historical moment.

PREPARING THE GROUND PLAN

There remains one more important preparation for your first design meetings, and that is to formulate your ideas about the configuration of the stage space. This should be done with special care because second only to your casting, the determination of your ground plan is the most influential decision you will make in your production process. While the final determination of the ground plan will be made in collaboration with your scenic designer, you must prepare by developing a clear sense of the spatial implications of the dramatic action.

We began this chapter speaking of the organic interrelationship of action and environment: The stage environment, as a translation of the landscape of the play, should invite the action to occur in a naturally effective way. As the actors begin to experience the action of the play, the set should assist them in forming expressive relationships and finding the best placement within the space. "Blocking" is really this spatial manifestation of the action within the configuration of the environment; if the configuration is correct, the blocking will emerge naturally from the actors as they experience the action. For this reason I say that it is the ground plan—not the director—which truly blocks the show; I know the ground plan is right when I need do no blocking at all.

For this reason, you will begin by looking for the psychodynamics of your ground plan. Here are a few of the considerations which may be important:

Stage/Audience Relationship: Given the nature of the theatre architecture in which you will work, should we be close to the action, or more distant? Should we surround it, or should it penetrate us? Should our relationship to it change, being distant at some times and close at others (for instance, do Hamlet's soliloquies not call for a close-up)?

Configuration: Can the shape of the space reflect the shape of the action or rhythm of the play? Should it be basically longitudinal or round (as perhaps for *The Glass Menagerie*, with Amanda at the center, the children "in orbit," and the Gentleman Caller coming from the outside)? Are levels important to help express supremacy, or aspiration? Is it a simple, open place, or are there lots of little nooks and crannies (as the frequent spying in *Hamlet* would suggest)?

Size: Is the space large or small? Do people get "lost" in it (as they do in *Hamlet*) or are they thrown upon one another (as they are in *The Glass Menagerie*)? Can the size and configuration support the largest number of people and the most violent action the play contains? In *Hamlet*, for instance, the capability to support the final duel between Hamlet and Laertes was a requisite for the ground plan.

Territories: To whom does the space "belong"? Who controls what aspects or areas of it? In *Hamlet*, for instance, Hamlet is made to feel like an outsider in his own home; in *The Glass Menagerie*, Tom and Laura are trapped by Amanda's influence like moons orbiting around a planet.

Axes of Conflict: What forces are at work in the scene and on what vectors should they operate? Could we establish one side, direction, or diagonal of the stage as "belonging" to one force, and the others to its opposite? Should these confront each other directly ("head to head") or more obliquely? Is there a character at the center of the action, into whom all the play's forces feed (as in Jean-Louis Barrault's famous staging of *Phaedre*, with the heroine at the center of a semicircle of doors out of which appeared all the other characters)? Are there obstacles between people that should be expressed spatially (like the gulf that separates Hamlet from his mother until the Closet scene)?

Placement of Crucial Moments: Can you reserve certain stage locations for moments of great significance? Can meaning be enhanced by putting certain things in the same spot, thereby unconsciously inviting a comparison of them?

Any or all of these considerations may be important in generating the ground plan. Consider each and be prepared to share your perceptions with your scenic designer, with whom you will make the final determination. While you might have some specific ideas to contribute to this discussion, avoid presenting your designer with a finished ground plan; give yourself the chance to benefit from his or her perceptions by using these ideas as a preparation for your collaborative effort, not as a substitute for it. The result of your thinking about the ground plan is not a completed design but a number of principles which will facilitate your work with the designer.

In *Hamlet*, for example, I reviewed each of the milestones in the map of the action: Hamlet's vow, the idea of the mousetrap, the choice not to kill the praying Claudius, the wrongful choice which kills Polonius, the choice to be ready at last, and the final choice to kill Claudius. I noticed that all these choices but the killings of Polonius and Claudius are made in soliloquy; these soliloquies have the function of bringing us close to Hamlet and his decision-making process. I decided, therefore, to reserve a special place, as much "within" the audience as possible, for all these moments; at the end, Hamlet would die in it as well.

I knew also that the action required the ability to separate conflicting forces and to express the gulf between Hamlet and his world; that the frequent spying in the play required hiding places; that the space needed to change instantly from one locale to another; that the final duel needed space and levels; and so on. From all these specific considerations, and from my overall desire to thrust the point of Hamlet's world into the laps of the audience, the ground plan was generated by my designer, as the production log will describe.

The important point here is that the ground plan is generated through a concern for the dynamics of the action, and not through a pictorial concern for the set as a static image. Good designers will understand this, but you will not always work with good designers; be prepared to share your sense of the play's dynamic and the way in which the stage environment can support it.

Exercise 13: Generating a Ground Plan

From your own understanding of *Hamlet*, prepare to generate a ground plan in collaboration with a designer; if possible, set up a simulation of a design meeting with a friend. Assume that you are doing the play in a specific theatre in which you might actually work, and review each of the spatial considerations which might influence the ground plan:

1. Stage/audience relationship
2. Configuration
3. Size
4. Territories
5. Axes of conflict
6. Placement of significant moments

When you have a rough outline of a ground plan, begin to envision each of the scenes in it: Does it invite the action to flow naturally into effective spatial images?

SETTING TO WORK

Your preparation is complete; you have embodied the play's system of norms in your own experience of the play. From this time on, you will be involved with the creative input of others. The work you have done so far has prepared you to share a sense of direction with them, to align their efforts with your perception of the play, and to synthesize their contributions in a unified production. This is the through-line of your work: Keep your eye on it despite the many distractions you will encounter. The life of the production depends on you keeping your center calm, and your eyes and mind open.

PART THREE
THE DIRECTOR
AT WORK

INTRODUCTION

Beginning directors are often eager to develop a method of work, a sort
of formula or sequence of steps for creating the production. While such
formulae do exist and can, in certain instances, produce results, the art
of directing can no more be reduced to a standard procedure than can
any other art. It is truer to say that all your study and skill are a
preparation to "make it up as you go along."

This is because once the actual work of design meetings and
rehearsals begins, you will be profoundly influenced by many factors
beyond your control. With each production you will find that the
process is never quite the same. As we said at the outset, directing is
not a matter of rules and formulae; it is a matter of principles and
strategies for problem-solving. Your understanding of the play and of
the techniques of directing must be applied in the precise way required
by each individual situation.

As in any problem-solving process, no amount of premeditation can
substitute for a clear sense of purpose and an open and inventive mind.
You hope that what you have done so far will contribute to your clarity

and your preparedness to respond to the moment. Here in Part Three, we will examine some of the principles and strategies which may be useful in the most basic directing tasks: generating a design, casting, dealing with actors, and staging in all its aspects.

ALIGNMENT

Your work in every phase of the process will have one superobjective, which was expressed by Jack O'Brien: "to give the company one story to tell." This requires that you assist all your fellow workers in experiencing the play's action for themselves, and in making an effective contribution to the life of that action through their own problem-solving efforts.

This does not mean that the members of your ensemble must all work or think alike, nor that they must somehow belittle their individual identities and creativity in favor of the group effort. Think of them not as a corporate mass whose individual identities are subsumed into your game plan, but rather as a group of co-equal and aligned individuals, their independent energies moving in the same direction toward the same goal.

Such alignment in no way diminishes individual creativity; on the contrary, since each member of an aligned group draws strength and inspiration from the whole, each can function at an enhanced level of personal accomplishment. In this way, the whole of an aligned group becomes greater than the sum of its parts, and each member gets more from it than he or she gives to it.

Your ongoing concern, then, is not so much to solve all the problems yourself, but to find the strategies which will facilitate the solving of problems by your fellow workers in a way that allows them to do their best work while also contributing to the unity of the whole production.

This happens best in an atmosphere of mutual respect and support. As David Emmes put it in answering my survey question, "what contributes most to a successful production,"

> . . . the people you assemble around you and whether you are able to create a working relationship that is characterized by the honesty and respect that permits us to be vulnerable.

THE HAMLET LOG

In order to tie our discussion to the realities of the practical situation, the log of the Oregon *Hamlet* will be more prominent in Part Three, serving as a kind of through-line. This is not because this production was "better" than some other, nor were its circumstances any more representative of American Theatre than some other type of production might have been; it is simply a detailed record of one real directing process.

I attempted to record the process fully and objectively, and my completed log was over three hundred pages. I have edited it to focus on the most representative details, so only one-fourth of it appears in these pages. I hope it will nevertheless give you some sense of the whole process.

NINE
THE DESIGN PROCESS

Your working relationship with your designers is critical to the success of your effort to find an effective translation of the play's system of norms. It is a relationship, moreover, which must be maintained in the face of several sources of pressure.

First is the pressure of time: Directors and designers are rarely given enough time to develop a satisfactory process of discovery—one or two discussions, a week or two to think it over, and the construction drawings must be done. Under the pressure of such deadlines, the director and designer are in danger of becoming adversaries, with the designer being forced to espouse the cause of expediency while the director resists the closing off of design options.

Even more difficult is the matter of timing: Construction schedules will often require you to make design decisions long before you have had a chance to discover the particular life the text will have given the actors and the space in which it will live. It is hard enough to communicate with a designer when you *know* what you want, much less when you are just beginning to understand it for yourself! If you are lucky, your designers will assist you in developing further your fledgling production concept, and this is the spirit with which the process should be approached.

Next is the pressure of territoriality: The respective territories of director and designer may be unfamiliar and intrinsically conflictive. Your designers may be working within constraints of time, space, budget, and personnel with which you are unfamiliar. On the other hand, you may understand the needs of the play and the production in a way that is impossible for the designer to share. Under these conditions, a great deal of trust, good faith, and communication is required.

Each pairing of director and designer must find its own set of territorial ground rules somewhere in the spectrum that ranges from the coldness of separate but equal powers ("After we've talked, I'll trust you to design it and you trust me to direct it") to the flexibility of continuous negotiation ("I know that your set will do some of the directing, and you know that my directing will do some of the designing") to completely mutual endeavor ("Let's just do the whole thing together.")

Any of these relationships can work, and any might be the best choice in a given situation. What does *not* work is to pretend that you are independent ("I won't influence your design if you don't influence my directing") or that you are not by necessity equals in the creative process ("Here's the set I want" versus "Here's the set you're going to get.") Not only is such independence an illusion in the face of the organic unity of action and environment, but it sacrifices the potential support which the aligned efforts of director and designer could supply to both.

THE DESIGN PROCESS:
FIRST DISCUSSIONS

The usual process by which a design evolves has several stages, each of which reflects increasing specificity and commitment to the idea on the part of both director and designer. In general, this progression is from the intangible toward the tangible: beginning with verbal images (discussions), then sometimes bringing in found images (such as pictures in books or magazines), to created images (sketches), and finally to a concrete object (a model). The increasing tangibility of the idea as it evolves from discussion to sketch to model involves more and more of the designer's effort and reflects a growing commitment. Beware of letting things get too tangible too soon: The initial discussions should define the territory to be explored and establish the strategy for exploring it.

Begin with what you understand best; allow what you see in the text to determine your strategy. For a play which features external action and an overt use of the theatre per se, such as a Restoration comedy, you might work from a sense of the play's original environment, and your fundamental design choice here might be to capture something of the social and architectural qualities of the Restoration playhouse. For a play which features an idea, like one by Brecht or Shaw, you might begin from an understanding of the structure of the argument and develop a design which reflects it. A play which features internalized action springing organically from the lives of the characters, on the other hand, might suggest beginning with a discussion of the psychology of the play and working toward a design which expresses this inner world. When Ming Cho Lee and Liviu Ciulei collaborated on their *Hamlet* at Washington's Arena Stage in 1978, for instance, they spent most of their time discussing the people of the play. Gradually a sense of the world inhabited by these people emerged from the discussions, and from this the eventual design.

In any case, allow the nature of the material to determine your initial strategy; begin from what is most clearly known and work toward the unknown.

SKETCHING: WORKING IN A DYNAMIC MODE

As we stressed in Chapter 6, plays are rhythmed events, a flow of modulated energy moving through time. The stage must be thought of as an environment for this event, not merely as a "picture." The design, therefore, must be conceived in four dimensions, not just three.

You have prepared to work in this way by thinking about your ground plan; you have come to understand the ways in which the action might live in space, and the types of spatial relationships which it requires. It is essential that your design process include this sense of the play's dynamism. Several strategies are available here. Most obviously, you can present your sense of the ground plan as a starting point for discussion. This runs the risk of placing the designers on the defensive, however; it would be preferable to develop a shared understanding of the action first, and allow a sense of the ground plan to emerge collaboratively.

One good way to do this is for you and the designers to simply talk through the play, telling the story and discussing the important moments as you go. As you develop a shared understanding of the story, you will naturally begin to generate a ground plan. When Jack O'Brien says that the essence of directing "is giving the company the same story to tell, to a man," he is clearly including the designers.

The idea of a *storyboard* can be extremely useful here. Think of designing in relation to the flow of the action: Select those significant moments which are the milestones of the action and work through them, allowing the needs of the space to be determined by them. This is a good example of the Bauhaus idea of letting "form follow function," and it was used by Brecht and his designers.

THE CENTRAL METAPHOR

Beside determining the configuration of the space in relationship to the action, you must also decide on the visual image the stage environment will present. Metaphors can be useful in this: It is a start when the director suggests that the play has the feeling of "a tribal initiation," or the designer sees it as a "black mass." Such an image may even become a *central metaphor*, which will motivate the entire design.

A central metaphor may be a reflection of some specific image suggested by the play. In researching my 1974 production of *Everyman* at the Guthrie Theatre, I came upon a medieval conjuring circle which eventually became the only set, and medieval anatomical drawings which became the costumes. The simplicity of this combination expressed the circular action of the play with its ritual vivisection of Everyman (Figure 9-1).

Sometimes the structure of the material can suggest a central metaphor. For instance, I have always been fascinated by the labyrinthian quality of

FIGURE 9-1.   *Everyman* at the Tyrone Guthrie Theatre, Minneapolis, 1975. James Harris at center. *Tyrone Guthrie Theatre.*

Kafka's novel, *The Trial*, and between 1967 and 1975 I developed a series of three environmental treatments of it: The first (at the University of Wisconsin-Milwaukee) resembled a wax works with audience seated among the figures in "jury boxes"; the second (at the Yale Drama School) was a three story maze in which the audience itself formed the outlines of the labyrinth; in the third (at the California Institute of the Arts), teams of "unit directors and designers" created a fifteen-room "fun house" through which the audience moved in small groups, each accompanying its own hero to his eventual execution.

In *Hamlet*, you will see that a "labyrinthian fortress" became the central metaphor for our design.

Beware: As useful as these evocative metaphors may be as the basis for a design, they are also extremely dangerous. An idea that seems exciting, and may even produce an interesting design, may easily wear thin over the two or three hours of the performance and eventually become a stale and rigid image that "traps" the show. I have seen many a show diminished by a scenic metaphor that went stale or became inoperative.

You must take care, then, that the metaphor remain an active element in the show and that it has somewhere to go. There are two qualifications which scenic metaphors must meet: First, can the metaphor, as a concept, be sufficiently submerged in the design so that it ceases to call attention to itself, or at least reveals itself gradually throughout the action; second, does the metaphor pay off at moments of significant crisis and climax? If these conditions cannot be met, you should discard the metaphor.

THE MODEL

Once the scenic concept has been developed, it is finally given a tangible form which serves as a sort of contract specifying your agreement on the design. This usually takes the form of either a final rendering or a scale model. While different designers prefer one or the other, I urge you to request a model whenever possible. Renderings are wonderful in portfolios or lobby displays, but as a specification of the set, they leave too much to the spatial imagination.

A good rendering or model should always include a human figure (or several) for scale, and even model furniture, if any. Such a model can be tremendously useful for checking the dynamism of the design before giving final approval. Go through the show in your mind (or if you must, use cutouts or toy figures) and see how various scenes might live within the design. This is only to check the possibilities, of course; do not block the show this way, unless you want your show to look like an enormous mechanical toy.

I have also found a good model useful during rehearsals and try to have one always present; the actors benefit a great deal from having a clear sense of the space, and I find that they frequently consult it (Figure 9-2).

A model is not necessarily the end of the design process, of course. Some

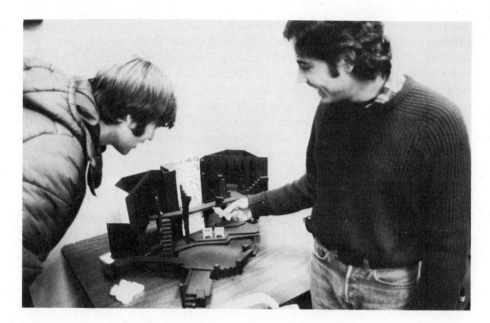

FIGURE 9-2.   The *Hamlet* Model in Rehearsal: Mark Murphey (L) working with fight choreographer Chris Villa. *Robert Benedetti.*

scenic concepts cannot be communicated, even in a preliminary way, in less than three dimensions, and in these cases rough models are a useful kind of three-dimensional sketching. One such case was my production of Pirandello's *Henry IV* at the Pacific Conservatory of the Performing Arts in 1976; the initial discussions developed the central metphor of "a luminous nursery which turns into a concentration camp." The designer's solution to this problem was a latticework of metal arches surrounding the stage like a huge birdcage which, with changes in the lighting, could change from a toy to a prison. The designer and I worked entirely with models, on which we experimented with lighting and which we happily destroyed and rebuilt as the specific set evolved. (In the Oregon *Hamlet*, something of this same procedure was followed, though the degree of change was smaller.)

CHANGES DURING REHEARSAL

The establishment of the final scenic and costume designs is not at all the end of the process. Throughout the rehearsal period, unforeseen questions will arise, construction difficulties will be met, and the need for adjustments will be discovered by you and the actors. Be clear about the degree of latitude for change available to you in the given circumstances: If certain issues clearly cannot be determined until after rehearsals have begun, perhaps your design needs to have some measure of flexibility built in. In general, try to keep your options open and avoid making decisions any sooner than absolutely necessary.

Even without such planned flexibility, some changes may be possible as work progresses. Stay in close touch with your designers and be sure that they visit rehearsals at regular intervals—and make them welcome when they do! If any problems with the designs arise, share them with the designers instantly. Make the problems *common concerns* and enlist the aid of the designers in finding solutions. Let them know that their participation in your ongoing work is eagerly invited.

COSTUMES, PROPS, AND LIGHTS

So far we have discussed the design process with special concern for the set, since the scenic concept is usually the first to be determined. If you are fortunate enough to meet with all your designers together, at least at first, (as in the *Hamlet* Log), you will help ensure the integration of design elements.

Eventually, however, you will have separate working sessions with your costume designer and, in some situations, your prop master. These people will need special information from you about the characters and their relationships, especially any contrasts between characters or groups of characters that are important to the underlying conflict of the play (the preparatory work you have already done should be sufficient for this purpose).

One thing is crucial about costume designs: Remember that you are designing the *body under the clothing*! Realizing this, you can see at once that the actor who will wear the clothing *must* be a factor in the design. Good costume designers prefer to work this way, of course, but in those rare and unfortunate situations when costumes must be designed without knowing the actors, then you will have no choice but to consider the predetermined image of the character during the casting: The actor and the image must be able to coalesce.

Best, of course, is the situation in which the actors can work for a time and then have input into the costume design process. It is sad to see an actor work on a role for weeks and then have much of the characterization modified or nullified by the costume.

In any case, you will be wise to give your actors the earliest possible idea of their clothing so that their work can head in the right direction. I keep copies of the designs in the rehearsal hall for their reference, and make absolutely sure that they begin using rehearsal clothing early, especially anything that will affect their relationship to gravity (such as boots or high heels) or their body line (such as skirts, capes, or constricting garments) as well as any hand props (such as canes, fans, or purses). The aim is to do all you can to make the actor and the clothing go together naturally.

Lighting and sound are usually not even discussed until rehearsals get under way, so we will put these topics off for a later chapter. Do assure yourself, however, that there is considerable coordination going on among your principle designers on such matters as color, texture, and overall visual style.

THE HAMLET LOG, PART 4: FIRST DESIGN CONFERENCE—SEPTEMBER 9

I fly to San Francisco for the first design conference with scenic designer Richard Hay and costume designer Jeannie Davidson. We are happy to be working together again since our *Taming of the Shrew* at Oregon ten years ago.

Richard and Jeannie have read the edition of the play I have specified (the Signet Classic edition, chosen for its inclusion of material from both the Good Quarto and the First Folio). I have brought with me three copies of my revised cutting in which I have marked the locations of potential major lighting and/or sound cues. Copies will be passed on to the lighting and sound designers for future meetings, and will be given to the actors playing Hamlet and Claudius as well.

In order to discuss the setting, I have gone through the play scene by scene to identify the various locales in which the action occurs. I have broken these down to the fewest number of different locales possible, with a listing of the scenes which occur in each location. In a real sense, I am making a "map" of the action (which, in the case of *Hamlet* means making a map of the castle of Elsinore and its adjoining churchyard). It appears that seven locales are essential:

1. The Battlements (scenes 11, 14, 15, 46)
2. The Throne Room or Great Hall (scenes 12, 22, 31, 43)
3. The Main Courtyard or "Lobby" (scenes 32, 43, 44, 52)
4. Claudius's Apartment or Chapel (scenes 33, 45, 47)
5. Gertrude's Closet (scenes 34 and 41—which I've combined into one scene)
6. The Graveyard (scene 51)
7. The Plain (scene 44)

I am eager to keep the action moving without interruptions of any kind. Shakespeare's plays work best when one scene flows directly into another so that the momentum and values of one scene carry over into the next. This clearly was the strategy in Shakespeare's own theatre, and his stage made such an unbroken flow easy to achieve.

For this reason, I've asked that we consider a "unit" set with an overall Elizabethan configuration. Moreover, the set should provide, as permanent elements, whatever places to sit may be necessary (as well as such elements as the arras in the Queen's closet) so there is no need for any break between scenes for the movement of furniture. Dick Hay has already considered the problem of furniture, and thinks there will be no problem except in the large court scenes when Gertrude and Claudius will have to be seated within the central playing area. He suggests the creation of two low "thrones" which can be set and struck as an integral part of the action of these scenes; I decide to create the character of a steward for this purpose.

The locale breakdown gives Dick a sense of the different "looks" of which the unit set must be capable, and how the action might move from area to area within the unit. We discuss briefly the qualities of each locale, with special attention to the scope of action it must contain, the entrances and exits required, and the general feeling of the scenes which occur there.

Next we discuss the feeling of the set as a whole. I describe briefly my sense of the operative elements of the environment as Shakespeare has suggested it. First, the coldness and hardness of Denmark, an inhospitable and lonely environment. Claudius is surrounded by very few people compared to other Shakespearean kings (only Macbeth is also forced to call several times for his bodyguard, as Claudius does in Act IV), and this sense of isolation must be reflected in the set.

Second, there is a strong labyrinthian quality to this world, with so many comings and goings, so many chance encounters in the hallways, so much hiding and spying. The set should imply a maze of corridors and passages leading to other spaces beyond the stage proper. I mention my recent visit to Cheyenne Mountain in Colorado, the vast underground command center for NORAD; it seems like an apt analog for "this warlike state."

Third is the omnipresence of war: The moment Claudius has chosen for his murder/seduction is made ripe by the imminent invasion by the powers of Norway, and the court will have no choice but to hastily elect a new king and to support the marriage which will make Gertrude "the jointress to this warlike state." Clearly, Claudius knows what Hamlet has yet to learn, that "the readiness is all."

Last, I mention the intimacy with Hamlet which the set must permit. The ground plan must allow his soliloquies to be delivered in the very laps of the audience. Luckily, the auditorium of the Angus Bowmer Theatre (which Dick himself designed) is a warm and hospitable space and, while fairly large, does give a sense of closeness for its size. But I want to go further and to literally thrust Hamlet into the audience so as to make them feel for the moment that he is one of them. To this end also, I want to de-emphasize the spatial division of stage and auditorium in every way possible. Dick is intrigued by this idea.

After a bit more discussion about the set's texture (cold and wet), tonality (generally dark), and weight (massive), the discussion turns to the costuming. I have brought a preliminary cast breakdown, but before we discuss the major figures, Jeannie asks that we discuss the period in which the production is to be set.

It seems to me that the play shows us a world in a moment of profound change. Hamlet stands pinned to the fulcrum of this change, torn between two irreconcilable value systems: the medieval on one hand and the first glimmerings of humanism on the other. For this reason, the choice of an historical period seems to lie between the Renaissance and our own time as the two moments in history which feature this radical and rapid shift in moral values, with all the conflict such a shift brings.

As E. M. W. Tillyard points out, the Elizabethans were fully aware of the new scientific and moral thought of the Renaissance, but they were also perfectly content to live their daily lives according to the time-worn values of the Middle Ages; someone faced with the unavoidable necessity of Hamlet's situation would find the inherent contradiction of these two positions insupportable. How alike is our own time with its tumultuous conflict between old, familiar values and new, frightening perceptions of the universe, and global, national, and interpersonal politics.

This is a powerful argument in favor of a modern-dress production, but I have chosen instead to leave the play in the original period. As Brecht pointed out when he argued against the modernization of older plays, the intrinsic distance of older plays helps us to see how the play's meaning relates to our own time; it heightens what Grotowski calls the "confrontation of values" between the world of the play and our own. It will mean more if the audience recognizes for themselves the underlying identity of Hamlet's world with our own, rather than being shown the point through techniques of staging.

Since the essential aspect of the historical period is its shift in values, I suggest that we emphasize the change in fashion from the old court under Hamlet's father, to the new court under Claudius. This idea sprang from my thinking about that odd character who appears at the end of the play, Osric. That he is a foolish dandy, and probably outlandishly dressed, is clear from the dialogue, but it is important to remember that he is also a wealthy man, "rich," Hamlet says, "in the possession of dirt." He is the kind of "beast" who, a "beast being king of beasts," has come "to feed at the king's mess." We must not dismiss Osric as mere "comic relief," then; the fact that the fatal challenge is borne by someone so unlike anyone we have met before is meant to emphasize the change in the court under Claudius. He has begun to "poison" the body politic, peopling the court with "beasts" like Osric—easily led, spineless, concerned with appearances more than with substance. Gone are the bluff, strong, career-warriors of the old Hamlet's court. How galling it must be to Hamlet to see what has become of a once-noble and honest court; how heavily he must feel the weight of responsibility for things having come to such a pass. No wonder he vents himself by making Osric look like a fool.

What is wanted, then, is a strong, military, functional look for the old court, and a precious, rich, ornamental look for the new. Jeannie notes that this difference is inherent in the shift from the Gothic to the Renaissance styles, and so the matter of period is settled.

Jeannie next asks about Hamlet himself; since I see him as "set apart" from the other characters, should he look different? There is, of course, his "customary suit of solemn black" and "inky cloak"; we examine these references in the text. It seems to me that Hamlet is maintaining the customary period of mourning as a visible protest against the marriage of his mother; soon he will abandon his mourning by assuming "an antic disposition," so he needn't remain in black throughout. Here I mention the idea of one critic that Hamlet is in fact dressed as a jester throughout his madness; we leave this idea hanging as one extreme possibility. In any case, we are agreed that Hamlet is meant to stand out in Scene 12 like a "black hole" against a background of color and dynamism.

Just what, Dick wants to know, *is* happening in Scene 12? Are they just coming from the wedding, or from Claudius's coronation, or what? I am excited by the image of a full-blown festivity, perhaps the reception following the double ceremony of wedding and coronation, wild and bright, with banners and high spirits (just the sort of public display Claudius would love and which a country on the brink of war would need to be properly "jointed"). Moreover, this might be only the first in a long sequence of parties by which Claudius will celebrate his triple victory—over the kingdom, over Fortinbras, and over Gertrude. We know for certain that the "carouse" will continue the next night, when Hamlet is on the battlement awaiting the Ghost, and is continuing weeks later, when the players arrive for their part in the festivities.

The image of a jubilant wedding scene against which stands a dark, skulking Hamlet gives me another idea; perhaps Hamlet has actually refused to attend his mother's wedding. I imagine an empty stage with the sounds of a great ceremony going on offstage; onto this empty stage wanders a solitary Hamlet, who stands for a time listening. Suddenly there is an ear shattering pealing of bells, and with a blaze of light the royal party bursts onto the stage, engulfing him. This seems like an excellent idea and I adopt it at once.

The meeting has been long but productive. There is some urgency about the set design since, although the show will not open for nearly five months, it is the first of five shows to be built and the drawings are due in the shop in three weeks! Costumes can be planned in a much more leisurely fashion, and lighting will not even be discussed before rehearsals begin. We adjourn with the promise to keep constantly in touch and to meet again in a couple of weeks.

TEN
CASTING

I have a sign hanging over my desk which says, "Directing is the art of correcting the mistakes you made in casting." Most of the directors who answered my survey agree: John Dillon says:

> . . . a director who is a poor acting coach may end up with a brilliantly acted production if he has a real flair for casting. Putting the right combination of people together in a room for four weeks of rehearsal may be sufficient genius to breathe life into a production.

Mark Lamos refers to the stakes in the "gamble" of casting:

> Correct casting is 90 per cent of a successful production. Sometimes I cast actors who seem rather "wrong" for the part, but in whom I sense a kindred spirit. Casting is, unfortunately, a big gamble.

Incorrect casting, on the other hand, can never be made quite right, and even after considerable effort can actually distort the life of the play. As Jack O'Brien puts it,

> With the wrong casting, you are reduced to "making it work" in spite of itself.

There is another choice, of course, and that is to replace the actor who has been wrongly cast; but that is usually very difficult if not impossible, and in any case seems unfair, since the actor is, in a sense, being made to suffer for your mistake (they may suffer more, of course, by remaining in a role which isn't right for them).

The stakes in the gamble of casting, then, are no less than the success of the show; in this chapter we will look at ways of improving your odds.

THE CRITERIA FOR CASTING

When you considered the relationship of dramatic action and character in Chapter Seven, you saw that there are two ways in which character and action are inextricably linked. First, individual characters serve as the agents for the action (that is, they may appear to cause the action through the choices they make); second, these choices are made in relation to the other characters, so that the action flows because of the action/reaction chain of stimulus and response that passes between the characters. For this reason we said that relationship was the conduit through which dramatic action flows.

This means that you have two criteria for casting a given actor: (1) Does he or she have the potential to make the choices the character makes, and (2) will the potential relationship between this actor and the actors being considered for other roles fit into the network of relationships in a way which will cause the action to flow naturally between them?

We can truly say, then, that *we are casting relationships rather than individual roles.* When the individual actor has the ability to create the character who makes the necessary choices, and when that created character interacts properly with the other characters, there is not a great deal left for the director to worry about: Blocking, the shaping and pace of the action, all will arise naturally from the action itself. The flip side of the sign over my desk is, "The better the casting, the less the directing."

THE CASTING PROCESS

By tradition, the casting of a play is usually divided into three steps: *Auditioning* the available actors to assess their ability and appropriateness to the production; *callbacks* of the most promising candidates for more work and, if possible, to test their relationship with the other choices; finally the *casting* itself. Casting sometimes is done in collaboration with a producer, artistic director, or, in repertory, the directors of other shows in the season, so that in these cases compromises may have to be made on economic or logistical grounds.

The specific conditions and techniques of casting may be entirely different from one theatrical context to another, and in some cases the director may have little control. In an experimental group, the collective may sort the casting out for itself; in a commercial production, the producer may control the casting of principals through negotiations with agents; in a resident company, the artistic director may determine significant casting in the contracting of the company. In general, however, you should do all you can to maintain control of the casting and to make sure that the nature of the casting process is suited to your needs.

The first question is that of time: Will you have enough time with each applicant to judge them accurately, and will you have enough time for callbacks to experiment with different combinations of casting? Remember that casting involves too many variables to be left only to the conscious mind; you *must* have time between phases of the process to "sleep on it," and to let your mind sort and sift the possibilities. In my experience, the entire process requires a minimum of three days even in highly organized situations.

Besides adequate time, you will need to determine the form of the auditions so as to get the information you most need. This involves selecting the nature of the material to be seen, having the time and flexibility to request adjustments or to work improvisationally with candidates, and so on. Such flexibility can maximize the effectiveness of the time you spend in auditions.

Even more important than time or flexibility is your frame of mind during auditions. Too often we go into auditions with a set of premeditated images of the characters; we spend the audition sifting the actors amongst these images, hoping that someone will coincide with each. This may make us think we know what we're looking for, but the truth is that we probably aren't really seeing the actors who are auditioning.

If you can put your immediate concerns aside and take a more inquisitive, open-minded approach, you will find not only that you can see each actor more clearly, but that you also start to get exciting ideas about the play itself from the qualities and associations suggested by the auditions. As we have said, you will ultimately "discover the text through the actors" and this actually begins with the auditioning process!

PRELIMINARY AUDITIONS

Your first priority at a preliminary audition is to meet the actors as people and as potential fellow workers. Since auditions are, at best, a threatening situation for the actor, the tendency of most is to hide behind a premeditated veneer, both in their personal demeanor and in their audition work. You must do all you can to help them relax and find the confidence to open up. You must also give yourself the opportunity to be a fair witness, to clear your mind, shut off the buzz of other concerns, take a deep breath and find a calm center, then let yourself simply "be" with each candidate.

This is extremely difficult in the most common preliminary audition format, the "cattle call" involving a rapid series of four-minute auditions. I have never found this a valuable auditioning situation and you should avoid it if you can. The importance of casting is so great that you can afford to "waste" considerable time in giving the actors a fair hearing, and yourself a fair oppor- tunity to assess each. If it is at all possible, then, try to budget at least ten minutes with each candidate; if there are too many to be seen, then ensure that you will at least have ten minutes for each callback, and use the prelimi- naries only as a coarse screening.

Assuming that the form of the audition is decided, there remains the question of its content. The prepared audition, in which the actors bring in their ready-made pieces is the most common preliminary form, and again it is perhaps the least desirable because it gives so little sense of the actor's process. If you must use this form, do all you can to get a sense of the actor as a worker. You will find yourself watching many things besides the audition itself, such as the way they conduct themselves in the business of auditioning, their preparation, even whatever impression you can get through informal social contact.

When someone's prepared audition seems interesting but stiff or rushed, try requesting a simple adjustment, such as "try that again as if you were pleading your case before a tribunal of judges"; or even suggest an irrelevant activity, such as "try that again while stacking up all these chairs"; anything to break their mindless pattern and force them to experience the piece anew.

Preferable to the prepared audition, when it is possible, is having the actors read from the play itself. However, the cold reading situation penalizes some very good actors and rewards some superficially glib ones, so it must be avoided. If it is at all possible, request that the actors read the play, or at least supply them with some capsular information about it. Either ask them to select their audition piece, or give them several choices; you will be interested to note their response to the material.

The best form of audition in my experience is scene work. Since your aim is to cast relationships rather than single roles, you must find out whether an actor plays well with a partner; this is nearly impossible in the monolgue audition. The logistical difficulty in setting up scenes is so great that we usually just do the best we can to guess at the actor's ability in this regard, or we wait for callbacks to make sure. However, since most monologues assume the pres- ence of another person, I like to encourage the actors to enlist an impromptu scene partner from one of the other auditionees, and to give them a few moments of preparation. The scene partner needn't do anything more than receive the awareness of the auditionee. (You will be fascinated to notice how much you learn about actors serving as scene partners; their feeling of being "safe" and "in service" often opens them up wonderfully—hence the old theat- rical cliché about the partner getting the job!)

JUDGING THE AUDITION

Whatever the form of the preliminary audition, you are really asking yourself three questions about each of the actors you see. First, is this someone with whom you want to work, what Mark Lamos calls a "kindred spirit"? This is not, of course, a matter of "liking" someone; you are forming a creative ensemble, not a social club. It has much more to do with an actor's seriousness of purpose and openness to the input of others, both fellow actors and yourself.

One of the qualities I look for in actors is their commitment to their own artistic development: Have they approached the audition as an opportunity for growth? Have they selected material that means something to them? Are they in touch with their surroundings? Are they eager for the input of others? By and large, I have found that actors who are serious about their own growth turn in better performances than those who are merely eager to please.

The second question in the back of your mind is "does this actor meet the basic requirements for this specific work." In a Shakespeare play, for instance, you might be especially concerned with the actor's sensitivity to language and ability to handle verse; in an outdoor festival, projection might be a special concern; for a Brecht play, you might want a sense of the actor's degree of political awareness; for a gutsy realistic play, you might watch for the actor's ability to deal with highly personal emotional material. In your preparation for casting you have isolated this agenda of essential concerns.

The third question is "what are this actor's potentials; which roles might he or she play." As we have said, this is not so much a matter of judging external qualities (though in specific cases these may be important), it is more a matter of sensing the potential of the actor to be driven by certain needs, to react in certain ways, to make certain kinds of choices. You might find yourself thinking something like "he seems like someone who is capable of great love," then considering that "he also seems capable of violence," and put them together to form "he could be so maddened by grief over a lost loved one that he would do anything for revenge" and so have found a good candidate for Laertes.

These kinds of associations form freely and almost unconsciously if you stay calm, and open to the actors. As the associations form, I record them by a simple method: I divide a large sheet of paper into boxes, one for each character. Then, as I think about the actors with whom I would like to work, I simply write their names under every role they might possibly play.

When I divide the characters among these casting boxes, I sometimes notice that one box will suffice (at least at first) for several characters. In *Hamlet*, for instance, I used one box for the Ghost, the Player King, and the English Ambassador, and another for Polonius and the Gravedigger. This is not so surprising in Shakespeare, of course, since we know that he wrote for a company of sixteen and that many roles were therefore doubled, most likely including those I doubled into my *Hamlet* casting boxes.

CALLBACKS

Once I've seen all the preliminary auditions, I sort out my sheet. Some roles will have a great many names in their boxes, others only a few. Using this record, I set up my callbacks to test all the likely combinations of relationships suggested by the possibilities for each role. In preparation for casting, I have selected a number of short scenes which feature the central relationships or "teams" into which the cast can be broken; I then simply set up as many repetitions of these scenes as necessary to try the various combinations.

Whatever system you use, the real function of callbacks is, to my mind, the testing of relationships. Even if the situation unfortunately requires that callbacks be individual rather than group sessions, you will be doing your best to make imaginative comparisons of the various relationship possibilities.

Of course, you will also be learning more about the actors as workers. Some will turn out to be rigid and dull and will fade away with repeated viewings, others will blossom and reveal unsuspected depths and excitement. Beware of commiting to an actor without the test of such repeated viewings and, as we said before, at least a night to sleep on it. You are forming a relationship that will, for a while, be as intense and as time-consuming as most marriages.

This is also the time when you will learn even more about the play; you may have whole new interpretive possibilities thrust into your consciousness. In fact, when the casting situation makes this kind of prolonged callback workshopping impossible (as in the Oregon *Hamlet*), I find that I miss it throughout the rehearsal process. The turmoil of casting is a time when you are forced to think about the play afresh in the face of the available talent, and it is the relationship callback which does this best.

CASTING AGAINST TYPE

One casting strategy that bears special mention is casting *against* the obvious quality demanded by the text. This is especially useful for "ambivalent" characters who possess both positive and negative qualities: The fascinating villain is one such type, of whom Richard III, Edmund the Bastard in *Lear*, and Iago are good examples. In such cases, the problem is to find an actor capable of embodying the negative aspects of the character without alienating the audience.

A good Iago, for instance, would have to be believably honest and trustworthy; everyone calls him "honest Iago," and Othello will seem like a fool if Iago seems anything less than trustworthy. Moreover, if the actor playing Iago isn't essentially likeable, the texture and dynamism of the play will be greatly reduced. We see, in the contrast between his scenes and his soliloquies, two sides of Iago, and you will want to accentuate the difference between them. Our modern psychological point of view often urges us to justify or validate a character's behavior by making it consistent, but this can easily ruin a character whose inconsistency is crucial to the play (in this case, the inconsistency between the way Iago seems to others and the way he is "inside"). It would be wise, therefore, to cast an actor who seems inherently honest and to let the context of the play generate his villainous qualities.

Another situation which recommends casting against type occurs when a character undergoes a radical change, such as the collapse of hope which drives Willy Loman to suicide in *Death of a Salesman*. If the actor playing Willy begins the play on the brink of suicide, the arc of the action will be greatly reduced. We need to see, especially in the flashbacks, the optimistic Willy filled with energy and happiness, so that the tragedy of his eventual defeat is the more vivid. In such a case, it is wise to cast the actor who seems most attuned to the character's early condition, but who has the capacity to undergo the change required.

Even if the change in the character is not as specific as Willy's, you may enhance the dynamism of the play by casting against type: Laertes's treachery will mean more if he begins as a deeply caring and loving boy (it is, in fact, the depth of his love for Polonius and Ophelia which drives him to treachery). In *King Lear*, Edgar ends the play as a man filled with compassion for the pain of life; this will move us more if he begins as a callow, selfish boy. In *Hamlet*, Claudius should be cast more for his attractiveness to Gertrude than for his monstrousness.

Even if the earlier condition of the character is only referred to in the play, we must be able to sense the remnants of that condition in them: How much more painful is the spectacle of Blanche Dubois in *Streetcar* if we see in her also the gracious, elegant, wholesome young woman from Bellerive! Cast such roles with a sense of what the character once was as well as what she or he has become. It may be riskier, or require more intense work during rehearsals, to re-create the metamorphosis the character has undergone, but eventually the results will be worth it.

In all these examples, the principle is to cast for the beginning of the play as well as for the end. Out of our desire to ensure a successful ending, we sometimes cast the actor who embodies the outcome so thoroughly that the play is left with nowhere to go. Remember that *change* is the essence of drama, and in no way is change more deeply felt than in the manifold textures of a developing character.

FINAL CASTING

I subscribe to what might be called the "ripple theory" of casting: You start at the center of the network of relationships and once the central relationship is determined, you allow it to generate all the rest of the casting, moving out through the network like a ripple. Thus each casting choice becomes the logical extension of the central choice, and each role is cast primarily according to its function within the whole (and this, we hope, may aid each actor in experiencing his or her superobjective).

In *Hamlet*, for instance, you will see from the network of relationships (Figure 7-1) that once you have a Hamlet, you can determine your Claudius and Gertrude; once you have these, you can select the appropriate Ophelia, Polonius, and Laertes, and so on. Circumstances may force you to start your casting choices somewhere other than the center of the network; it may be that there is only one Claudius available, for instance. The question then arises: Should you pick the Hamlet that goes best with this Claudius, or should you pick the "best" Hamlet and do what you can to make the relationship work?

Sometimes, you will find yourself in this sort of situation *after* you have cast and have begun rehearsal: One of the actors will seem much different in the role than you had anticipated. In such a case, you are a little like a weaver who has run out of red yarn and is considering using blue instead: Should you alter your entire design to compensate for the change, or should you continue with your old design with the new element? This is a difficult choice. Ask yourself: "Does the whole make any sense with the new element?" If so, you can probably go ahead; if not, you must alter the basic design.

In most cases, of course, always cast the best available actor, whether "right" for the part or not. A good actor can make it right!

THE HAMLET LOG, PART 5: PRINCIPAL CASTING—SEPTEMBER 1

I fly to Ashland to discuss the casting of the production from next season's resident company, which is now being formed. During the past weeks I have studied the characters carefully and have done a scene-by-scene breakdown in order to determine possible doubling and consolidation of minor characters. I will be prepared to give Producing Director Jerry Turner a precise cast list which will guide him in forming the company.

Most important to Jerry is the decision about a Hamlet, and I am to audition several actors for the role. In my own mind, I am as eager to cast the roles of Claudius and Gertrude, since Hamlet will function most in these central relationships.

In preparation for the auditions, I consider the particular acting skills the role will require: Certainly sensitivity to Shakespeare's language will be a primary consideration, as will the sheer stamina necessary to sustain a role of this size. Also crucial, however, will be the actor's ability to reveal himself through his performance, his capacity to make us feel close to him. We must be able to sense his passion, both intellectual and sexual.

Three actors in the present company are under consideration (though I am free to suggest others if I wish), and I am able to see all three in performance or rehearsal (this is one of the tremendous advantages of a resident company). While I am careful not to let these performances prejudice me unduly about their potential for Hamlet, I am able to assess their technical capabilities; and there is no doubt that all three have the language, the physical presence, and the sheer stamina to support the role.

I next meet them individually, and with each I discuss the play in general, eager to get a sense of their ideas and to get to know them as people. As I envision it, the role will involve the actor's own feelings of mortality; I am therefore interested in their beliefs and feelings about death, and in each case this topic comes up naturally. The three actors are very different from one another and I become fascinated by the interpretative possibilities each opens in my mind. Each brings a unique energy to the role which would slant the entire production in one direction or another.

The first is an actor of enormous intelligence. He brings with him a number of critical commentaries (from among the many he has already read) which express ideas about the role he finds especially attractive. He speaks of the play with great fervor and in amazing detail; his preparation clearly rivals my own. Together, we read each of the great soliloquies in sequence and discuss the progression of thought which flows through them. He is particularly excited by the suggestion of one critic, based on the references to Hamlet's "antic disposition," that Hamlet "acts the fool" fully, even to the wearing of motley.

I value this actor's intelligence and his commitment to the play as a whole; certainly he has the rich intellectual life the role requires. It remains to be seen if he can embody also the passion needed.

The second actor I interview surprises me by the quietness of his personal bearing: He is someone you might easily overlook in a crowded room, and even in this private conversation he has an almost humble quality. He asks a few pithy questions about the role, but in the main he seems shy about advancing an opinion of his own, preferring to let me determine the course of the conversation. And yet there is something of great interest lurking here. Together, we go through the major soliloquies; his readings are also reserved, but far from dull. Rather, they communicate an effort to search the material out, to examine it *viva voce*. I greatly appreciate this approach, but I wonder what the performance might be like once it has been found. I will need more information before I can comfortably make up my mind.

I have heard much about the power of the third actor, and that night I see him give a stunning performance in Strindberg's *The Father*. We meet after the performance in a local pub. We discuss the play generally, and it is clear at once that we draw the same values from it, perhaps because we are precisely the same age (to the day) and are both experiencing a mid-life crisis. From a purely subjective point of view, working together on *Hamlet* could be an experience of great potential value.

There is an objective consideration, however: His age cannot be ignored. The text specifies that Hamlet is thirty, and he has always "felt" younger to me. Nevertheless, we discuss the interpretive possibilities of an older Hamlet, and there is much that is intriguing about the idea, especially the "existential weight" which an older actor can bring to the part.

Balanced against the positive value of an older Hamlet, however, is the difficulty in casting the relationships; Gertrude and Claudius would have to be at least in their late fifties, and then there is Ophelia . . . questions of interpretation aside, are the older actors available in the resident company?

The next day, Jerry Turner and I meet to discuss casting in general. We first go over the possibilities for Laertes, Ophelia, and Polonius. I've seen several possibilities for the brother and sister in the present company: Bruce Gooch, who is currently playing Henry V, would make a fine Laertes. Gayle Bellows (whom I have seen in *Spokesong*) has the kind of vulnerable-but-sexy quality I want in Ophelia; moreover she and Bruce could easily pass as brother and sister. We agree on this choice.

I am delighted to learn also that Bruce is an accomplished swordsman. The climactic fight between Hamlet and Laertes must be tremendously exciting and skillful; I am hoping that we can have a resident choreographer who can work over several weeks to develop the dramatic potential of the fight as rehearsals progress, though it will probably not be wise for Bruce to take this task on himself since he will have other roles.

We turn next to the question of Polonius. I explain that I want Polonius to be more an opportunist than a fool, and that the love of Polonius for his children, and they for him, must be genuine and strong. Ophelia's suicidal madness must be engendered as much by her father's death as by Hamlet's rejection. Likewise, Laertes will join Claudius's deceitful plot out of the depth of his grief over the deaths of his father and sister, so the actor playing Polonius must engender these feelings from his children. Jerry suggests Richard Elmore, whom I have seen in *Blythe Spirit*, and I agree.

There is only one possibility for Gertrude in the present company, and she is unavailable due to other assignments. I describe my preference for a voluptuous Gertrude who is clearly driven by her physical passions, and Jerry says he has some possibilities in mind.

The casting of Claudius is a more complex issue and is, in my mind, as important to the success of the production as is the casting of Hamlet. I have become steadily more and more fascinated by the complexity of Claudius: He is similar to Iago and Richard III as a study of innate evil and yet capable of remorse in a way they are not. Three actors in the present company might be considered for the role. Of the three, the best choice is clearly the oldest of the three actors I have auditioned for Hamlet; he would realize the inner conflict which so fascinates me in Claudius. Moreover, I sense that he would be an excellent foil to the second actor's Hamlet.

I am clearly leaning toward the second actor as Hamlet. I find that my impression of his work has been enhanced by the passage of time, and by the warm feelings for him expressed by other directors who have recently worked with him.

Still, this is a choice that needs to be slept on, and Jerry is leaving it entirely up to me. I leave with the agreement to make my decision within a few days. Contracts are in the process of negotiation, and the needs of the other productions must be considered as well. The remaining roles will be cast when I return to Ashland for rehearsals.

SEPTEMBER 4

After envisioning the various actors in the parts for a few days, my choice is made: I want the second actor, Mark Murphey, to play Hamlet, and the third, Denis Arndt, as Claudius.

I telephone Jerry Turner, and he is delighted. This solution, it seems, would also have been his personal choice. He will present the situation to both actors for their consideration. I know that Denis will have reservations about playing Claudius rather than Hamlet, and I decide to write him a personal letter explaining my choice.

THE HAMLET LOG, PART 6: SECOND DESIGN CONFERENCE—OCTOBER 1–2

I fly to Ashland for the second design conference. At Dick's request we have given ourselves two full days to work interactively until we have established the final design, since the construction drawings are due in a week. Although the costume designs are not due for months, Jeannie will also attend the meeting to ensure a close coordination of the design elements.

I again read through the play several times, looking for clues about the environment; I want to have a fresh impression for the conference. I am struck once more by the omnipresence of war and the sense of impending danger from the outer world creating an atmosphere of paranoia and an incestuous "turning inward." There are several references to cannon in particular.

I notice again how much spying happens, and that twice an arras is used to conceal the spying Polonius. In the first instance, it is possible that Hamlet suspects his presence when he pointedly asks Ophelia, "Where is your father?" I plan to mention this prominence of cannon, tapestries, and hiding places to Dick.

I arrive for the first meeting in Dick's studio. We have not so far done any of the sketching by which a design is usually developed, but I know from our past work that Dick prefers to work in three dimensions throughout the process. I am not surprised, then, to find that he has created a quarter-inch scale model of his proposed design, which sits within a model of the auditorium with two small lamps arranged to simulate stage lighting. Dick assures me that this design is only a starting point and is open to radical alteration. Accordingly, we treat it in the spirit of a three-dimensional sketch, laying hands upon it and moving things about (see Figures 10-1 and 10-2).

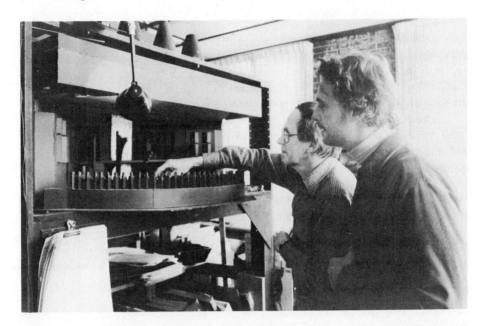

Figure 10-1.   Working on the Model; Richard Hay (L) and the Author. *Robert Benedetti.*

Figure 10-2.   The *Hamlet* Model. *Robert Benedetti.*

I am immediately excited by Dick's concept. The stage is thrust well out into the auditorium, with an extension running into one of the vomitoria and the architectural decor of the auditorium has been continued around behind and into the set so that the house and set "embrace" one another. I am especially delighted to notice how well the set provides an area for soliloquies "in the laps of the audience," as I had hoped.

The basic configuration of the set is that of the Elizabethan stage, but rendered in a Gothic style. The overall visual impression is that of a fortress, with three large cannon (!) guarding the central area like silent sentinels. Surrounding the main playing area on all sides are raised walkways, open stairs, and ramps which give a sense of the battle scaffolding erected in medieval castles during a siege. These walkways give the sense of a maze, and extend offstage in five directions and on various levels, leading to other spaces beyond.

The most startling element of the design is an an enormous tapestry standing in front of the central tower, running the full height of the stage opening. On it stands the gargantuan figure of the old Hamlet, brooding over the scene below. Dick explains that this tapestry could be used in various ways: He has prepared cutouts of it swagged back to either side, or split down the middle and opened to both sides. He runs through various scenes inserting first one cutout, then another. For the appearance and disappearance of the Ghost, he suggests using it as a scrim and having the Ghost emerge through it on the upper level.

The design has captured all the major points raised at our first design conference and has anticipated the images of cannon and tapestry which had struck me on the plane. I sit in front of the model and begin to run through the play in my mind, exploring the possibilities it offers for each scene. After some time, I feel certain that the set will work splendidly.

I have some specific questions about sightlines and the relationship of certain areas to the audience, so Dick and I carry it into the auditorium. There we outline the precise location of the set and check sightlines from various points; I am delighted with the way it penetrates into the house, and have only a few alterations to suggest.

First, I think the downstage edge of the forestage could be advanced even a few feet further into the house, creating a slightly larger downstage playing area in which some two-person scenes could be played. This downstage area suggests to me a wharf: There is a block at its front edge extending down to the auditorium floor which reminds me of a piling, and I suggest creating a second piling at center. This will both extend the image of a wharf and add a down-center sitting place for some of the most reflective soliloquies.

The idea of a wharf intrigues me; the castle might believably have its own adjacent harbor. I run through the locale breakdown and see at once three scenes which concern people embarking: The farewell of Laertes in 13, that of Reynaldo in 21, and Hamlet's own embarcation for England in 44. Another possible wharf scene is 46, when Hamlet's letters are delivered by the sailors. In all these cases, I love the effect created by the nearness of the sea; it carries the feeling of what Jung called "the Oceanic Feeling."

My last suggestion concerns the tapestry: I fear its prominence. It stands as the central point of focus and tends to draw the eye away from the action below; moreover, it is a static metaphor that might wear out after a few scenes. It also obscures the useful center portion of the upper walkway. I suggest that we move it behind the central walkway, so that the horizontal line of the catwalk cuts its massive vertical. Moving it upstage in this way will also separate it more from the central playing area, and will reduce the amount of key light which will hit it.

We modify the model to reflect this change, and we both like the effect. We go through the show, dropping the cutouts in place to see how the curtain will look in various positions, checking entrances and exits. We pay special attention to the stabbing of Polonius and the problem of his falling so that Hamlet cannot see whom he has killed.

In our first design conference, Dick had mentioned that the killing of Polonius in other productions had never seemed horrible enough to make us feel "that Hamlet has done something really awful." As one solution, he has designed a separate curtain, hidden in the body of one of the central walkway supports, which would be drawn in front of the larger tapestry during the Closet scene. The dying Polonius could then tear this curtain down and stagger forward and collapse in its folds. I am not happy with the idea of a second arras, however. A scenic element as prominent as the tapestry must be justified by being integrated into the action, and using it as the arras is the most obvious instance of such integration; I would feel cheated if it did not pay off in this way.

Instead, I suggest cutting the lower portion of the tapestry into ribbons so that the sword can pass through easily; Hamlet can then pull the impaled Polonius through it as he withdraws his sword, though the problem of his not seeing who it is remains. It might be possible for Hamlet to hold the impaled Polonius on his sword until the moment of recognition. In any case, the ribbon curtain will make it easy for Hamlet to drag Polonius out.

We agree on these changes, and Dick sets to work revising the model. It is fairly late in the day, and we agree to sleep on the design and to meet with Jeannie the next morning.

SECOND DESIGN CONFERENCE, CONTINUED: OCTOBER 2

Jeannie, Dick, and I meet the next morning. At my suggestion, Jerry Turner stops by to take a look at the set; he admires it, but is concerned about the access to some seats being cut off by the vomitorium ramp. Dick agrees to check this out, and he has several ideas for modifications if necessary, such as inserting a drawbridge in the vomitorium ramp to provide access across the front of the house during intermissions.

After Jerry leaves, we begin to go through the show again, scene by scene. The alteration made yesterday to the tapestry still seems a good one and opens the first scene up considerably. By using all the walkways as battlements, the action can cover a great deal of space, with good distance between the soldiers below and the Ghost above. To enhance this sense of distance and mystery, I request the use of fog in all the Ghost scenes, and Dick notes the possible locations of ducts from which the fog can emanate.

Jeannie asks about the movements of the Ghost, since his maximum height will be established by the doorways through which he will pass; I trace several pathways he might take on the battlements and later in the Closet scene, and we agree that seven feet is the maximum. While we all want the Ghost to be a frightening figure, I am eager that his human scale not be lost; the scene between Hamlet and the Ghost must first of all be a scene between father and son. We discuss several treatments for the Ghost, including the use of a wireless microphone to make a subtle augmentation of his voice; an internal glow is also a possibility. We adjust the positioning of several escape stairs to allow for his passage.

To further enhance the sense of mystery, I want to use torches and lanterns in the Battlement scenes, and again in the Mousetrap scene. The use of animal masquerade masks to create a nightmarish quality for that scene still seems like an excellent idea. We go over the cast list to see how many torchbearers could be available in each scene, and find that five is the maximum. I must soon produce a detailed scene-breakdown chart listing the number of servants, torchbearers, bannerbearers, soldiers, and rabble.

While considering these extras, Jeannie points out the need for more ladies in this otherwise very male court. The presence of women will also help to strengthen the contrast between the bluff, military court of the old king and the elegant, ambassadorial court which Claudius will create, since the women's gowns make a stronger statement of a change in fashion than does the men's clothing. I agree to add at least two ladies to each of the court scenes.

The entrances and exits of large groups is a special consideration. Dick points out that the stage-right entrances are quite tall, permitting a banner or halberds to enter erect, while the stage-left doorways are lower: He had thought of the right as the "ceremonial" side and the left as the "intimate" side. I realize there is a sharp contrast in the play between the public and the private scenes, and I begin thinking of ways to emphasize this difference through the use of the ground plan and the lighting.

In the Wedding/Coronation scene, we consider the entrance of the wedding party and Hamlet's relationship to it. It occurs to me that a priest will help to place the event, and could reappear at Ophelia's funeral as well; in fact, the priest might accompany Claudius in a number of scenes, extending his preoccupation with the appearances of piety.

We next discuss the entrance of the Players. The down-left stairway from the vomitorium has emerged as the front door of the castle, so that the departing and returning ambassadors, the arriving Rosencrantz and Guildenstern, and the Players will all use this entrance. We consider how the Players can carry whatever equipment they might have. Dick suggests that some of their props might be used in the speeches performed at Hamlet's request, and that they can be left on stage for Hamlet's use during the soliloquy, which will close our first act; they can then be struck during the intermission. I find this an exciting idea.

The Mousetrap scene is discussed, and we agree that the main focus should be the battle of wits between Claudius and Hamlet. I opt to place the Players' peformance downstage so that we can watch the assembled court behind it. The bringing on of the thrones and the Players' equipment will make excellent activity during the Advice-to-the-Players scene; Dick suggests the use of a rug to define the "stage."

The Graveyard scene raises serious issues: A trapdoor must serve as the grave, and it must be placed to provide sufficient space around it for the mourners. The entrance of the Gravediggers will be from within the grave, and we check the problem of access for them, and of escape for the coffin. Jeannie asks about the body of Ophelia in the Funeral scene; will she be visible or in a closed casket? It seems more dramatic if she can be seen, yet if she is simply carried on a bier, can we imagine Laertes and Hamlet jumping into the grave atop her exposed body? I suggest a casket which is open during the funeral procession, then closed and sealed as she is lowered into the grave.

The depth of the grave is a concern, and we check sightlines. The grave must be deep enough for the casket to pass out of sight, but not so deep that the Gravediggers cannot extricate themselves; we agree on four feet. We discuss dirt, and agree that there will be no actual digging by the Gravediggers, their work being nearly done when the scene starts. Whether or not the Gravedigger should remain on stage during the funeral is discussed; I think he must.

The fight between Hamlet and Laertes is discussed at length; I reserve judgment as to whether Hamlet and Laertes ought to fight inside or outside of the grave.

The next scene which takes our attention is the breaking in of Laertes in 45: Should he be accompanied by a rabble, as indicated by the text? Should the rabble be seen or only heard? I opt to have a sizeable crowd fight its way up the vomitorium behind Laertes. The political unrest of the kingdom under Claudius is important, for by now his rule is beginning to slip (he has to call twice for his "Switzers," mercenaries who may have been hired as personal bodyguards because he cannot trust his own soldiers). I make a note to include as many actors in the rabble as are available for this scene.

The final scene is discussed, and the set seems to support it very well. I voice a concern about the downstage cannon; it may be in the way of scenes played on the vomitorium ramp it occupies. I suggest the possibility of moving it off a few feet during the first intermission, but we will reach no decision on this until the blocking has been determined.

Last, we discuss the sky cyclorama which surrounds the set, and the way in which it might be used to indicate changing spaces and times, as well as the nature of the backing for the center entrances, agreeing that both the lower and the upper should open into blackness.

The meeting has been long and productive (only the highlights have been reported here). Dick will now produce a half-inch scale model for the guidance of the shop, and he and his assistants will produce the construction drawings immediately. The questions of color and texture will be discussed after rehearsals have begun, since the set would not be painted until then. I ask Dick to send me the quarter-inch model for my use in the weeks before rehearsal.

Jeannie will not actually begin the costume designs for several weeks yet. Jeannie hopes to bring her first sketches to me in Los Angeles when she comes in to shop for the other productions. With a great sense of accomplishment, we adjourn.

MEETING WITH HAMLET: OCTOBER 3

I have breakfast this morning with Mark Murphey, who is eager to get my thoughts about Hamlet, and I his. We speak generally about the play first, and I pose a number of the questions that intrigue me most, avoiding any conclusions. As Mark prepares to attack the role, I can help most by assisting him in identifying the most meaningful issues. If I short-circuit his problem-solving process by supplying premature answers, I will have deprived him of a crucial step in the gradual transformation by which a good actor enters into the consciousness of his character.

The conversation centers around the issue of readiness. When does Hamlet get ready? What is stopping him from being ready sooner? What is the precise nature of his readiness, once it is achieved? We discuss this at some length; I suggest that Hamlet's readiness is not the readiness to initiate action, but rather, readiness to react to whatever fortune may bring, to live "in the moment." It is, in short, the readiness of enlightenment. This, I believe, will be the heart of our production; it will be Mark's superobjective to find how each moment of his performance will lead him to (and then from) this "getting ready."

Mark has a number of questions springing from this idea; I encourage him to think personally, to bring his relationship to his own mother, father, and wife to bear on the problem, as well as his own sense of mortality. I am surprised to learn that he is thirty-six (he seems younger both in person and on stage), and I am glad to learn that many of the concerns of the mid-life crisis are already at work in him.

I let him know that I want to work in an exploratory manner, and that his ideas are welcome and will be put to work in rehearsals. We leave in high spirits, and I am feeling better than ever about my casting choice.

Before flying back to LA I meet once more with Jerry Turner. He is further along in planning the resident company, and it now appears that we won't have as many men available for *Hamlet* as we had hoped. Now that I have added Torch Bearers, Claudius's Priest, and a Steward, however, twenty-one men is the minimum. Since four of these are very small roles, we agree to use townspeople if necessary.

I drive to the airport with Pat Patton, the production manager. He has a concern about the running time of *Hamlet*: There are some days when *Hamlet* plays a matinee, with a changeover to a different show in the evening. The crew will be pushed to strike and set up before the house opens at 7:30. Pat is concerned that the two intermissions I am planning will increase the overall length of the show, and he encourages me to consider only one intermission. I explain that the shape of the action makes three acts a preferable structure, and that there is no good place for a single break to fall. Still, I agree to keep the possibility of one intermission alive until I can see enough of the show in rehearsal to make a firm judgment.

THE HAMLET LOG, PART 7: COSTUME AND SOUND MEETINGS—OCTOBER 5-7

I spend three days making up the master scene/character/time/place chart, deciding who will carry banners and torches, and so on (see Appendix One). I make a final determination on the doubling (with only a few minor changes from my initial list). I usually resist committing myself to this much staging detail so far in advance, but it seems necessary; I am being careful to leave plenty of room within this staging context for the exploration of meaning.

I am especially interested in exploring the "climate" of each scene; I read through the play carefully for indications of time and place, noting them in my script wherever they occur. Working from this evidence, I fill out the time line of the play, choosing to keep the action continuous (that is, in "real time") as much as possible. I am noting also any necessary sound or lighting effects, furniture or curtain movements, or costuming notes.

This master chart will undergo constant revision throughout the rehearsal period, but it will serve as an important anchor to the work, and as the main basis for communication between me and the design staff.

FURTHER SCENIC NOTES: OCTOBER 20

Dick calls with an idea for the appearance of the Ghost. By using a rear-projection screen, the image of the Ghost can be made to merge out of the figure on the tapestry. It would require tight cueing, but could be quite magical. I encourage him to pursue this idea.

The center tower is now being built. As originally designed, it had two hidden exitways on either side, but it would be easier to build without them. Will I need them? I assure him that I've been thinking over the "geography" of the set and that I won't.

Dick reports that the matter of audience access and the vomitorium ramp has been settled. The ramp has been widened to connect with the aisles on either side, and it will contain a trapdoor which can be dropped in an emergency to allow access across the front of the stage. These are good solutions and I am glad that we have headed off any possible disruption of our ground plan.

Dick is still concerned over the death of Polonius: The unit which would contain the second arras is about to be built; am I quite certain that we ought not to use it? I assure him that I will find a way to curdle his blood without it.

FIRST MUSIC AND SOUND MEETING:
OCTOBER 22

Todd Barton, the resident composer for the Festival, is in LA for a recording session; we arrange a meeting. Todd has read my cutting, which indicates locations of possible sound and light cues; he has also examined the master scene chart, which is explicit about the time, place, and atmosphere of each scene and also listed those sound effects which were specified by the text or necessitated by the action. Those cues which are specifically musical in nature will be Todd's responsibility; sound effects, such as the tolling of bells, or the sound of wind under a scene, will be created by Douglas Faerber, the Festival sound designer.

Todd and I had spoken briefly during the summer and I had suggested that bells should be the central motif of the show. We run through the text and find the possibility of bells in nearly every scene: A tolling bell that I want to bracket the play, the ringing of the hours, pealing bells for the coronation, ships' bells in the port, chapel bells, and a live bell tree for the Players. I had suggested that we might use at least one large live "killer" bell for emphasis, but Todd has decided that we can do the job best on tape.

Todd proposes to use a bell ensemble with percussion as the basis for most of the music (the flourishes as well as the songs; we agree to avoid all trumpets). Todd suggests a simple, Teutonic sound for the melodies, with Ophelia's mad song being the main melodic motif. We will also use synthesizer enhancement for such effects as the ghost.

I hope that we can use sound to create a sense of environment in each scene, and we examine each locale to see what its acoustical properties might be: a moaning wind for the battlement scenes, the sound of water and ships at the wharf, distant chanting for Claudius's chapel, and night sounds for the graveyard are all obvious choices. We consider as well the echoing of the hollow hallways in the chase, and sounds of partying offstage in several scenes. We agree that these environmental sounds will be omnidirectional, surrounding the audience in the same way that the set is intended to "wrap around" the entire auditorium.

We then go through the script chronologically, discussing the placement and nature of each specific cue. We note those cues which require a sense of direction; speaker placement may have to be considered as part of the set construction process. We discuss also the use of a wireless microphone for a subliminal enhancement of the Ghost's voice.

I express the hope that as the environmental cues are developed, the rough tapes can come into rehearsal so that the actors can begin to work within the acoustical environment of each scene. This could be a powerful element in the rehearsal process. We adjourn, and Todd promises to communicate this information and to begin work soon.

EARLY COSTUME CONCEPTS:
OCTOBER 31

Jeannie writes thanking me for the master scene chart, which she has found most helpful. She suggests a meeting in Los Angeles in two weeks while she is there shopping for fabrics, and gives me her initial thoughts:

> My notions of *Hamlet* and how it looks begin to shape up like this—costumes are heavy, focus is on mass and color rather than a proliferation of small detail. Silhouettes are strong, expansive; fabrics largely thick, rich, light-absorbent—lots of velour, wool, even fur; the place is cold, dank. This is not to say that riotous color is not admissible where it is appropriate. Gertrude may appear in a smashing red, hugely brocaded gown at some point, but it is very thick, rich, sumptuous and decadently "bare" at the same moment. Sleeves are large, I think, and cloaks enveloping. Ornamentation exists as either an elaborate total pattern in the fabric (perhaps a brocade pattern painted on velour with metallic gold, for instance) or as a single large brooch on an otherwise plain costume; sharply contrasting linings peek out.
>
> My ideas about color are, as usual, emotional; somehow I want to restrict this palette a lot—for the strength of the statement that will make, perhaps. Black/red/white and the attendant extensions of those colors (black into browns and greys, white into beige and creme, red into rust and wine).
>
> I get from you a need for a "real-clothes" sense, especially in the more casual "undressed" moments. I prefer a sense of layered garments myself, and this suits the real-clothes feeling well.

I write in response at once, enthusiastic about her ideas.

SECOND COSTUME MEETING: NOVEMBER 21

Jeannie is in LA buying fabric; we meet downtown to examine her preliminary pencil drawings.

We discuss several general matters first. The show, because of its size (seventy-four costumes), will be a mixture of entirely new costumes and elements pulled from stock: it is presently budgeted to be about 50 percent new and 50 percent stock. Basically, all the principal costumes will be built anew, and designs have been created for each. Some characters have a number of changes (Gertrude amd Claudius, for instance, have five costumes each, and Hamlet four). Those costumes to be pulled from stock are indicated by a general description.

Jeannie's color ideas are as she described in her letter: The coronation will be mainly white (beige, creme) except for the black Hamlet; the Mousetrap scene will be mainly red (wine, rust); and the final Fight scene, with the court in mourning for Ophelia, will be mainly black (brown, grey), except for a now white-shirted Hamlet—this an interesting reversal of the Coronation scene.

Details will be avoided except for large three-dimensional patterns and ornaments, and the painting will be restricted to spattering with metallic paints to provide texture and movement. The period will be on the cusp between medieval Gothic and German Renaissance, with the old court in the Gothic style and the new court, under Claudius, in the Renaissance style.

The Ghost will be in Gothic armor that is rotting away, so we get gaping holes revealing a black interior. He will be large (with a built-up helmet) and will carry his own light sources so that he appears to be phosphorescent (as rotten things sometimes are). It is especially important to Jeannie that he seem to float, so his skirt will cover his feet.

The Party scene will, as I suggested, be a masquerade. Jeannie wants to select animal masks which will make a comment on the person wearing them, for instance, a monkey and a fox for Rosencrantz and Guildenstern. Hamlet, however, will not be in mask but instead will wear a jester's coxcomb and carry the traditional jester's stick. The dumb show will be done in tall, totemic masks, white robes and cothurni, so that they seem like Viking figures.

We next discuss each of the characters, looking at the designs for each and paying special attention to any practical onstage activity (like dressing or undressing, pockets and purses, the raising of the Ghost's beaver).

Hamlet begins in a very simple mourning outfit in 12, then a mussed look in 22 (as described by Ophelia); at the party he is well dressed, though again the most simple of all the court figures. When he returns from England he is caped, with a blunt, honest look.

Ophelia is in a courtly gown in 12, then in her nightgown in 21; after a lovely party dress, she will appear in a "ruined" version of this nightgown for her Mad scene.

Gertrude has a progression of five costumes; in all she is a mixture of sexy bareness and regal splendor, with a heavily layered look. We agree, however, that she will not be too sexy in the Closet scene, and her nightdress here is demure. The "picture" of Claudius (which Hamlet contrasts to his "picture" of his father) will be a portrait cameo around her neck, and Hamlet will tear it from her.

Claudius is a clotheshorse and goes through five changes as well, each quite stylish and tasteful, though elaborate (nowadays he would dress like Tom Wolfe). His preoccupation with the appearance of piety is carried out in a necklace of crosses.

Horatio has a scholarly look, very simple, with an armhole cloak and skull cap. Voltemand, Cornelius, the lords and ladies, will provide lots of color for the coronation and party; Osric will be the most outrageously dressed, and his hat will literally be the only hat in the show, though it will not appear until the final scene.

I am pleased with these preliminary drawings, and Jeannie goes ahead with final designs and the shopping for the show.

FURTHER COSTUME AND SCENIC NOTES: DECEMBER 7-9

Jeannie calls with some bad news: her shop manager's estimate of the required work time is too high; we have to cut about fourteen costumes. This can be done by eliminating costume changes for the minor court members in the large group scenes, which may reduce the single-color dominance in each somewhat, but the statement will still be made. The principal costumes are unaffected by this choice; the final designs are in the mail.

Dick Hay calls about the Funeral scene; he has realized that the down-left vom is the only entrance wide enough to accomodate the funeral procession, and is worried about that limitation. This is actually the way I had been thinking about the scene, though, since in my sense of the geography of the set the down-left entrance is to and from the "outer world."

It appears that the scenic demands of the season have created problems for the scene shop, and that the applied texture we had considered for the set is impossible. Dick suggests simply painting it to match the walls of the theatre so as to carry the sense of the environment around fully, and this is fine with me.

Dick also asks me to consider the specific uses of the tapestry (when and how it will be opened and closed) so he can design the necessary operating devices. I demur, saying that I need to rough through the show in the first two weeks of rehearsal before deciding on these details.

He also needs a preliminary prop list; it needn't be definitive, but the prop master needs some idea of the scope of the show. Using my master scene chart I am able to produce a preliminary list fairly quickly, and mail it off the next day.

FINAL COSTUME DESIGNS: DECEMBER 10

The final sketches from Jeannie arrive in the mail, and we talk on the phone after I have examined them; I have only a few minor questions. By eliminating costume changes for the supporting characters we have not only reduced the number of costumes but also assisted the audience in character identification. The idea of a dominant color in each of the three large crowd scenes is now restricted to the principals, and can be supported by banner colors as well.

Two days later, Jeannie calls again: Having finished pulling materials from stock, she is satisfied that all our ideas will work. She has decided to use a lot of primitive textures—furs, monk's cloth, and the like. She tells me that the prop master from the American Conservatory Theatre in San Francisco has been commissioned to create the Ghost as a special project. This costume will be so difficult to get into that I must avoid doubling the Ghost as a soldier, which I had originally planned.

ELEVEN
FIRST REHEARSALS

In Chapter Three I suggested that the seed of a plant was a good metaphor for the system of norms of a play, and that gardening was therefore a useful metaphor for directing. If we extend this metaphor to the specifics of the rehearsal process, we can see that the director, like the gardener, must first prepare the soil and plant the seed properly. In order to sprout, the seed must be given the best conditions in which to grow. While the plant is developing, it may need temporary support. At last it can stand on its own and can be strengthened and shaped by pruning. Throughout the process, the gardener's efforts are aligned with the growth of the plant, and this gives the work an overall rhythm with a logical flow from one stage of development to another.

If we translate the gardener's process into the traditional progression of rehearsing a play, the various stages look something like this:

1. *Preparing the climate of growth*: preparing the cast to work together effectively and establishing a growthful rehearsal atmosphere;

2. *Planting the seed*: first readings and discussions to give a sense of direction;

3. *Cultivating*: early explorations of the action, looking into the given circumstances, breaking the scenes down, locating crises, finding the through-line of action, beginning character development;

4. *Shaping and pruning*: establishing the tempo/rhythm of the emerging performance (scoring), and developing pace through detailed work on choices to solidify the connections that transmit the action;

6. *Harvesting*: the addition of the actual set, costumes, props, lighting and sound, and the synthesis of all the elements in a rhythmically unified performance.

While there is a logic to this sequence as a general outline, it is not necessarily right in every detail for every situation. You should give some thought early on to the strategy which might be best suited to the demands of your particular play and theatrical circumstances, knowing that you will make adjustments as the work progresses; for like the gardener, you must align your efforts with the emerging energies of the play as it grows.

In the remaining five chapters of this book we will look at each of these phases in the rehearsal process.

PREPARING THE WORK CLIMATE

The atmosphere in the rehearsal hall is the climate in which the play will grow; you must be sure that it is hospitable, though not indiscriminately idyllic. What is wanted is a *creative state*.

For most of us, a creative state implies a spirit of enthusiasm and almost child-like abandon. Several of the directors answering my question about an effective rehearsal environment specifically mentioned laughter as a sign of the creative state, as in Jack O'Brien's statement:

> I know that I am at my best when I'm full of enthusiasm, both for the material and for the people themselves. I like an "up" free-wheeling rehearsal atmosphere in which everyone feels supported and able to release whatever they want to bring out. I think it's terribly important to laugh, because the tension is dissipated, and the simple truth can emerge. It's the strain, the dark tension that I try to avoid, because it is self-important, self-conscious, and self-involving. When the rehearsal process makes it possible to "give it away," it is at its best.

How do you help to create such an atmosphere? Directors sometimes use games, exercises, or parties to break the ice and to establish a rapport within the cast. While such activities can be useful, they must be natural to the situation; if they are imposed self-consciously or as a kind of emotional bribery, they can can be irrelevant and even counter-productive. You may want your actors to be as uninhibited as children, but you must treat them like the adults they are and avoid a "summer camp" mentality.

Most important is your personal preparation and discipline, since the mood of the group will usually reflect your own. Do whatever you can to put yourself into the state you would prefer for the entire group. Tom Haas describes the process this way:

> When I am best in rehearsal, I am most at play, although the work necessary to achieve this state is a long and sometimes arduous process. I find when I have time to prepare myself for the production and time to put all that preparation on

a back burner in my mind, then I am most free to be on the floor and be available to what comes up, trusting my own impulses and the assessment of others. Whether the play be tragedy or musical comedy, I find I am working at my best when there is a genuine sense of humor and laughter on the rehearsal floor.

It should be noted that a few directors disagree with this emphasis on laughter: In his early work with The Polish Laboratory Theatre, Grotowski actually prohibited laughter from the rehearsal hall. Charles Marowitz and Richard Schechner both argue that a good rehearsal process *must* pass through a period of unpleasant tension, a sort of "birth crisis" or "test by fire," which tempers the work and burns away superficiality. Marowitz, in fact, will sometimes engineer a crisis if the rehearsal process seems too placid or playful.

Whatever atmosphere seems most creative for the group and for the demands of the play, you mustn't invest too much in it: The best of ensemble spirits is no guarantee of creativity. Remember that a good group does not necessarily create good work: It is far truer to say that the work creates the group. The alignment of the creative ensemble derives solely from its true purpose, and that is the exploration and development of a work of art; whatever social life the group may have is a byproduct of that effort. Energy directed primarily toward the social life of the group is off purpose; stay on purpose and help the group to find its own identity through the work itself.

Remember the concept of alignment which we discussed earlier: Each member of the ensemble is a sovereign individual with a unique contribution to make; it is part of your job to assist them in aligning their efforts toward the group's purpose, and to see that they have the conditions they need to do their best work. Those conditions include a clear sense of the shared objective, the active support of their fellow workers, and honest and considerate communication during the work itself.

All this having been said, however, remember above all that the real source of a creative rehearsal environment is *you*. When you are tense, frightened, and confused, so will it be; when you are enthusiastic, interested, and daring, so will it be. When things go wrong, you will know where to look first.

FIRST CAST MEETINGS

In describing the most important element of an effective production process, Michael Leibert says:

> The single most important element is the collaborative effort, but it must have a firm beginning if it is to have a successful end.

Your own preparation has given you a firm beginning in your embodiment of the play's system of norms; in your early rehearsals you will assist your actors in sharing your perception of the play, and in experiencing the play's norms for themselves. This is how alignment in the deepest sense will be achieved. Insofar as the actors can embody the norms of the play, they will be better able to contribute to the group purpose without constant supervision from you. In a sense, you are trying to get things underway so as to make yourself unnecessary later on.

One traditional way for you to share your perception of the play is by opening remarks at the first rehearsal about "what this play really means." This sort of speech may be useful in sharing your perception of the play, but it is not a very good way of giving the actors their own experience of the play's system of norms. A director's opening statement about a play must be used with great discretion; to say nothing and allow the play to speak for itself is often the best policy.

Sometimes directors are guilty of using these opening remarks to make a good impression, displaying a weight of critical and historical preparation which puts the actors in a passive position. Nor should an opening statement be concerned with the form of the eventual production, as in "here's how we will do this play." A cast will be considerably put off by the sense that the director is laying the journey out for them, step by step, as if they are simply to recreate the production the director can already see in his or her mind. This makes them feel like puppets (because in such a situation they are), and they rightly resent it.

How then should you begin? Think of these first rehearsals as the beginning of a journey of exploration into an unknown land, with the text as a kind of cryptic map. The business of these first meetings is to prepare for the trip:

1. Organize the expedition and ensure good communications (a common vocabulary and the beginnings of a shared methodology);
2. Be sure everyone knows how to read the map and has a general sense of the direction in which you will begin;
3. Assemble whatever provisions you may need (remembering that you don't want to carry anything you can find along the way).

In other words, begin by thinking not about rehearsing the production, but about preparing to develop that which will be rehearsed later. Think the way an athletic coach does: The athlete must be prepared to make the play, both intellectually (by understanding the rules, strategy, and objective of the game) and physically (in terms of the fundamental skills and techniques needed for success), but finally the play itself cannot be rehearsed; it must be executed on the spot.

From this point of view, we theatre people spend entirely too much time rehearsing and far too little preparing. In my talks with Lee Breuer, he emphasized further that we spend too much time perfecting performances of concepts and stage images which have not themselves been sufficiently explored or tested; out of our eagerness to produce and to meet deadlines, we devote too much effort to form and not enough to content!

If you give an opening statement at all, then, it should have the spirit of marching orders, providing a sense of direction and the means whereby you will proceed into the world of the play, and perhaps some sense of what you hope (at least initially) to find there.

Helping everyone to learn how to read the map may require some work on special techniques such as scansion or figures of speech; or special information such as definitions of colloquial or archaic speech.

Some of the most exciting preparatory work could be "the collecting of provisions for the journey"; ask yourself what might make your exploration more effective. Among the possibilities are:

1. Technical skills such as fencing, period dance, verse delivery, singing, and acrobatics;
2. Special information, such as an awareness of the moral, philosophical, theatrical, or psychological assumptions on which the play is based;
3. Experiences such as a sense of the historical moment of the play, a feeling for the theatre in which it was originally done, or an understanding of what it is like to live under the absolute domination of another person;
4. Direct experience of the play's norms, such as its rhythms, textures, and imagery.

Your research into the play (Chapter Two) has already provided you with a list of provisions. Select those items that will best enliven and support the work to be done, and provide them in the most effective form: readings, films, exercises, games, or simulations. I remember the first rehearsal for a play about life in a concentration camp; the director created a "sensorium" of music, pictures, barbed wire, clothing for the actors to wear, smells, food. The actors spent a day and night in the sensorium, under guard, eating and being made to behave as the inmates would. Over the weeks that followed, the actors themselves contributed to the sensorium—diaries, pictures, reports from their own families. The effect of this work on the production could have been achieved by no other means.

A note of caution about this kind of "provisioning," however: Avoid burdening your actors with excess baggage! Select only those experiences and information that are essential to the journey, and avoid carrying things that can be found along the way. It may be, for instance, that several weeks of speaking Shakespeare's lines will produce a better understanding of his scansion than would an introductory seminar on prosody, or it may be that such a seminar would be more effective at a later date. Try to supply things when they are truly needed; as Hamlet says, "the ripeness is all"!

THE FIRST READING

Of course, the most important job to be done in these early rehearsals is to introduce the cast to the play itself. This is traditionally done through a first reading, and you should do all you can to ensure that this first encounter is as effective as possible. A dull first reading that dampens enthusiasm for the material can be difficult to overcome.

The most common problem in first readings is that the actors tend to adopt a literary rather than a theatrical frame of mind, settling back and putting their noses into their books. Do what you can to keep this first encounter in a theatrical rather than literary mode: Help the actors to visualize the given circumstances and most of all to read in relationship with one another. You will find some important suggestions about this in the *Hamlet* Log, Part 8.

The idea of experiencing the text in a theatrical rather than in a literary mode is important. Voice specialist Kristin Linklater has pointed out that in literary perception there is a very short neurological connection formed from the optic nerve to the conceptual centers of the brain; an actor must literally lengthen this connection to include the deepest sources of the autonomous nervous system in the old brain stem and in the base of the spine, and thereby re-create the whole psychophysical experience of which the text is a residue. This gradual translation of the actor's experience of the play from the literary to the active mode is one of the underlying processes of rehearsal; you can feel it at work as the script finally gets up on its feet and starts to work under its own power.

Some directors like to hasten this process by requiring actors to report to the first rehearsal with their lines already memorized, ready to begin experiencing the action on their feet. If you choose this strategy, be sure to caution the actors against building interpretations into the learning of their lines, or you may find yourself at the first rehearsal confronted by a number of entrenched characterizational choices which will be difficult to dislodge.

It may be that there are better ways of introducing the text which avoid the literary mode of experience altogether. If time permitted, you might consider beginning by improvising around the themes of the play, or by exploring physical imagery (as Stanislavski sometimes did), gradually working toward the text. Such a process would be intended to give the actors a chance to "substitute" themselves "for the dead dramatist and re-create the play," as Saint-Denis suggested the director do.

A less time-consuming strategy might be to set up the given circumstances and the scenario of the action, then let the actors improvise the dialogue until the need for the text arises. Since not all actors are good improvisers, however, (and since not all good improvisers are good actors) I prefer to avoid extensive improvisation; instead, I have sometimes encouraged actors to use their own paraphrase of the text in early rehearsals (rather than reading from the book) until the action starts to make itself felt. The use of paraphrase also forces the actors to become clear about the thinking behind the lines, and to own those thoughts by speaking them in their own words and voices.

Another concern for these early encounters with the text is the tendency of actors to characterize and emotionalize too soon. Instead of coming to understand what the playwright has provided and allowing it to influence them, actors will sometimes (usually unconsciously) try to impose some premeditated image or idiosyncratic response of their own onto the material. This will often manifest itself by the adoption of an artificial voice. Encourage the actors to speak the text in their own voices; the material will have no chance to work upon them until they actually let it in, and they do this by first letting the words in.

Of course, a good actor's initial response to a role is not necessarily off the mark; don't resist the truth when it arises, even if it comes sooner than you expected.

YOUR FRAME OF MIND IN REHEARSALS

One day I asked the Master: "How can the shot be loosed if 'I' do not do it?

"'It' shoots," he replied. . . .

"And who or what is this 'It'?"

"Once you have understood that, you will have no further need of me. And if I tried to give you a clue at the cost of your own experience, I would be the worst of teachers and would deserve to be sacked! So let's stop talking about it and go on practicing."[15]

As shown by this quote, the Master in *Zen in the Art of Archery* used the kind of rehearsal strategy advocated by a number of the directors who answered my survey. My question to them was, "How would you describe your frame of mind when you are at your best in rehearsal?" There were many different answers, of course, but common agreement that it is important to "stop talking about it and go on practicing." Dan Sullivan says:

I know things are going well when I don't feel the need to talk too much.

And Michael Leibert agreed:

I'm at my best when I'm not doing anything; the actors... build upon our starting point, they discover and change, and if I'm smart I keep my mouth shut.

This is not to suggest that the director is passive; the silence being advocated is rather a watchful silence, like that of a cat in front of a mousehole. Richard Foreman calls it "free floating attention, like a psychoanalyst," and Mark Lamos described it as "being open to all possibility, but on guard for the truth."

The important point is that the life of the play must be allowed to develop; the actors must be allowed to find it for themselves. Effective direction facilitates this process but cannot substitute for it or even hasten it. However good the gardener, it is finally the plant that must do the growing.

THE HAMLET LOG, PART 8: FINAL CASTING AND FIRST REHEARSALS— DECEMBER 28-31

My first day in Ashland is a very full one. After brief opening remarks and the introduction of the company and staff, the directors see the new company members in short prepared auditions.

Before the auditions I meet briefly with Jerry to get an update on casting. Jerry reports that he has hired Megan Cole as Gertrude; Megan played Katherine in my *Shrew* here eleven years ago. In forming the rest of the company, Jerry has cast (beside the principals we discussed earlier) the Player King, Rosencrantz and Guildenstern, Marcellus, and Osric; luckily, I am pleased with his choices. I have ten roles left open, but only seven male actors left in the company (we had agreed that three nonspeaking males would be cast from townspeople later). I will cast Voltemand, Cornelius, Fortinbras, Reynaldo, and the Player Queen from today's auditions.

The prepared audition pieces are not all Shakespeare, so I make callbacks for all seven men to check their handling of the language. Afterward, the four directors meet for what would usually be the "repertory slave market," in which casting conflicts between shows would be negotiated; here, however, this has already been done by the artistic director in his formation of the company. I decide to alter one or two of my doublings because of the body type of the actors cast, and this information is sent to Jeannie.

When I enter the auditorium, I get a surprise: The *Hamlet* set is on the stage, complete except for the main stairway; due to its complexity it couldn't be built anywhere else! I am very glad to see it in the flesh; I walk it, testing various locations and movement patterns. The positions for the soliloquies feel very good indeed. My only reservation is that the steps breaking up the central playing area feel higher than they seemed on the model. I go back to the model to check, and when I lay my face down and look with my eye at stage level, I see that it is correct; I had been looking at the model from too high an angle before. I am worried about the actors being able to flow over these steps in the course of playing intimate scenes, especially because they break the space at an odd diagonal. Luckily, though, the actors will have a chance to work on the set early.

Dick and Jeannie want to discuss the safety considerations raised by the open and narrow catwalks on the set. Dick suggests small railings, and plans to inset small LED lights along their edges (like airport landing lights), which will guide the actors but will be invisible to the audience. I don't like the look of the railings, but agree to them on the proviso that they may be dropped if the actors, having once gained confidence on the set without them, agree.

The special problem of the Ghost's safety is discussed: His helmet will give him limited downward visibility and this could be dangerous on the steep central stairway; I agree to block him without ever using these stairs.

My first rehearsal is scheduled for 9:00 a.m. the next morning, so after spending some time staring at the set, I go home to rough out a rehearsal schedule strategy and to prepare.

FIRST REHEARSAL: DECEMBER 29

The final casting for the festival was posted at 8:30 a.m., and the cast of *Hamlet* gathered at 9:00 a.m. for our first rehearsal.

I have been in my usual quandry about the best way to begin. I have sometimes used exercises or other devices to let everyone know that their creative participation is not only welcome but expected; but with a cast which knows one another well and which is involved in the preparation of five other plays, I don't feel that this is necessary. The traditional opening statement and first reading seems the best choice. Considering the limitless possibilities of this play and my own tendency to ramble when speaking extemporaneously, I do something I have never done before: I write a short essay in which I express my view of the main action of the play, the point of its crisis, and the thematic focus I have selected. I estimate that I can present these ideas in about twenty minutes, leaving enough time for the reading itself.

Before anything else can be done, however, the actors must get the cuts I have made in the script. Giving cuts aloud is a dull and time-consuming task, as is distributing a written list. Instead I ask the stage manager, Peter Allen, to lay each page of his prompt script out in sequence on several long tables; as the actors enter, they are given scripts, and they move along the tables, copying the clearly marked cuts from the prompt script into their scenes. Since not everyone is in all scenes, as many as ten or twelve actors are at work at one time and we are done in a half-hour.

At 9:30 the stage manager makes a few housekeeping remarks, and I rather sheepishly begin my prepared introduction. The group is surprisingly attentive, and I finish in the twenty minutes I had allotted myself. I ask for questions or comments but (not surprisingly) there are none.

The remainder of the four-hour rehearsal will be devoted to the first reading. To help make the first reading as dramatic as possible, I have prepared a brief preface for each scene, outlining the given circumstances of time and place (with special emphasis on the time-line of the play). My hope is that the actors will thus be able to visualize the scenes and begin "playing" them at once.

We begin the reading, but some of the actors are speaking "Shakespearean," an artificially elevated enunciation and tone; I instruct them to speak in their own voices. This is crucial; the text must become their own words expressing their own thoughts, and this will never happen if they do not begin speaking it in their own voices.

I notice too that some of the actors have settled back into their books and are adopting a literary frame of mind; I ask everyone to read in relationship, to get their noses out of the book and speak directly to the others in the scene; those who are being addressed are asked to help by reacting as fully as possible.

Happily, my instructions are taken at once. Polonius even begins to move from seat to seat so as to sit near his scene partners. As a result, the reading proceeds with good pace and with a strong sense of dramatic action. I take notes as I listen, and after each scene I briefly note any important questions, items of information, or clues about relationships or motives; I am also checking pronunciation and scansion.

Peter has clocked our reading of my proposed first part at sixty-four minutes, discounting the time taken by my comments and a few brief discussions. The action in this sequence is interrupted by Hamlet's inability to take action during Shakespeare's Act II; there is danger of a slump about an hour in if we do not find a strong through-line. A short break is called, the rehearsal being now nearly three hours old.

We return with an hour left and read our second act in fifty minutes. As I expected, the second act has a strong natural pace, containing as it does an intrinsic acceleration from the preparations for the play-within-the-play, and the Recorder, Praying, and Closet scenes, the murder of Polonius, and the veritable chase sequence leading to the capture and embarcation of Hamlet.

I mention my hope that we can keep the show down to three-and-a-half hours, and encourage everyone to look for cuts in their parts.

The rehearsal is adjourned with the call to finish the reading tomorrow. Peter and I meet to plan the next day's work: We decide to allot one hour to the reading of the remaining act. I ask that the costume and scenic designs then be presented by the designers; we will have the advantage of meeting in the auditorium on the actual set. The remaining two hours will be spent in the first work-throughs of scenes 11 and 12. Costume fittings are already underway and will be scheduled around our calls.

The remainder of my morning is spent listening to tapes of some melodies by composer Todd Barton; the main theme to be sung by Ophelia is exquisite.

FIRST LIGHT MEETING: DECEMBER 29

I meet Bob Peterson, the lighting designer, for the first time; Dick Hay is also at the meeting, as is stagemanager Peter Allen (who will attend all future meetings with me).

I have enough sense of the geography of the set that I have blocked out the playing areas involved in each locale of the play; the master chart already gives the time of day and any special effects required. We move through each scene, discussing its atmosphere and placement on the stage, as well as the location of the sun, moon, torches, and other motivating light sources.

We pay special attention to the transitions between scenes; I am eager to avoid any blackouts in order to keep the action flowing. There are a few places where the movements of the tapestry, or the opening or closing of the trap for the graveyard, may require special adjustments.

Each special effect is discussed. Whereas we have been thinking that our big effect, the emergence of the Ghost from the figure on the tapestry, would occur in the very first scene; I now suggest that we save it for the Ghost's appearance to Hamlet in the second Battlement scene (14). This appearance can be "set up," we decide, by having the Ghost disappear through the tapestry in the first scene when Horatio and the soldiers attack it. We consider follow spots or some special lighting for the Ghost, but agree to depend on his self-contained light source. I suggest a hand-held dimmer (like a slot-car control) which will permit him to control his own lights.

The overall coloration of the show is not discussed, since Bob needs to meet with Jeannie on costume colors first.

Later that night I prepare a chart for the movements and positions of the tapestry, necessarily thinking more specifically about the transitions from scene to scene. I am happy to find that the tapestry can be moved within the reality of each scene by soldiers or servants; I don't really want the set to do anything on its own.

SECOND SOUND MEETING:
DECEMBER 30

The next morning I meet with Todd Barton, Douglas Faerber (sound designer), and my stage manager. Peter has prepared a complete list of those sound cues which I had initially outlined in my cutting of the script, plus several I had missed. There are three types of cues in *Hamlet*: environmental sound effects to create an atmosphere for a scene, musical cues such as flourishes or incidental music for performances, and realistic sound effects such as cock crows and bells marking the hour. We discuss each according to four qualities: its emotional or atmospheric quality, its placement in the text, its duration, and its directionality.

The responsibility for each cue is divided between Todd (music) and Douglas (sound effects), with several cues being a mixture of both. We also consider which cues will be taped, which live, and which a mixture of both We pay special attention to transitions that will have to be timed to a tape, such as the coronation entrance; we agree that in two weeks Peter and I will supply an exact timing for these cues.

The Ghost's wireless microphone is discussed; I make it clear that I want to hear the actor's live voice as the primary sound source, with the augmentation (by reverb or synthesizer) being almost subliminal. We discuss also the Ghost's voice from beneath the floor in scene 15; we decide to do this through the wireless microphone, feeding the live voice of the actor through speakers.

I encourage them to bring environmental cues into rehearsal as soon as possible; Todd has already finished Ophelia's songs and has sheet music and a rehearsal tape for her.

SECOND REHEARSAL: DECEMBER 31

We meet to resume the first reading of our Third Part, using the same format as before. It is read in fifty-four minutes; I hope we can eventually trim another ten minutes from it. A few of the actors have already found some minor cuts they want to make in their parts, and these are checked and approved. A few of the more zealous actors are even comparing the various editions of the play to select those readings most attractive to them, and Allan Nause (Horatio) has a few substitutions from the Good Quarto. I encourage all this; I have found that if actors are given some control, however limited, over the words they speak, it enhances the process of personalization.

The reading concluded, I spend a few minutes describing the way I like to work: I encourage an exploratory attitude, pointing out that the opening night is not the sole objective of our process, rather we are preparing the show for a long run during which its depths can be plumbed in earnest. Specifically, I encourage everyone to concentrate on the choices made by his or her character; each choice is to be understood in terms of what stimulates the need for a choice, what needs or attitudes the stimulus arouses, and what alternatives are considered by the character. The aim is to live through the choice as fully as possible, for this is both the best means toward transformation and the way in which the action of the play is moved forward.

The main business of our rehearsals, I explain, will be the establishment of moment-by-moment connections of action/reaction; we want to give each actor what she or he needs in order to be compelled to make the choices required by the the scene; this is the true source of *pace*. I encourage them to be open about their needs, with me and with their fellow actors.

At this point, the designer would normally present the set through a rendering or model, but we are fortunate in having the set itself under construction. We move to the auditorium to examine it; it now has a partial base coat of paint. I explain the principles behind the ground plan—up left for ceremonial entrances, the left vom for access to the outer world, the right vom ramp and forestage as the wharf and lower battlements, the up-center tower as the castle proper, and the catwalks above as the upper battlements.

I describe the playing axes that are native to the ground plan, with special attention to the steps in the central playing area. Dominance of one character over another, for instance, may suggest who is up and who is down. The set will be down soon, and I have everyone get up and walk the set; the taped lines on the floor of the rehearsal hall will mean more after this experience.

The stage manager explains the terminology we will use to indicate locations on the set, and discusses the escapes and backstage conditions. There are some questions from the actors about safety considerations on the ramps and escapes, and I explain about the possibility of railings if needed. The crews are returning for work, so we adjourn to the rehearsal hall to begin working the first two scenes.

In the rehearsal hall, the stage manager explains the marks on the floor and placement of small posts representing doorways and pillars, using the set model as reference. We are now ready to begin rehearsal in earnest.

Since it involves the largest number of people, we begin with the first court entrance in scene 12. I have spent some time looking at the set and have a rough idea about how people will get on and off. I had already decided that Hamlet should enter first, alone, while we hear the sounds of the ceremony offstage. After a moment of his looking at the figure of his dead father on the tapestry, the crowd will enter explosively.

As I looked at the set early this morning, I decided that the up-left entrance was the strongest for the court entrance; this naturally pushes Hamlet down right onto the vom platform; this will be a perfect place for him during this scene, standing literally in the audience's midst (I hope to identify the audience with Hamlet and this first position will help do this).

Claudius would surely choose to take the most dominant position, up left center; with him here, a considerable gulf separates him from Hamlet as they face each other across the sunken pit of the main playing area. The question at once arises: Who will cross the gulf first? Will Hamlet be a good boy and come to papa, or will Claudius eat crow and go to him? The public nature of the scene (as I have defined it) adds to the potential embarassment. I give the actors these opening positions and let them begin exploring the scene with no further suggestions from me.

As they work the scene, important questions arise and are discussed at some length: Did Hamlet get back in time for his father's funeral (no), how long has it been since then (about a month), have Gertrude and Claudius been adulterous prior to the murder (yes), what is the precise quality of incest in their relationship (the Old Testament accounts a marriage with a brother-in-law as incestuous); in each case, the answers come from the actors, not from me.

The exact nature of the ceremony is at last established: Laertes points out his line, "To show my duty in your coronation . . . now . . . that duty done," and we decide that this has been a double ceremony, both marriage and crowning, and that Gertrude has "come with the office." Claudius is delighted with this definition of things, and is playing the scene in a triumphant and jovial mood, he and Gertrude being overtly affectionate; perhaps too much for a state occasion, but I say nothing for now.

The gulf between Hamlet and Claudius works well; I am surprised when Gertrude is the first to cross, and a tender private moment between mother and son, in which she appeals to Hamlet to behave, results. Soon Claudius himself crosses over. Denis at first is a bit threatening, making his recognition of the danger Hamlet represents obvious; but after a few tries he switches strategy and attempts to be fatherly. We agree that this is the better approach to the scene.

Denis is approaching Claudius as a consummate improviser rather than as a methodical schemer; he is quick to seize the opportunity and to recognize the potential advantage in any situation. While this is quite different from my own initial ideas about Claudius, I recognize at once that this approach has two strong advantages over my own: First, it will produce more lively and suspenseful scenes, and second, it will create a sharper contrast to the unimpulsive, cautious Hamlet. I begin to adjust my thinking about the other relationships to take this new quality into account.

Laertes suggests that since his sister is present (I have blocked Ophelia into the wedding party as Gertrude's bridesmaid), he would like to see something pass between her and Hamlet to help motivate his later cautionary comments to her. This is a splendid idea and will help establish the relationship of Hamlet and Ophelia; I decide to have Ophelia lead the wedding procession and be the first person to confront Hamlet; a moment can pass between them until Laertes, next in line, parts them.

The first four pages of scene 12 take more than an hour to work through in this manner; we stop when we reach Hamlet's first soliloquy. Much of value has been established.

We have forty-five minutes to work scene 11: The blocking here is largely determined by the set, so the scene falls together at once. The same kinds of questions about the given circumstances arise: How much do the soldiers know about the political situation (not much; Horatio has to explain it); how do they feel about Claudius (they mistrust him and mourn the passing of old Hamlet, their warrior king); how do they feel about the Ghost (they have a childlike awe and fear of it). One of the actors brings up the importance of their decision, at Horatio's urging, to report the Ghost's appearance to Hamlet rather than to Claudius (as they would normally be required to do); I had never noticed this crisis in the scene before, and the exit takes on a special value as a result.

The rehearsal is broken; I am relieved and pleased with this first taste of real work.

I must make an important decision regarding rehearsal strategy. I would normally prefer to spend this first week rereading each scene and discussing its action and relationships before putting it up on its feet; however, the set will remain onstage for only two weeks more, and won't be available again until just before technical rehearsals.

I decide, therefore, that we will continue to work the play on its feet, moving quickly through the play chronologically and roughing in the broad outlines of the action in time for a run-through on the set at the end of the third week. I check with the production manager and my designers to see if this is possible. Construction of the stairway is not scheduled to be finished before the set is moved out, but in a meeting with the technical director, I win agreement that the set will be functional by then, and that the construction schedule will be coordinated through my stage manager to maximize our time on the set before then.

This means that we will try to rough block the entire show in two-and-a-half weeks! The idea scares me: Will we short-circuit our process of discovery? I weigh this against the value of working on this complicated unit set early, and I decide that we can use the time not so much to block as to rough out the action in spatial terms. We will still have three weeks left before technical rehearsal to return for detail work and to reexamine our choices.

This will be our strategy, then: To rough in the broad outlines first, then return to examine details. I make out a rehearsal schedule accordingly, then spend a few hours staring at the stage, thinking about the four large crowd scenes. We have a total of only 120 hours of rehearsal before dress rehearsal; I would prefer a minimum of 180 (about fifty hours of rehearsal for each hour of playing time), but this much time is simply not available in repertory (or in the American theatre in general, for that matter).

FIRST PROP MEETING: DECEMBER 31

The design of props is divided among three people: Jeannie is responsible for costume props such as masks and necklaces; Dick designs the set props such as banners and furniture; Paul Dennis Martin, the prop master, designs the hand props and weapons, and oversees all the prop construction.

Dick brings in designs for the banners and furniture; colors and fabric have been coordinated with Jeannie. We then discuss the costume props, particularly the party masks, and we check each actor for the type of mask he or she will wear: Full head masks for supporting characters, partial masks for those who speak, and stick masks for Claudius, Gertrude, and Ophelia, since we want to watch their reactions to the play.

We next go over the weapons, deciding exactly who will wear what in which scene. The fighting is taken into account; some of the weapons are purely decorative. Besides the soldiers on guard, only six will wear swords throughout: Rosencrantz and Guildenstern, Voltemand and Cornelius, Osric and Laertes. Claudius will carry a dagger, and Hamlet will have a sword in some scenes but not in others. The dueling weapons are discussed: There will be four from which the antagonists will choose (Laertes having to choose twice to get the "unbated" sword) and the fight will be rapier-and-dagger style as specified by Osric's lines.

We go through each scene to specify the design of all hand props. The torches are discussed for the quality of their flame, their smokelessness, and their burning time. We decide on three classes of torch: a "standard military issue," a "court" or "civilian" torch, and lanterns for Ophelia and Polonius.

The design of Ophelia's bier is presented: It is a simple, flat litter without handles. The problem of moving up the stairs from the vom is considered, as is the lowering of the bier into the trap: The Gravedigger will bring the support poles and ropes in with him, then remain onstage to help throughout the scene.

To safeguard the costumes, we agree to use no liquid for wine (except for the poisoned cup at the end), so the design of the wine pitchers will have a snout that will conceal this fact when glasses are "filled." Ophelia's flowers and other expendables conclude our business. At two-and-one-half hours, this has been the longest meeting so far.

TWELVE
EXPLORING THE ACTION

As the play gets up on its feet, the actors begin in earnest to search for the action. In order to assist them in this search, you must remember that an action can't be experienced unless it's happening; anything that stops the flow of action (like endless discussion) impedes the search. At the same time, the individual connections through which the action flows must be fully experienced; anything which short-circuits this experience (like "playing results" or rushing) must also be avoided.

The action is found gradually: The readings of the play have given an idea of the whole action, and now individual moment-to-moment connections are explored. As these connections form, the action begins to flow through them as a living event. As more and more of these connections are found, the whole of the action begins to come into focus; this, in turn, reveals more about the significance of each momentary connection, and so on, each detail revealing more of the whole, the emerging whole giving significance to each detail.

What is being formed in this process of discovery is the network of transactions through which the through-line of the action will eventually flow. Each actor is beginning to see how each of their transactions contributes to the entire network, and this is how they come to understand what Stanislavski called their superobjective, "understanding how each moment of the performance contributes to the reason the play was written."

This network of transactions consists of two kinds of connections: the external connections of stimulus and response between characters, and the internal connections between reaction and objective within each character. These external and internal connections alternate, one provoking the other, so that the momentum of the action depends on the reality, specificity, and appropriateness of both: They are merely different modes of the same energy.

Since the external connections are visible and audible, they are the ones that tell the story to the audience; but the reality and human significance of the external connections depend on the completeness and depth of the inner connections from which they spring. It is as foolish to say that one is more or less important than the other as it is to say that the notes in a piece of music are more important than the silences which separate them.

CHOICE AND THE FLOW OF ACTION

We can describe a segment in this network of transactions like this: An *event* stimulates a *reaction* in someone who makes a *choice*, which gives him or her an *objective* toward which he or she directs *activity*, which produces another *event*, which in turn stimulates a *reaction* in someone else who makes a *choice*, and so on. We could reduce this even further:

EVENT - reaction - choice - objective - EVENT - reaction - choice - objective - EVENT

Each link in the network allows the whole action to flow, and the flow of the whole establishes the requirements for each link.

From the actor's point of view, each significant choice made by the character results in a new objective (even if it is only a change in strategy), and we call each of these choices the begining of a new unit of action or *beat*; each of these beats is, as Stanislavski phrased it, "like a vertebra in the spine of the play."

Since the playwright created each character to make the particular choices required to advance the action, the actors begin to find their characters naturally by experiencing the flow of the action, that is, by doing what the character does within the given circumstances. The actor playing Claudius starts to experience himself as someone who makes choices based entirely on self-interest, manipulating others with no regard for their fate. The actor playing Hamlet begins to experience himself as someone whose choices are between moral concerns on the one hand ("conscience doth make cowards of us all") and the passionate desire for revenge on the other.

Your job, then, is to help the actors find *for themselves* the external connections of stimulus/response through which the action flows, and to begin experiencing *for themselves* the internal choices of reaction/objective which produce those connections. If this is done, all else—character and emotion—will begin to follow naturally.

THE SHAPE OF THE ACTION

As we discussed in Chapter Five, the action of a play does not merely flow in a steady way: it rises and falls with the "ravelling" of the plot, and sometimes even changes direction in a reversal. These turning points (crises) are the milestones of the map of the action which your cast is exploring, and it is useful if you can assist them in recognizing these milestones as they are encountered.

This is where the preparation you did in Part Two will really pay off; your sense of the scenario of the play will help you to recognize these pivotal choices, thereby giving you a sense of which of the character's choices are the most significant and why; this, in turn, prepares you to assist the actors in focusing on those choices as they arise. By experiencing these crucial choices fully, the actors will find the emotions which arise from those choices and be led toward an understanding of the qualities of character which most influence them; the process of transformation will have begun.

This, then, is the process of exploration by which the actors make the transition from concept to reality, from the potential of the play's literary norms to the specific life of an event occuring between people. Your part in this process is to monitor the formation of the network, watching for the possibility of connections, testing the strength and validity of those which form, bringing attention to the gaps which remain unfilled; you will also make sure that each turning point moves the action toward its eventual destination.

THE STRATEGY OF EXPLORATION

The action of a play can be explored in several different ways, and you will have to decide which is the best approach for the particular play at hand. Basically, the choices are:

1. To work first in sequence and in large chunks, trying to experience the broad outlines of the whole action first, then gradually filling in the individual connections;

2. To work first on details, scene by scene or even beat by beat, examining each connection and allowing the longer arc of the action to gradually become clear;

3. To work out of sequence, exploring certain elements of the action before putting it all together; this could mean working on crucial scenes first so that the scenes which lead to them or follow from them have a strong sense of direction; conversely, it may mean working toward crucial scenes, setting them up so completely that they can eventually happen under their own power.

Any one or a combination of these choices may be useful in a given circumstance. One traditional rhythm is to work on the broad outlines for a time, with read-throughs and even walk-throughs; then to switch to moment-by-moment detailed work for a few weeks; finally to put it all back together with run-throughs as the dress rehearsals approach.

This traditional rhythm is not always the best: You may choose to let the structure of the rehearsal process reflect the structure of the play. For instance, I recently rehearsed *The Time of Your Life* by simply running through large segments of the show in their entirety, usually without stopping, day after day, until all the details had filled themselves in. On the other hand, I'm working now on *A Midsummer Night's Dream* by rehearsing the subplots of the fairies, lovers, and rustics separately at first, then intertwining them. In each case, consider your options and see what fits the play best.

As you plan your rehearsal strategy, remember that an efficient use of the available time and space, and a considerate use of your actors' energy, should be important factors in your rehearsal planning. Of course, I do not argue that efficiency and consideration per se necessarily produce better results; but as they say in the Yiddish theatre, "it couldn't hurt." It is part of my ethic as a director to avoid waste and to treat the time and effort of others with respect; I urge you to adopt these ideals as their own reward, remembering only that efficiency must never become an end unto itself.

GUIDING THE EXPLORATION

In the last chapter we discussed your frame of mind as a fair witness, "open to all possibility but on guard for the truth." This is not a passive frame of mind; you must respond to what is happening. If the truth appears, you celebrate it; if you catch only a passing glimpse of it, you invite it to stay and visit; if it refuses to appear at all, you send the actors in search of it. How do you guide the exploration without merely manipulating the actors like pawns? How do you help actors find things for themselves?

There are a number of techniques from which you may choose in responding to any given instance, ranging all the way from brute force to benign neglect. Most of the directors I queried opt for a moderate approach. Mark Lamos speaks for those who prefer an active exploration:

> I work as a benevolent dictator, forcing as many different hats on a moment as I can before discarding everything and attempting to come to terms with the essence of it.

David Emmes takes a gentle approach:

> I am at my "best" in rehearsal when I am able to be caught up in the flow of imaginative and creative energy of the actors as they explore a scene, and by a

process of coaxing, reinforcing, and gently spurring, I am able to keep this artistic momentum going for a time.

In a talk at NYU, Jerzy Grotowski advocated strong but indirect means of influencing the actor's experience:

> The director's purpose is to create a condition which leads another (the actor) to a new experience; a thousand times it won't work, but once it will, and that once is essential.

To "create a condition" is a very useful technique: You can do so by reinforcing an aspect of the given circumstances ("remember that you've got to persuade her before they all come back in") or by suggesting an adjustment in the circumstances ("what if the walls are so thin that you can be easily heard in the next room?") You might even impose a physical condition on the rehearsal: I remember overcoming an impasse in a scene from *King Lear* by lowering the imaginary ceiling of the room so that the actors had to play the scene on all fours. What all these techniques have in common is that they manipulate external conditions in order to bring about an internal adjustment.

It is also possible (and in fact more common) to suggest internal adjustments in order to generate a change in externals. In order to work in this way, you need to understand the specifics of the internal process that allows an incoming stimulus to result in an outgoing response. This process begins with a perceived *stimulus*, which gives rise to a need or *attitude*, which causes a *choice*, which (as you have seen) generates an *intention*; as the intention is acted upon, there is the adoption of a *strategy* directed toward the external *objective*. (For a full discussion, see *The Actor at Work*, Lesson 16).

An adjustment can be made at any step in this internal process: Instead of supplying the adjustment ready-made, however, I prefer to ask a question that brings the actor's awareness to some particular stage of this inner process while allowing the actor to find his or her own answer. Here are the types of questions associated with each phase of the inner action:

1. What happens that makes you (do, say, think) that?
2. What does it mean to you? How does it make you feel?
3. What do you decide to do? What else might you do? What did you decide *not* to do?
4. What do you want from her?
5. How are you going to try to get it?
6. What change do you want to make in her? What do you want her to do?

It often doesn't matter what answer the actor supplies; the simple act of bringing awareness and encouraging them to fully experience what they are doing can be enough to solve many problems.

Of course, you may sometimes want them to find a new value in order to move the action in a different direction altogether; in this case, I usually extend the questioning strategy and, by the Socratic method, help the actors to find *their* understanding of the moment which leads in the right direction.

In any specific instance, then, you may choose to deal with the actor in terms of an adjustment in the external condition, or through an adjustment in the internal process. Whichever way you choose, remember that your aim is to maintain the congruence of the inner and outer phases of the action, so be sure that a change in one is allowed to cause the necessary change in the other. As Stanislavski put it,

> Every physical action has an inner psychological action which gives rise to it. And in every psychological inner action there is always a physical action which expresses its psychic nature: The unity between these two [inner and outer] is organic action on the stage.[16]

COMMUNICATING WITH ACTORS: DISCUSSION

There are three main ways you may communicate with actors in the formal rehearsal situation: discussions, side-coaching, and notes. Each has its own purposes and requirements, and we will examine each briefly, beginning with discussions. These may occur at any time throughout the rehearsal process; they are enormously valuable, though care must be taken to maximize their effectiveness and to avoid some common pitfalls.

Perhaps most important for the effectiveness of rehearsal discussion is the creation of a "ground" from which it can naturally spring. Every member of the group should feel the right to initiate discussion, and the group should treat all concerns and ideas appropriately without regard to source: Beware that a pecking order not be established; the truth can arise from anywhere, at any time. At the same time, you must be on guard against the individual who tends to unnecessarily monopolize the floor: If you fail to restrain such a person, resentment will develop in the group and the freedom to discuss will actually lessen; on the other hand, if you restrain such a person too forcibly, it will have a chilling effect on everyone. A middle course is best in most cases, with private talks and negotiations in difficult instances.

Some issues lend themselves to group discussions, and in general, you should think of the work of every member of the team as being of concern to every other member. Actors are necessarily interdependent, and it is impossible for an actor to isolate his or her creation from the created whole; often the problems and concerns of one actor will be related to the work of others. For this reason, I tend to give notes in the group context as much as possible. Nevertheless, some things are primarily of individual concern, and you should be careful about using the group's time for such talks. There are also times when an actor needs the support of your individual attention, or when you need to communicate some concern of yours privately.

Discussions tend to generate a momentum of their own and can easily become an end unto themselves. Discussions within the formal rehearsal situation should be focused on a specific issue which has arisen in the natural course of work, and these should be kept as brief as possible without creating an atmosphere of suppression. On the other hand, open-ended discussions of a free-wheeling and general nature are also extremely valuable; these are appropriate to social situations, and the pub or lounge can be the most fertile ground of ideas available to you. Spend time with your cast in these informal situations—many a show has been best directed in the local pub!

Discussions sometimes short-circuit the problem-solving process when they are used in an effort to avoid problems before they arise. Discussions should always be held in reaction to the effort to play the scene; beware when you find yourself rehearsing in reaction to your discussions!

Another danger is that discussions have a tendency to become a substitute for actual creativity. Remember that rehearsal is a problem-solving activity: Discussions can identify and specify problems, consider the possible means of their solution, and evaluate the results of those efforts. But problems are rarely actually solved by discussion, and every idea must be tested on its feet.

Perhaps the greatest danger of discussions is that they tend to kill the natural momentum of the work. There is a great difference between the creative and the analytical frames of mind; the best ideas often arise from the actual playing of a scene when the creative imagination of the actors is fully engaged, rather than in the more analytical mode of discursive thought. The best discussions are an opportunity to share and align your creative impulses and, as such, flow naturally out of and back into the work on the scene; keep the flow going!

SIDE-COACHING

The need for discussion can often be greatly reduced through the use of side-coaching—brief comments you insert into the flow of the scene without stopping it. To see side-coaching at its best, watch a top athletic coach in action: A careful study of basketball great John Wooden's technique revealed that some 70 per cent of his sideline comments during practice were *immediate responses* to the play in progress accompanied by *specific corrections*. This combination of immediacy and specificity is the key to side-coaching effectiveness.

You can achieve these qualities mainly through your own rhythmic participation in the work of the actors. When you feel in your own body the action of the scene as it is emerging from their interactions, your responses will naturally begin to flow with it, encouraging the moments that are in line and inhibiting those moments which deviate from the path. These responses need be no more than simple approvals and encouragements like "good," "that's it," "go for her," or adjustments like "not yet, wait until she's ready," "listen to what she's saying," "stop and think about that!" Once you have established rapport with your actors and they have become familiar with your side-coaching style, you may find that simple exclamations and noises are enough; the purpose of side-coaching is not to give information but rather to provide immediate feedback on the effectiveness of specific choices and activities.

Perhaps the most useful function of side-coaching is to encourage an actor to release a suppressed impulse. You will begin to sense when an actor is censoring an impulse, and if it seems potentially valuable you will naturally encourage her or him to follow it, with comments such as "go ahead," "yes, take it!"

Normally, side-coaching is most effective after a scene is somewhat established and has begun to play under its own power. Too much coaching too early can have a chilling effect on the actors' work by making them feel like puppets; be sure that your comments are in reaction to the actors' work rather than a manipulation of it. Sometimes, of course, you will have an idea or recognize a potential in the work which you will explore immediately through comments like "try catching her off guard with this," or "what if you see what he's trying to do?" If such an idea is inserted at the right moment and is indeed consistent with the flow of the action, the actors will experience its rightness and will pursue and extend it without further instructions.

Side-coaching should be used appropriately and economically. As the scene develops, the need for side-coaching gradually diminishes, although in later phases of rehearsal it may be useful for the polishing of details. At some point, however, you must begin to wean the performance by gradually withdrawing your input.

NOTES

As the performance develops and you begin to let it run entirely on its own, you will begin to take notes which you will share with the actors after the segment of action has run its course. There are many different ways of taking notes: I have experimented with dictating to an assistant, recording comments on a tape which I then played back to the actors, writing notes on ditto masters which were then run off and distributed, and writing individual notes on separate pieces of paper for each actor (see "Sample Notes to Hamlet" in Appendix Four.)

Likewise, there are many ways of giving your notes to the actors: Some directors prefer to speak individually to actors; some deliver brief group lectures at the end of rehearsal; others let notes mature for a time and give them at the beginning of the next rehearsal; some even give the actors written notes, post them on the callboard, or have certain kinds of notes delivered by the stage manager or assistant director. Different techniques may be useful in various situations or at different stages of the rehearsal process.

By far the most common technique, however, is the group note session at the conclusion of each rehearsal; this can be either a unilateral session in which you simply give your notes, or an open session in which everyone has an opportunity to share problems and ideas, and to suggest solutions. I prefer this sort of interaction among the actors because it encourages everyone to think in terms of the entire production. You must guide such a session carefully (as discussed above) and should reserve the right and responsibility of final judgment.

The greatest danger in group note sessions is the wasting of time while purely individual notes are given; try to segregate those notes of individual concern and give these after the general session has been dismissed.

Whatever system of taking and giving notes you adopt in a given instance, remember that the greatest advantage to a note-taking procedure is the ability to edit and screen the notes before the actors receive them. As we said in Chapter Nine, your ideal aim is to assist the actors in experiencing the scene for themselves; like the Master in *Zen in the Art of Archery*, you do not want to give them "a clue at the expense" of their own experience. Before giving a note, then, you should first consider whether it will contribute to the actor's process of discovery, or whether it needs to be given at all; the notes you do *not* give are as important as the one you do.

As a general rule, I avoid giving a note the first time it comes up; if it comes up a second time (many do not), I consider whether the actor's work is leading toward self-discovery, and if it is, I refrain again. Thereafter, I give the most useful note I can as if it were the first time: Beware of covertly blaming the actor for not finding the solution to a problem of which he or she is unaware.

At the end of a rehearsal, you may find yourself with several pages of detailed notes; consider whether there is a pattern underlying some of them. There may be one fundamental note which will, in fact, clear up many specific notes. Devote some time and attention to finding such notes before you burden your actors' minds with a clutter of specific details. Remember, every note you give is a piece of baggage for the actor to carry and will be a distraction until it is assimilated into the score of the performance; every note must therefore pull its own weight, or it is better not given.

Over a period of time, you may find even larger patterns underlying your notes: There may be certain types of problems recurring for certain actors, or as a result of special qualities of the material. In these cases, consider the creation of a corrective mechanism that can be built into the given circumstances of the scene. For instance, if you see that many of your notes in a given scene tend to be the result of poor pace, or of an insufficient energy level, look for a way to apply a deadline, or some other source of urgency or significance which will raise the stakes. In *Hamlet*, I had the problem of pace in the crowd scenes when group reactions tended to be sluggish; I gave the cast a list of "Deadlines and Urgencies" for each scene, which helped a great deal (see Appendix Five).

A corrective mechanism can also be an adjustment in the methodology of the actors; when someone habitually fails to listen to a partner, for instance, I ask him or her to simply repeat (mentally) everything said to them for a time. The Camera Game, in which the actor pretends to be photographing everything, can be useful in the same way. Actors who fail to think their way through important choices can be assisted by verbalizing their thought processes through an inner monlogue exercise, and so on.

Of course, none of these these devices and principles guarantees success. You may have been patient, insightful, and skillful in your communications and the actor may still not have gotten it; the work of the other actors is being impeded and the action of the play is failing to develop properly. In this case, sometime before everyone has gotten hopelessly frustrated or you have lost your temper, you simply tell the offending actor what to do—by the numbers. There may even be certain situations and/or certain actors with whom this is the best means of communication, so long as it contributes to their experience of the action of the scene. We will discuss this further in the section on blocking.

CUMULATIVE EXPLORATION

The process of discovery is oriented toward the evolution of the production; it must not become an end unto itself. As Dan Sullivan says in his questionnaire,

> Go for "results"; that's ultimately what a production is—a series of results.

You are responsible for the accumulation of the "series of results." Ideally, the rehearsal process should have a momentum of its own, with each day's work building upon the day before and leading toward the day to come. This is not to say that you don't sometimes hit fallow periods and even impassable barriers. At such times you may need to back up and start afresh, or, like Jerry in *The Zoo Story*, go "a long way out of your way in order to come back a short distance correctly."

The cumulative momentum of the rehearsal process is produced by your selectivity as the work evolves; as the truth arises, it must be acknowledged or it will tend to vanish. At the same time, flexibility is required so that yesterday's truth may lead to something even better today. As Michael Leibert puts it,

> It is crucial to make choices quickly and firmly, and to let go of moments as better, newer ones are discovered.

What do you do when a moment works? Caution is required; if too much fuss is made, the actors may try to capture it by mechanically re-creating it—this will lead only to frustration, because a living moment cannot be stuffed and mounted like a hunting trophy. The moment was a step in the whole journey of the scene; its life came from the flow of the action, and you must identify those conditions from which it arose. If those conditions can become a regular feature of the score of the scene, it is likely to happen again, probably in a slightly different way according to the way the scene is living in that instance.

This is an important recognition: You and your actors are searching for the life of the play at a level deeper than superficial form; a living thing cannot happen exactly the same way twice. You are looking for the structure and sequence of action that will, within the boundaries of a relatively established form, eventually drive the event of the play anew in each performance. For the actor, this means constructing a "sequence of stimulating actions" which become what Stanislavski called the "score of the role:"

> The law of theatrical art decrees: Discover the correct conception in the scenic action, in your role, and in the beats of the play; and then make the correct habitual and the habitual beautiful.[17]

During this phase of rehearsal, you are the midwife at the birth of the score.

HAMLET LOG, PART 9: ROUGHING OUT THE SCENIC ACTION—JANUARY 1-7

There is a New Year's Eve party in the rehearsal hall tonight; Mark and I talk informally about Hamlet's capacity for action. Mark is struck by Hamlet's insistence on having just the right conditions for action: "Now is the very witching time of night . . . now could I do it," and again behind the praying Claudius when he chooses "a fitter time and place." Mark is inclined to think that Hamlet is willing to act but insists on having things his own way; he won't accept the opportunities as they are. In this sense, one could say that Hamlet is actually willful.

I encourage this idea; it will be splendid for Mark to think of himself as fully willing to act but needing to create the perfect situation for action: This will give momentum to Hamlet's actions and help to avoid passivity; Mark will be understanding things in the way Hamlet understands things. Of course, one might argue whether Hamlet's insistence on the "perfect moment" for revenge is willfulness or the mere rationalization of a weak will, but our aim is not literary interpretation, it is performance; if Hamlet misunderstands his own motives then it will be fine for the actor to misunderstand them in the same way.

Figure 12-1. An Early Rehearsal. *Robert Benedetti.*

THIRD REHEARSAL: JANUARY 2

This is our first eight-hour rehearsal day and a great deal is accomplished. During the morning session we work through two-thirds of the first act, continuing to rough out each scene and then running the entire sequence.

My procedure is simple: Yesterday I sat for hours in front of the set, planning entrances and exits which will be consistent with the geography of the set and which will ensure a good spatial flow. I also chose an underlying spatial principle for each scene which could express the action, and established opening positions for each character which set up this relationship. In rehearsal, I simply give the actors their entrance, first position, and exit, then let them begin to explore the action on their own. I hope I have chosen an initial pattern that allows the subsequent choices to flow naturally; if not, we adjust.

These actors are very sensitive to spatial relationships; I need only encourage their impulses and edit the results. I watch the actors closely and try to sense when they are inhibiting a reaction; when they do, I try to bring it out and extend it. Gradually they stop censoring themselves and become self-motivating, and I am able to simply watch and edit the results as the whole begins to emerge.

Of course, it is not just any impulse which I encourage and extend; there is a natural selectivity in my responses to those things I sense may be useful in leading the scene in the proper direction. I have, for myself, broken the scenes

Figure 12-2.   **Blocking a Group Scene.** *Robert Benedetti.*

down into units of action and have identified the crisis of each, and this sense of the architecture guides my choices. I do not, however, give the breakdown to the actors, preferring that they discover the structure for themselves.

Relationships are beginning to emerge already and this is the best sign that the action is beginning to flow. I pay special attention to people's attitudes toward one another in specific situations, and give notes or ask questions.

An important discovery is made by Megan (Gertrude); she notices that Hamlet's first soliloquy establishes that it is "not quite two months" since the King's death, and the marraige of Claudius and Gertrude was "within a month" of that—so we are wrong that the opening ceremony is both wedding and coronation, since the wedding occured some three weeks ago. I send word to the designers about this; some changes in costume and prop design will be necessary.

From this recognition, we realize that Hamlet did indeed rush home for his father's funeral only to find his mother's wedding instead. The fact that Hamlet has been around for three weeks since then is also intriguing: What has he been doing? What's been going on with Ophelia in that time?

At lunch, Megan and I discuss privately the feelings of Gertrude toward Claudius and Hamlet. She feels that she is crazy in love with Claudius and that the relationship is a very sexual one; the old Hamlet was probably a stern and unromantic man who left Gertrude very unsatisfied and ripe for the picking by Claudius, so she definitely *did* commit adultery prior to the murder, although she does not suspect that her husband's death was anything but natural. Megan feels that Gertrude is a product of a highly chauvinistic world in which women have little significance in anything but a sexual way.

These ideas coincide with my feeling that Gertrude is essentially a good person. We discuss the the Closet scene and agree that Gertrude is truly repentent and won over to Hamlet's side. When she reports the death of Polonius to Claudius, she maintains her boy's cover of madness; I suggest we even consider the possibility that she suspects the poisoned pearl in the last scene and drinks the wine in order to save Hamlet.

In the afternoon we spend several hours in a first examination of the Closet scene, approaching it gradually. First we read it, and I ask about their initial objectives: What "daggers" does Hamlet intend to speak to Gertrude; what does she hope to achieve with him?

We examine also Polonius's position in the scene. Although it has been my assumption that Gertrude has summoned Hamlet, Dick (Polonius) points out that he is the real author of the encounter: In scene 31, after the rigged interview with Ophelia has failed to reveal Hamlet's true feelings, it is Polonius who suggests that Gertrude meet with Hamlet after the play and that Polonius spy on them.

The fact that Gertrude is "following orders" makes a tremendous difference in the scene. It takes several hours to trace it through, but at last we find that a loving alliance is forged between them. We decide that Gertrude will actively help in the removal of the body and even help cover Hamlet's tracks by adjusting the arras.

We spend some time trying to decipher Hamlet's last speech, but none of us can make head or tail of it; I make a mental note to get an expert critical opinion on the matter. (What I eventually got was agreement that the speech makes no sense in its present form.)

I have decided to combine this scene with the following (41) by having Claudius burst in looking for Hamlet. I came to this idea because I wanted to avoid breaking the flow of action with a scene shift, but this is impossible as it is written because Gertrude is the last off in 34 and the first on in 41. I like the change also because having Claudius come chasing after Hamlet expresses his growing desperation.

At each rehearsal more information has been found in the text; despite my numerous readings it is finally through the actors that many discoveries are being made. Perhaps I have been reading too much between the lines; so much turns on such minute details! I am more and more humble before the genius of the play.

HAIR AND BEARDS, MASKS:
JANUARY 3

The next morning, Jeannie, Peter, and I meet to discuss the haircuts and beards for the show. We discuss the style of hair for each character, deciding where we can use the actor's own hair and where false beards and wigs will be necessary. Some choices are specified in the text: Hamlet says that the Player King, for instance, has come "new-valenced" to "beard me here in Denmark"; his gibing of Polonius about "old men with white beards and weak hams" suggests Polonius's own white beard. Other choices are based on the personality, age, and class of the character, and on design considerations.

Jeannie adds that the distinction we wish to make between the old and the new courts (Gothic and Renaissance) implies beards for the Gothic style and beardless for the Renaissance; thus Claudius will have no beard.

We also work through all the doubling, using the addition or the removal of beards to enhance the double whenever possible. All our decisions must be coordinated with the needs of the other shows, and these require that all our beards be false.

Jeannie shows me the masks for the party scene, which are being rebuilt from stock items; these are stunningly nightmarish, as I had hoped.

WALK-THROUGH PART ONE: JANUARY 3

We finish roughing out the last scenes of our First Part; in these scenes, Hamlet is set upon in earnest by those who would plumb his secret: First Polonius, then Ophelia, then Rosencrantz and Guildenstern. At last the Players arrive. Despite his torment, Hamlet finds some freedom in his "antic disposition." Mark is beginning to find Hamlet's humor, though this is the aspect of the role that is most difficult for him. I am encouraging him toward lighter, more comedic readings and a more manic quality.

In the second hour, the entire cast is called for a rough walk-through of the entire Part. First, however, I take the opportunity to explain the strategy I have adopted, having decided to rough out the entire show this week, then have two run-throughs on the set late next week. I promise that after these rough run-throughs we will return to examine each scene in greater detail, and that we will be free to alter any and all blocking at that time.

Actually, these initial sessions have not really been blocking rehearsals as such, since we have mainly been exploring the action, with the blocking being generated by the actors' own impulses; but then, that is what blocking should be: a spatial expression of the action. Nevertheless, I am concerned that we not become locked into these early spatial choices and will do what I can to ensure a thorough reexamination of them later.

We run through Part One without stopping; a number of the actors are already working off-book and calling for lines from the ASM (there are two stage managers at every rehearsal, Peter and his assistant, Janna). I am watching the run-through to see if the movement patterns relate well to the action and the space; afterward, I give some acting notes, and alter one sequence of entrances and exits; we rerun the last fifteen minutes of the Part to set these changes.

After the rest are dismissed, I work with Mark on the soliloquy which ends the act. He tends now to begin with a burst of self-anger ("O, what a rogue and peasant slave am I!") and then turn reflective toward the end; the problem will be to find instead a way to play up into the act ending. I suggest that what he is really saying is that he is fed up with *words*, and needs desperately to find some way to *act*; the solution lies in the idea for the Mousetrap scene, which began dimly to form in his mind when the Players arrived (when he asks them to perform a speech about the fall of a king, he is really testing this idea). Now he develops the idea fully, and finally commits to it in the final couplet, "The play's the thing wherein I'll catch the conscience of the King."

After rehearsal I speak briefly to Polonius; I have noticed that as he works to learn and understand his lines, he is falling into a laborious tempo which I don't want to become habitual. I suggest that Polonius's complicated use of rhetoric and figures of speech are the result of his schooling and his college theatrical experience (I am thinking of B. L. Joseph's account of Elizabethan schooling); since this ornate way of speaking is second nature to him, it does not require much real thought: the words can tumble effusively out, as if his mouth is on automatic pilot.

Peter has been able to get a good timing on the transitional sound cues for this Part, and we have run the whole in one hour and twenty minutes inclusive; once people are off book I feel confident that Part One will run under seventy minutes.

ROUGHING OUT PART TWO: JANUARY 5

In order to give Mark a chance to explore the ideas we developed yesterday about his final soliloquy, we begin by reviewing the scenes among Rosencrantz and Guildenstern, Polonius, and Hamlet leading up to the arrival of the Players. I want to get a sense of the fellowship Hamlet feels for the Players, and also to explore the use he hopes to make of them in his plot to unmask Claudius. The speech he requests begins to feel like an audition: Are they really as good as he remembers? Good enough to move Claudius to the point of betraying himself?

We then move into scene 32, the preparations for the performance itself and the famous "advice to the players." The need for this advice is now very great: In order for the performance to have its desired effect on Claudius, it must have the realistic impact Hamlet desires.

Hamlet has probably had a hard time keeping his preparations for the performance secret from Polonius, Rosencrantz and Guildenstern. We decide that Hamlet may have posted Horatio as a lookout, so that he warns Hamlet of their approach; this establishes an active sense of conspiracy between them.

For the remainder of the afternoon I sit with Claudius, Gertrude, Polonius, and Hamlet and talk through the Closet scene. This discussion leads us to consider the background of the relationships in the court, and we all (including the stage managers) express our sense of the situation. After much give and take, the consensus emerges that Polonius has been counsellor to the old King and is now fighting to keep his job under Claudius; that there has been some tension in the past between Gertrude and Polonius, as Polonius considers her too lax in the rearing of Hamlet (he being an almost paranoically stern parent); and that he may even fear she will try to influence Claudius to get rid of him.

For her part, Gertrude is not happy about the ideas proposed by Polonius for dealing with Hamlet. She doesn't like the idea of setting Ophelia to spy on him, nor does she like having Polonius spy on them in the Closet scene. Polonius enjoins her to be stern with Hamlet, but what she really wants is a private and tender moment alone with her son. I suggest that when Hamlet enters, she take him downstage, away from the lurking Polonius. After the Closet scene, Gertrude—who realizes that Hamlet is not crazy and has to face her own guilt—becomes Hamlet's accomplice; from this moment on, she will indeed no longer sleep with Claudius.

Denis suggests that Claudius has encouraged Polonius to spy behind the arras because he hopes that Hamlet will indeed kill him; in this way Claudius gets rid of his troublesome accomplice and puts Hamlet in the wrong, effectively killing two birds with one stone. This is consistent with Denis's view of the entire play as springing from the original sin of the poisoning of the old King. At first this first poisoning unleashes a euphoric sensuality, long suppressed under the old Hamlet, which sweeps the entire kingdom; eventually, however, the weight of the sin comes crashing down upon them until they are all poisoned in earnest—Gertrude by the wine, Laertes and Hamlet by the tainted sword, and Claudius himself at Hamlet's hands. It is the growth of this poisonous cancer ("the imposthume of much wealth," as Hamlet puts it) which Hamlet is called upon to excise.

I question my earlier decision to incorporate 34 and 41 by having Claudius come to Gertrude's closet; we agree that it would be better, given our new understanding of things, to restore the original. That night I spend much agonized time trying to find a way to do this, but unless these two scenes are separated by an intermission, or unless I create a new beginning to 41 which doesn't involve Gertrude, there will be an intolerable interruption in the show's momentum just at the time when events should be rushing toward the crisis. I see no solution but to combine the two scenes.

I am uneasy; we are entering the most difficult part of the play.

CONTINUE ROUGHING OUT PART TWO: JANUARY 6

I meet first with Claudius, Gertrude, Polonius, and Hamlet. After thinking over yesterday's discussion about their relationships and reviewing in my mind the emerging characterizations, I have prepared careful notes for each of them. For each I have an "attraction" and a "reservation."

Denis has brought tremendous energy and dynamism to the role of Claudius with his interpretation of the man as an "improviser"; I fully support this choice. I suggest that he also move in the direction of greater elegance; his sexuality is a bit too Falstaffian at present. I like his image of "the poisoner" as a spiritual as well as a physical metaphor, and suggest that he think more in terms of a serpent than a bear.

Megan is giving Gertrude great dignity and a clear need for intimacy and love; I urge her to develop even more of a carnal drive, letting us understand that she is driven by a great hunger in her womb, both as mother to Hamlet and as lover to Claudius.

Dick's Polonius is loving and likeable, as I had hoped; he need only get the salesman or huckster quality in terms of a less philosophical and more theatrical personal style.

Mark's Hamlet is likeable, loving and, best of all, active. I encourage him to continue making the most active possible choices and to continue finding every opportunity to express his basically loving nature; he needs also to develop more the man's great sense of humor and occasional zaniness.

When the rest of the cast arrives, we continue to rough in the rest of our Part Two and by the end of the rehearsal we are able to walk through it. A break in the construction work allows us to use the set for a time, and we experiment with the placement of the Praying scene especially: I had planned to have Hamlet enter on the catwalk above, but this puts him too far away from us; the staging of this scene continues to elude us.

Ophelia and Hamlet work through the Nunnery scene; this scene, the Closet scene, the Praying scene, and the final Duel will receive the most rehearsal time of any scenes in the play.

The little scene in which Hamlet is nearly captured by Rosencrantz and Guildenstern (42) has become a chase sequence in which Hamlet is gradually surrounded by five people, each cutting off one route of escape after another, until Hamlet must at last leap nearly into the audience to get away on, "Hide fox, and all after!" We spend over two hours working this through.

By contrast, the scene in which Claudius banishes Hamlet (43) works quite well at once, as does the Fortinbras scene which ends Part II. This whole Part is beginning to have excellent momentum.

The terrific pace at which we have been working is exhausting us, but I am driven by the limited availability of the set. I must be careful that we do not outrun our emotional supply lines and pursue form at the expense of exploring content; we are on the very edge of doing so.

EVENING WALK-THROUGH FIRST HALF
ON SET: JANUARY 7

This is my first opportunity to see if what we have done in the rehearsal hall works on the set itself; the special way this set relates to the auditorium is difficult to visualize in the hall. We run Part I without stopping, though I encourage the actors to take their time, working their way through the coordination of movements with lines. I am glad to see that they are feeling the logic of the space and are making the adjustments in placement which are natural to the action.

The overall flow of the action within the space is good, but there is one major adjustment which needs to be made: I have over-used the down-center wharf area, and under-used the up-right center area; this not only makes the mass of the set seem useless, it also blurs the distinction from one locale to another. I hope to have each succeeding scene take place in a different area of the set, or at least to establish different playing axes from one scene to the next.

Accordingly, I move some scenes out of the downstage area, and adjust portions of some other scenes upstage. This reserves the downstage area for the battlement and wharf scenes, for Hamlet's and Claudius's soliloquies, and later, for the vow by Claudius and Laertes to kill Hamlet. I am pleased to see that this vow will naturally occur in exactly the same spot on the stage as does Hamlet's initial vow to kill Claudius.

The first two scenes of Part II are then run for the first time; we stop and start, fixing things as we go. The large group entrance into the Mousetrap scene is working well, and the performance by the Players is beginning to take shape. Composer Todd Barton has come to rehearsal to watch this scene so he will have a sense of the kind of music that should accompany the play-within-the-play.

We have come now to the Praying scene (33) in Claudius's chapel. This is the only locale in the play for which I have not been able to find a good stage location and spatial basis; I have been puzzling over it for days, and have asked Dick Hay to come into rehearsal to help me with it. We consider using the up-left area with the addition of a curtain across the Gothic arch there; unfortunately, the exit from the previous party scene must go through here, so it cannot be used now. We try using the up-center entrance with the tapestry swagged to one side (the only scene for which it would be so used); the Priest might bring in a candleabra to put on the down-left block as an altar. This would work, but I dislike the fact that the Queen's Closet scene, which follows next, will use the same area and the same playing axis.

I decide finally that the down right vom ramp would be the best place for the praying Claudius; this would give him the same proximity to the audience for his soliloquy that Hamlet had for his; it also places him with his back toward Hamlet, who could enter from up left to center for his decision to postpone the killing.

I am eager to give Hamlet's choice not to kill Claudius at prayer full weight. Up to this moment, the play has proceeded as a traditional revenge play: Hamlet has taken action to prove Claudius's guilt (with the mousetrap) and to penetrate his defenses (with his feigned madness), just as he does in the German source play, *Fratricide Punished.* Now the revenge is at hand, and if Hamlet did kill the praying Claudius, the play could end in the expected way. But, instead, Shakespeare moves his play fully into the realm of psychological action: in the German play, Hamlet was restrained by bodyguards and other external factors; Shakespeare's Hamlet refrains for purely internal reasons.

We decide to bring Hamlet close enough to actually do it: I ask Mark to start drawing his dagger in the same spot that the Player King had raised his sword while enacting Pyrrhus, who also pauses at the fatal moment; Hamlet raises his dagger ("send his soul to heaven"), creeps to within inches of the kneeling Claudius, and remains for a moment, reconsiders ("That would be scanned") then must quickly withdraw to work things out.

This solution having been reached, however, I must deal with the cannon which now occupies the right vom area in which Claudius will pray; we need a more usefully abstract scenic element which could become the chapel altar. Dick and I discuss it; we agree that the cannon is useful in the battlement and crowd scenes in Part I, so we decide to use it then, and to replace it during the first intermission with another unit. This also opens the right vom area to greater usefulness in the last act.

THIRTEEN
EARLY STAGING

When you determined your ground plan, you were already thinking about the ways in which the action could be manifested in movement and spatial relationships. Now that the actors are discovering the action for themselves, they are beginning to feel impulses to move within the space you have defined. Assuming that your ground plan is effective in giving them natural modes of movement and inviting them to take stageworthy positions, you will easily be able to extend, refine, and edit these impulses into an expressive pattern. This is the process of blocking the show.

Since blocking is the spatial manifestation of the action, and since the action lives through the relationships and specific transactions of the characters, the evolution of the blocking will arise as an integral part of the the actors' exploration of their roles; their movements and spatial relationships should have an organic connection to their reactions, choices, and objectives. For this reason, it is preferable for the blocking to emerge from the actors' impulses rather than for it to be imposed a priori from your premeditated design.

Blocking generated from the impulses of the actors will better express the specifics of action, character, and relationship as they live within the unique psychodynamics of a particular cast. Moreover, this sort of blocking will more directly express the particular shape and rhythm of the action; changes in beats, crises, and climaxes will, through the movement impulses of the actors, result in the appropriate changes in spatial relationship. As a result, I have found that blocking generated in this way, once it is edited and refined, tends to flow better than anything you might design on your own.

This is not to say that your spatial and pictorial ideas are unimportant, nor are you entirely passive in this process. Rather, your aim is to create the conditions in which the actors can generate the blocking impulses which you then extend, edit, and refine according to the same spatial principles which generated the ground plan. In this way, the blocking will be organic to the action, to the emerging characterizations, and to the set.

When you work this way, the emergence of blocking is a continual part of the process of exploring the action. Blocking ought not to be set apart as a separate activity; nor should it mean freezing the action into an immutable form; rather, the gradual development of the spatial pattern of the show should itself be a mechanism for exploration of the action.

Think of blocking, then, as a continuous activity which grows naturally out of the tendency of human beings to place themselves in expressive relationships whenever they are engaged in significant interactions in a specific space. When the interaction becomes clear and forceful enough, trust that it will block itself; when it does, the ground plan and your editing will shape it into stageworthy pictures.

GENERATING THE BLOCKING

Your first task is to free the actors physically so they begin to express the action in coherent movement. If you merely put the actors on their feet with no guidance whatever, some will either freeze up or wander aimlessly about. You must supply three things to your actors before the blocking can begin to emerge in a free and logical way:

1.   A strong sense of their action and its specific shape, especially in terms of their objectives;

2.   The entrances and eventual exists for each scene, and perhaps the initial stage position in each scene as well;

3.   A firm understanding of the geography of the set as it relates to relationship and action.

Let's examine each briefly.

The action is already developing, and through your work on the inner phase you are encouraging the actors to begin experiencing both their objectives and the sequence or through-line which those objectives form (this is the foundation for the score of the role, and we will discuss this at length in the next chapter). Putting the show on its feet will greatly enhance the actor's experience of the action by translating these inner impulses into larger outer actions. For this reason, many directors like to get a show on its feet as soon as possible.

Not all directors use this approach, however. Gil Dennis, for instance, prefers to have his casts sit and read the play for days and not get up until they are fully off book. By reading repeatedly—in a dramatic mode—the cast begins to develop impulses to move; when these impulses to move are repeatedly suppressed, they actually grow stronger and stronger, so that when they are finally unleashed the blocking erupts quite spontaneously as a release of this pent-up energy. This method has the further virtue of pre-screening the impulses of the actors: Only the strongest movement impulses survive the prolonged period of suppression.

The second item, the outline of entrances and exits, is usually determined by the logic of the ground plan (which doors lead to what places); you will also do some preplanning of entrances and exits with a concern for the action and the effective use of the stage space. In *Hamlet*, for instance, I did both: Each locale was given its own entrances and underlying spatial configuration (specifically each had its own major playing axis); these choices, however, were also influenced by the sequence of scenes, so that the transitions between scenes were interesting and kinetically logical, and so the area of the stage used from scene to scene had a pleasing variety. Consider this aspect of your work to be a kind of subtle choreography as the large patterns of the action, scene by scene, "dance" within the space of the set.

The third consideration is the spatial logic or geography of the set. This may be determined by realistic considerations, such as the ownership of the room (for example, the kitchen is mom's domain, so dad is a visitor when he's in it) or even of territories within the room (the chair by the fire is dad's, but the alcove belongs to the kids), or of the beaten paths or unexplored territories (the whole neighborhood cuts through the kitchen on their way to the pool, but no one except a stranger uses the front door).

In a less realistic way, the geography of the set may be expressed in terms of different functions for different spaces (the down-left area is for intimate scenes, while the center area is reserved for the violence with which the play ends).

It may even be possible to set up patterns of movement and axes of relationship that express different qualities (the traditional "Grand Diagonal" from up left to down right for the intimate scenes within a family, while the intrusion of strangers cuts perpendicularly across it). I recall a production in-the-round of *Ulysses in Nighttown*, for instance, in which almost everyone moved in clockwise patterns except poor Bloom, who swam against the current by moving counterclockwise.

These ideas, and more, were considerations when you planned your ground plan (Exercise 13); now you will communicate the geography of the set to the actors in terms which will generate an underlying logic in the emerging blocking.

This spatial logic will also form the basis of your selection and editing of the actors' impulses for movement. When I establish the choreography of entrances and exits, I also select opening positions which express the initial set-up of the scene flowing from those initial positions; I then have in the back of my mind a basic pattern that expresses the action. Often, the actors fall naturally into this pattern, or one even better than I had conceived; if not, I can offer a few adjustments based upon the sequence I had envisioned, at least as a starting point for further exploration.

Sometimes, however, I will actually rough block a scene, giving the actors a basic movement pattern designed to help them experience the action for themselves. For instance, in *King Lear* there is a scene in which the two daughters gang up on the old man to strip him of his retinue; I set up the entrances so that the two daughters came in from opposite sides, trapping Lear between them; I then suggested that they gradually circle and move in on him, forcing him further and further downstage, until at last they came together and literally drove him off the stage. While this was not the ultimate blocking of the scene, it did assist the actors in experiencing the action of the scene and got the process of blocking underway.

This sort of provisional blocking, then, can be a useful rehearsal device. Martin Platt, who is one director who uses blocking as a way of communicating with actors, says,

> I find "blocking" almost the most important tool. By giving the actors patterns and spatial relationships on stage, it is possible to communicate to them the emotional content of a scene or relationship.

If you choose to use blocking in this way, be careful that the actors understand what you are doing; encourage them to reexperience the blocking for themselves, and to allow your initial pattern to evolve into new and better patterns if necessary.

SPECIFYING THE MIS EN SCENE

As the action comes into focus, you will exercise greater and greater selectivity and will begin to edit and refine the blocking. Sometimes, specific stage arrangements will emerge which capture the action in a special way, and you may be moved to extend and refine such stage pictures by the adjustment of certain elements, the supportive addition of lighting and sound, and so on. Such total staging is called in Europe the *mis en scene*. Note that this kind of staging is done not as an exercise in your own picturization, but rather in the spirit of extending the nature of the action in the direction in which it is already going.

As an example of how a moment may emerge from the later stages of rehearsal and be refined by the director, here is Stanislavski at work as described by his assistant, Gorchakov. During a run-through of a scene, one of the actresses makes a spontaneous movement, and from the auditorium,

Stanislavski interrupted: "Hold this mise en scene. This will be the final point in the second act. Gorchakov, please make a drawing of this mise en scene: half-open door, Marion standing on the threshold with one hand resting on the door post and the other pressing her handkerchief to her bosom."

Without taking his eyes from the stage, Stanislavski moved a piece of paper in front of me and handed me his pen.

"Konstantin Sergeyevich," I said, "I can't draw."

"Draw as well as you can," he said. "Don't talk, just draw, and later we will discuss it. The director must know how to sketch the design of any mise en scene in his notebook during the rehearsals. Sketch Clemency in front of Marion with her hand outstretched, as if to say 'Don't come any nearer!'; Warden standing in a kind of demon pose (I have in mind Vrobel's picture, *The Demon*); a moon, a strong blue spotlight will be directed toward Warden's back, lighting his figure in silhouette—dark and somber. Marion and Clemency lit by direct light seem much paler. There is scarcely any fire left in the fireplace. It would be good to contrast the silence of this pause with some sound, perhaps the cricket's chirp, and then have the curtain come down slowly. Have you made this sketch? . . . Very good. Now let's test it."[18]

PLANNING THE TECHNICAL ELEMENTS

Given whatever planning you have already done for the technical elements of the staging (principally lights and sound), this is the stage of rehearsal when the precise location and nature of technical cues will start to become clear; they should be allowed to emerge in the same way as the blocking. Lighting and sound are rhythmic energies in the production just as the characters are; they should likewise be motivated at each moment by the superobjective of contributing to the reason the play was written, and need to be choreographed so as to express and enhance the flow of the action.

The elements of light and sound can be used to fulfill several functions:

1. For realistic effects required by the text, such as the sunrise which drives the Ghost away in *Hamlet*;

2. To establish environment in a realistic sense—the ships' bells and shimmer of light from the surface of the water we used in the Wharf scenes;

3. To enhance the emotional tone of a scene—the blue leafless tree light pattern and the funeral bell that tolled throughout the Graveyard scene;

4. For punctuation or emphasis of the action—the way each of Hamlet's crucial choices was made as some bell or other was ringing, or Shakespear's call for a "drum-trumpet-cannon" sound effect at each crucial point in the final Duel;

5. For continuity: lighting and music changes have traditionally been used to support transitions from one scene into another; the flourishes in Shakespeare often serve this purpose. In *Hamlet,* the environmental sound for each scene was started just as the previous scene was ending, so that sound always preceeded and overlapped the scene transitions (a technique borrowed from the movies).

In addition to these five functions, which may be served by both sound and lights, lighting has three additional functions of its own:

    6. Illumination, which on the stage means specifically the ability to see the actors' eyes;

    7. Modeling for three-dimensionality and figure-ground relationship;

    8. Tonality or coloration, which is also related to emotional tone.

As the show gets up on its feet, watch for the needs of the action and the environment in these ways; this is not only a matter of enhancement, it is actually the extension and completion of the stage environment into a total sensory milieu.

Indeed, these technical elements will only extend, and never substitute for, the power of the action; except for required effects like telephones ringing, your show must be able to stand effectively on its own without such effects. It is an old TV axiom that if the acting in a scene is bad, you simply add background music; the whole process of adding such enhancements is appropriately called "sweetening." Make sure your show doesn't need sweetening; technical effects should grow out of the need to complete the intrinsic qualities of action and environment, not to compensate for a weakness in them.

In the same way, avoid effects that merely duplicate some aspect of the scene which is already sufficiently strong; such redundant effects may actually obscure the action (some of the environmental effects we had planned in *Hamlet*, for instance, had to be cut after the show opened for just this reason).

Assuming that you begin to feel the need for effects on a legitimate basis, however, have your stage manager begin to note possible cues, and communicate with the designers on a regular basis; invite them to have input into this early evolution of the lighting and sound.

This is also the time for you and your stage manager to begin noting the properties and costume implications as the actors begin to find "business" and to interact with their environment. Continuous communication at this early stage will pay big dividends later on.

THE STAGE MANAGER

Your Stage manager (usually called the "SM," sometimes as in "sado-masochist") is many things to you: social director, police officer, general contractor, tactician, conscience and alter ego.

The SM's primary responsibility during the rehearsal process is to facilitate the work itself: this means making sure everything needed for an effective rehearsal is ready when work is to begin: a substitute set, furniture, props, whatever. He or she will also police the actors and deal with problems of lateness, incorrect line memorization, and rehearsal deportment. In these ways, the SM greatly influences the atmosphere in the rehearsal hall, and you must make sure that she or he understands the kind of atmosphere you want.

Take time to work with the SM and go over the specifics of your rehearsal strategy and style; don't work these things out in front of the actors.

The SM is also your main channel of communication with the design and technical staff and with the theatre management; as such, the SM is like the general contractor who coordinates the efforts of many workers so that the entire project comes to fruition smoothly. Keep your SM informed of your thinking every moment of the time, and ask for daily reports on the work going on outside the rehearsal hall.

The SM is also a tactician, in charge of planning scenery shifts, the backstage choreography of quick changes and prop handling, perhaps even (if you choose) elements of the production such as battle sequences. Coordinate on these matters early so that the SM's planning is coherent with the objectives of the whole show.

If the chemistry between you and the SM is right for it, you can even use her or him as a sort of conscience, to give you an objective sense of how you are handling things, and to offer observations about the conduct of rehearsals, the needs of certain cast members, and such. SM's are often privy to feelings which are concealed from directors.

In any case, your SM will finally be the coxswain for the show: Beginning at the first technical rehearsal, the SM will actually run all the logistical and technical elements of the show and, in an Equity situation, take over as surrogate director once the show opens. For all these reasons, treat your relationship with your SM with loving care; it is nearly as important as your relationship with the cast.

THE HAMLET LOG, PART 10: FIRST RUN-THROUGHS—JANUARY 7

Having worked very quickly to roughly block the first two Parts, I feel the need to briefly return to a more reflective approach in the more emotionally complex second half of the play. Accordingly, we spend this afternoon sitting in a circle and reading through the play from the end of the play-within-the-play. We stop whenever anyone has a question or an idea to share.

Many interesting details come up: We notice that Hamlet's sea voyage was interrupted on the second day out; even assuming that the pirates did not bring him directly home, he is still gone only about a week. This establishes the right time span between Polonius's death and Ophelia's funeral, for Polonius, we know, was interred "hugger-mugger," and Laertes rushes home from France immediately (a journey of only several days). So Ophelia goes mad only days after the funeral of her father; Gayle Bellows (Ophelia) points out how everyone, including her father and brother, questions her honesty (even though she herself is totally honest); add to this the harsh treatment she receives from Hamlet in the Nunnery scene, the death of her father, and it is no wonder that she goes over the edge.

Megan decides that Gertrude has fallen into a deeper and deeper depression since Hamlet's departure, and is feeling more and more hopeless. She can see no happy outcome to any of this; though she feels sympathy for Ophelia, she hasn't the margin of strength needed to cope with her, and so she doesn't want to see her in 45. When Ophelia reenters later, however, Gertrude will be moved to follow her off and will, therefore, witness her death first-hand; she rushes back with the news, almost mad herself.

It seems odd that through all this, Horatio is present: Is he watching out for Hamlet's interests in his absence? How does Claudius feel about his being there? Does Gertrude accept him as an ally in Hamlet's absence? We follow Horatio as he watches after Ophelia, then is called away from her by the arrival of Hamlet's letter.

Laertes's instantaneous acceptance by the mob (which cries "Laertes shall be King!") is explained by the growing dissaffection for Claudius (provoked by the announcement of the death of Polonius and the banishment of Hamlet) and the fickleness of the mob (a frequent theme in Shakespeare.) When he breaks in, Laertes is beyond reason in his grief and is easy prey for Claudius's wildest improvisation so far. They withdraw to the privacy of Claudius's chapel—I continue the irony that Claudius's darkest scheming is done in this holy place—so that Laertes does indeed swear "to cut his throat in the church."

These are a few of the details we have discussed during our reading of the text; this kind of occasional review of the evidence is my favorite rehearsal strategy, and I'm sure this session will make these scenes easier to work on during the next two days.

WORK-THROUGH SECOND HALF: JANUARY 8

Tonight on the set we work through the first of the scenes we reread yesterday afternoon.

This sequence of scenes occurs in real time; only about an hour passes from the play-within-the-play (32), to Claudius's futile effort at prayer and Hamlet's choice to delay killing him (33), to the Queen's Closet and the killing of Polonius (34), to the Capture of Hamlet by Rosencrantz and Guildenstern (42), to the shipping of Hamlet to his doom in England by Claudius (43), to the crucial scene in which Hamlet becomes ready for action (44)—which signals our second intermission. It is my objective to stage this entire sequence with maximum flow and momentum, so I pay special attention to the transitions between scenes and the way in which they flow in the space of the set. The shape of this sequence must propel us into the play's crisis.

There are really two major crises in this play: The first occurs when

Hamlet hesitates in the killing of Claudius. At that moment Hamlet has over-come all external obstacles between himself and his revenge, but at that moment, the internal obstacles assert themselves. From there until the main crisis in 45 ("Henceforth my thoughts be bloody or nothing worth") the events of the play hurtle out of Hamlet's control (as in the killing of Polonius); I want the pacing of this sequence of scenes to have this "hurtling" quality.

We begin with our first walk-through of the Praying scene. Our choice of the extreme downstage position for the prayer works beautifully: Hamlet now enters behind the kneeling Claudius, and we try several routes and posi-tions. Mark follows his impulse to creep very close to Claudius, letting his dagger hover inches above the kneeling figure (I have decided to give Hamlet a dagger instead of a sword here and in the killing of Polonius—for safety reasons and because the dagger blows can be more brutal).

Can Hamlet speak at such close proximity? These speeches are an unusual use of the aside, and they function as if they were voice-overs in a movie; by convention, Hamlet can speak while standing directly behind Claudius and not be heard. Denis suggests that once Hamlet has paused, however, he runs the risk that Claudius will sense his presence and turn on him; he must strike or withdraw at once. Mark seizes on this idea: He creeps in for the kill, but then pauses and rushes silently away, flattening himself against the wall as he says "That would be scanned."

We go next to the Closet scene, which moves well, having already been rehearsed several times; next is the chase scene blocked last night; I am not pleased with it on second viewing, and we spend another hour and a half reworking these thirty-one lines! Finally, Hamlet is able to escape his pursuers with a sensational leap, and poor Rosencrantz straggles off last in pursuit.

This rehearsal is the loosest we have had so far, with much laughter and joking. I fall into the spirit of it—we have all been working very hard and need the release.

The Banishment scene goes together quite easily at once; during Hamlet's final speech to Claudius, in which he calls him "mother," I suggest that Hamlet kiss Claudius a sarcastic goodbye. This outrages Claudius, who sends Rosen-crantz and Guildenstern after him with the fatal letter; alone with his Priest for his final speech, Claudius says that he will have no joy until Hamlet is dead.

We are out of time and energy, but we will be ready for a run-through of Part II before we lose our set.

ROUGH BLOCK PART THREE: JANUARY 9

Today in the rehearsal hall (the crews are busy on the set) we do the first blocking work on Part Three. These are the events during the few days following Hamlet's sea voyage: Polonius has been interred "hugger-mugger" (probably a day or two after his death), and it is now three or four days later; Laertes has received the news and has returned home, raising a sympathetic mob in his wake as he rushes to the castle; Ophelia has gone completely mad.

The time we spent two days ago reading and discussing these scenes pays off, and we work well through each. I set the entrances and exits and opening positions, then we follow the actors' impulses to establish the blocking pattern, then run it again to set it in people's memories.

Ophelia's mad scene goes particularly well. She is struggling with the melody of her song, but I encourage her to forget the music for now and to examine the meaning behind the lyrics; what I believe she will find is that there is great subtextual bitterness in them, that Ophelia uses them to blame Claudius and Gertrude for depriving her of both her father and her lover, and even threatens them ("My brother shall hear of it.") Of course, she may be only dimly aware of these feelings herself; her surface quality is one of a fey lightness. I am thinking of the song of the nightingale which tradition says is sung as it flies up to meet its death (the "swan song"). Gayle is beginning to discover all this with only the barest suggestion from me.

Laertes and his mob break in, and I have Osric rush in with the news; Claudius calls for his Switzers, but only Voltemand and Cornelius dash in and skirmish briefly with Laertes, while Osric cowers safely to one side. The rabble, an important image of the poison spreading through the kingdom, fights its way up the vomitorium until Laertes stops them. They are to have rural weapons like pitchforks and scythes; we will do the specifics of this after our fight director arrives, but I want it to be ugly and violent. If greater numbers of actors were available I would be tempted to make this encounter a full scale skirmish to show the disintegration of social order in the kingdom.

The confrontation between Claudius and Laertes is going strong when Ophelia appears on the catwalk above, singing. Her long, unsteady walk across the catwalk is frightening. She comes down and distributes her flowers and herbs to the appropriate people: rosemary and pansies to Laertes for remembrance and thought (of Polonius), fennel and columbine to Claudius (for flattery and cuckoldry), rue to Gertrude (for sorrow and repentence). She and Laertes come together for her last songs, which are of their dead father, and as she goes off (followed by the solicitous Gertrude), the shaken Laertes is left alone with Claudius. Claudius, of course, seizes the moment to take Laertes aside for his wildest improvisation yet—the use of Laertes to kill Hamlet.

We shift to the wharf, where Marcellus (the last of the old court) leads Horatio to the Sailor to receive Hamlet's letter. This scene goes together quite easily, and with a little adjustment of the final lines, Marcellus is given the letter to deliver to the King, while Horatio and the Sailor rush off to the waiting Hamlet.

Claudius and Laertes enter the chapel alone. The main problem in this scene is to keep the momentum going up into the crisis, which we agree is

Laertes's choice to go along with Claudius's plan on the line "I'll do it." Denis suggests that this moment be the first physical contact between them. It is natural for this to occur in front of the altar unit, the same spot on which Hamlet swore to kill Claudius.

We skip the Gravedigger scene for now, since that threesome can be called for a separate rehearsal, and go into the complex Funeral scene. The large number of people involved would make it difficult to generate the blocking in process, so I have planned a detailed blocking pattern in advance. We run the scene three times, making several adjustments for relationship and pace.

I am still pursuing our early design decision to have the body of Ophelia visible on her bier; but Laertes's climbing into the grave onto her body seems too grotesque—even silly—and Hamlet wonders why he doesn't recognize Ophelia sooner. It takes very little discussion to convince me that a closed casket is best. This would permit the fight between Hamlet and Laertes to take place in the grave proper.

We block this; Hamlet is outraged at Laertes's climbing into the grave, and rushes forward to drag him out, but Laertes pulls him in on the line "The devil take thy soul!" Everyone pulls them out while they continue fighting, until Claudius, Gertrude, and Horatio part them, Claudius because he wants Laertes to wait until they can kill Hamlet without obvious blame.

We run the Funeral scene with this pattern twice more, but I'm not satisfied that it is at all correct. We will have to examine it from scratch again. The bulk of the cast is dismissed and we return to the Gravedigger scene. This scene can easily become too philosophical; we will have to find the way the action continues to flow through Hamlet's thought processes; my initial sense is that Hamlet is "making friends with death" because he feels the imminence of his own.

Allan Nause (Horatio) suggests that he is eager for Hamlet to leave this open place and get to safety, but Hamlet insists on lingering; this is a good extra source of pace for the scene, and we block it accordingly.

We're out of time, and we forgo work on the Osric scene until later.

WALK-THROUGH PART TWO: JANUARY 10

Tonight we will run our Part Two on the set so I can see how it flows through the space, and get a sense of the shaping of the whole. This Part has the strongest natural momentum, and the run-through flows very well. The only major disappointment is the first scene (31), which now makes no sense at all; I don't know what we were thinking when we first worked it, but we were wrong. There is no action being expressed by this blocking, and the actors are very uncomfortable with it; the scene will have to be redone from scratch.

The rest of Part Two having gone satisfactorily, we move on to Part Three and the scenes worked yesterday. When we come to the Graveyard, we work for over an hour on the fight in the actual grave using a rehearsal coffin. This is a difficult rehearsal; we are all tired and concentration is in short supply; I suspect that we will have to redo this scene when we next come back to it.

Later, I review the rehearsal in my mind; I feel that I had trouble organizing myself. I was in a very receptive frame of mind, but in too passive a way—perhaps it is the exhaustion of our heavy schedule so far. After all, we have put nearly the entire play up on its feet in two weeks! Tomorrow, thankfully, is a day off.

That night, I review the overall shape of the show as I have begun to experience it in these run-throughs. From the point of view of plot, our three Parts break down into something like the three movements of a symphony:

Part One (Statement): The command for vengeance and Hamlet's first ploys (the antic disposition and the play-within-the-play).

Part Two (Development): The outcome of Hamlet's plotting (his ruse is successful, but at the moment of vengeance he pauses, thus placing himself in mortal danger).

Part Three (Recapitulation): The plotting by Claudius (Hamlet has given up plotting in favor of acting in the moment). Because Hamlet is now ready to act, Claudius is undone when his plot goes awry.

Each Part has its own crisis at the very end, and it is the momentum up to these crises that I am hoping to develop in these run-throughs; this momentum (or pace) is created by the actors' experience of the causal connections linking each choice they make to the whole, beat by beat, scene by scene, and Part by Part. A detailed examination of choice, beat by beat, will be the next major phase of rehearsal once we lose our set and return to the rehearsal hall; the spatial memory of the set should then be strong enough in the actors to permit us to make any changes in our blocking that seem necessary.

FIGHT MEETING: JANUARY 11

Chris Villa, our fight choreographer, arrives today and we immediately meet on the set. We discuss first the nature of the weapons. Chris points out that during the transition between the Gothic and Renaissance periods the weapons (and the style of fighting) were undergoing considerable change: The Gothic sword was broad, for hacking and slashing, while the Renaissance sword was slender and long, for thrusting. The size of our set makes a medium-length Renaissance blade the best choice.

I describe the blocking I have planned for the onlookers during the fight: The entire front of the stage is open, with Hamlet and his seconds (Horatio and Marcellus) on stage left, and Laertes alone on the stage right vom (in the same spot he took his deadly vow, and where he can easily poison his blade without being seen by anyone but the audience). Osric, as judge, and the King and Queen will be up center.

We plan briefly the choosing of the weapons; I don't want Osric to be complicit with the plot, since he will not be punished at the end of the play, so he can't force the choice of swords. Chris suggests that Laertes give Hamlet his own sword at the outset as a seemingly sportsmanlike gesture, leaving Laertes free to select the unbated sword, which has been marked in some way.

We read through the scene together to discuss its dramatic content: Laertes is hellbent on vengeance, while Hamlet has confidence in the "continual practice" he says he has had. As the fight begins, they feel one another out: Laertes is surprised by Hamlet's skill and loses the first point. Claudius is so alarmed by Hamlet's skill that he offers the poison cup immediately, though Hamlet doesn't drink. In the second point, Laertes tries harder, but again Hamlet bests him.

Now Laertes is desperate; he *must* win the next hit in order to deliver the poison. This last point, then, is extremely violent, launching us into the rapid succession of deaths which ends the play. The crisis of the fight is the exchange of weapons that leaves Hamlet with the poisoned sword; we talk about ways of achieving this.

I give Chris three requirements for this crisis: First, that it be easy for the audience to keep track of which sword is which; second, that the exchange be clearly accidental; and third, that Hamlet immediately go at Laertes ferociously (which is when Claudius cries "Part them, they are incensed"), but that Hamlet clearly not mean to kill him, but rather only to beat him soundly.

Chris suggests an idea from the critic A. C. Bradley, that Claudius cries "Part them, they are incensed" because he realizes that Hamlet now has the poisoned sword; we agree to pursue this assumption. We discuss also whether Hamlet realizes that Laertes's sword is "unbated," since he has been cut by it. A *bate* was a covering or blunting of the tip of a dueling sword; however, the edge could still cut; dueling scars are still a proud mark of the Wittenberg swordsmen. What is important to me is that, like Polonius's death, Rosencrantz's and Guildenstern's condemnation, and Gertrude's drinking of the wine, the killing of Laertes be the result of an accident. I don't want Hamlet to become so bloodthirsty that he knowingly kills Laertes.

Chris and I also discuss the other moments of violence in the play: the attack of Laertes and the rabble, the killing of Polonius, the end of the Nunnery scene when Hamlet throws Ophelia to the ground. Chris will check the safety and effectiveness of the action at these points.

ROUGH BLOCK FINAL SCENE: JANUARY 11

I have spent several hours planning the entrance of the court and their opening positions; I have had to think backward all the way from the final positions of the dead bodies to the entrance of the court!

It takes some two hours to work through the connections of this complex scene; at each point I am amazed at how Shakespeare has provided for the handling of the *entire* scene: Lines like "Guard the doors there," and "Treason, treason!" help to shift groups of people so as to establish a change in the situation and to prepare for the entrance of Fortinbras from above.

As we work through the deaths, Megan points out how alone they each are when they die; only Hamlet has the comfort of Horatio. Indeed, I have placed the four dead bodies as far apart from one another as possible. Denis has the idea that Claudius should die in his throne, pinned there by Hamlet's sword thrust. We can't actually empale him on the sword, but we block the thrust so that it drives him into his chair; Hamlet then bends his head over the back of the chair and forces the dregs of the poison wine down his throat.

To emphasize the love between Hamlet and Horatio, I have Horatio cradle Hamlet's body throughout his final speeches. He and Marcellus alone carry Hamlet off (we cut Fortinbras's reference to "Captains"), with soldiers carrying torches fore and aft.

We run the scene several times, then dismiss most of the cast. Hamlet, Horatio, and Osric stay behind to work the Osric scene. The bitterness Hamlet feels toward the entire court is starting to drive his comic treatment of "this waterfly"; Mark is beginning to get the size and looseness of the ready Hamlet in this scene.

After rehearsal, Chris, Peter, and I discuss blood: Will the various wounds produce bleeding? We agree that the bulk of Claudius's robes makes blood unnecessary for him, but Laertes and Hamlet should bleed, Laertes profusely. Peter will check with the costume department about this; the rigor of ninety-seven performances and the washing of shirts must be considered, but I am prepared to insist if necessary.

COURT SCENES: JANUARY 12

Today we work through all the court scenes in order: I am watching for the development of the relationship among Claudius, Gertrude, Polonius, and Hamlet. The actors are encouraged to stop and start, and to ask questions; we make some minor adjustments as we begin to clarify these relationships, but in the main our initial outline is holding up.

Ophelia makes tremendous strides today; the subtext of her mad songs (as an indictment of Claudius and Gertrude) has given them tremendous power; her contact with Laertes is touching, and gives him strong motivation to avenge his father's death.

I insist on reviewing Ophelia's funeral scene without the pallbearers and Priest present, so we can be clearer about the underlying action; I am still unclear about it. Denis suggests that the problem lies in a cut we had made earlier in one of Hamlet's speeches: during his fight with Laertes, Hamlet says,

I prithee take thy fingers from my throat,
For, though I am not splenitive and rash,
Yet have I in me something dangerous,
Which let thy wisdom fear.

These lines had been cut because of the difficulty of saying them clearly during the uproar of the fight; but as Denis points out, they make it clear that it is *Laertes* who attacks Hamlet, and that Hamlet avoids the confrontation. I recall the early design discussion, when Dick Hay had made this same point, and this is indeed the way I had originally understood the scene, but somehow it slipped away in the search for a more dramatic fight. We return to the original idea of Laertes leaping out of the grave at Hamlet, who then repulses him; we restore the cut speech, making it a warning from Hamlet to Laertes, but Laertes ignores it and attacks again; they are then pulled apart. The scene now works; our staging is at last aligned with the text.

At the evening session, Hamlet and I spend an hour alone working on his "To be or not to be" soliloquy. The main point here is the depth of his feeling of impotence and self-hatred, which leads him to consider suicide. Mark has many questions about Hamlet's thinking at this point and I answer them as best I can, but there is the danger that an intelligent actor like Mark may think himself into a state of paralysis with a role like this; there are really no a priori answers, and the role must be found by trial and error. I wish I could find more tangible ways of helping Mark into the experience; I hope that having roughed the play out quickly so as to get the scenes under way will help to find the long arcs on which the role is based. I decide that on the day after tomorrow we will devote a rehearsal to tracing his choices through the entire play.

Chris Villa arrives and shows me his selection of weapons for the show. He, Mark, and Bruce (Laertes) begin work on the fight; this first session will be devoted to vocabulary and the basic moves out of which the fight will be composed.

WORK-THROUGH PART THREE:
JANUARY 13

Tonight we work through Part III on stage. The first four scenes, which had been among those worked yesterday, go smoothly. We stop to work the details of the Rabble, which enters with Laertes; Chris Villa has designed some moves for the disarming of Voltemand and Cornelius, which is tricky because the audience is within two feet of the fight.

The Gravedigger scene is beginning to work; the Funeral scene is reworked in detail with the changes decided last night, and makes a great deal more sense.

The Osric scene is run twice; it is very tenuous still, and I note that we will have to spend some special rehearsal time on it next week.

The final scene of the play is worked through for the first time on the set; we spend over an hour running it three times, blocking the movements of the crowd around the fight as Chris describes it. Each time we work the scene the actors make stronger connections, and the action is beginning to flow within the entire cast (twenty-eight people are on the stage during this scene).

At the conclusion of rehearsal I call the cast together. We have now completed sixty hours of rehearsal, and the play is completely rough-blocked; the day after tomorrow we will culminate this phase of the work in a walk-through of the entire play with the sound, lighting, and costume designers present. This will help ensure smooth technical and dress rehearsals; this is especially important because there is a gap of one whole week between our technical and dress rehearsals (due to the final rehearsals for the other six shows in the repertory) and the show will have to be very sound in its staging to survive this erratic schedule.

I emphasize that this is only the first phase of the work, however, and that we will be going back over the play, scene by scene, for the next three weeks. We will review every choice and get much more deeply into the substance of the action.

All but Hamlet and Laertes are dismissed; Chris spends the remaining hour continuing to drill them on the movements from which the fight will be composed; I sit and watch.

I am relieved; in a sense, the hardest part of my work is over. There is enough structure in what we have done in these three weeks so that the action will begin to assert itself fully. When the show begins to pick up its own organic momentum, I can adopt the basically reactive stance toward the work which I prefer.

There is the real possibility, however, that our early staging could imprison the growth of the play; I will have to watch carefully that it does not, and prod whenever it seems that something is being done for form alone.

HAMLET'S CHOICES: JANUARY 14

Before we do our run-through for the designers, I call a rehearsal to examine Hamlet's choices throughout the play; Gertrude, Polonius, Ophelia, the Ghost, and Horatio are called to go through their encounters with Hamlet.

I've reread the play from Hamlet's point of view, and it still seems to me that he is trying to do all he can within his understanding of the situation. When, at the end of Act IV he finally says, "I know not why I have yet to say, 'this thing's to do,'" it is literally true; he's done all that he saw the possibility for, given his beliefs and understanding. For instance, his reasons for not killing Claudius at prayer are entirely sound: Hamlet believes that Claudius will go to heaven if killed in "a state of grace," and this will in no way be a quid pro quo for the torment the Ghost is suffering for having been killed "all unready." Crucial to this, of course, is Hamlet's deep religiousness, and of that we have numerous examples: at no time does he doubt the existence of God (or the Devil) or of an afterlife, though he knows not what form it may take.

With these underlying assumptions, we trace each of Hamlet's choices through the play, beginning with his choice to "hold his tongue" despite his outrage at what his mother and Claudius are doing. This inner tension is given the chance of release by the appearance of the Ghost.

Ivars Mikelson, our Ghost, has only just arrived due to an injury, but he falls in quickly with my desire for a strong father-son relationship in these scenes; Hamlet can easily choose to avenge his father, and will only in retrospect begin to consider that the Ghost may have been a devil.

Mark is exploring Hamlet's choice to adopt an "antic disposition"; we are agreed that this feigned madness is not only a ploy to disarm Claudius, it also permits Hamlet to give vent to his genuinely confused feelings; it is therefore a mixture of feigned and real madness.

After Shakespeare's First Act, however, there follows a delay of weeks—perhaps months—and Hamlet has done nothing, evidently beset by second thoughts and suspicions (and perhaps impeded by the precautions of the wily Claudius as well). He is probably feeling very alone: Confronted with his old friends, Rosencrantz and Guildenstern, he quickly chooses not to trust them; but this is nothing compared to the pain of his rejection of Ophelia in the Nunnery scene. His jibing of Polonius as "old Jeptha who had a daughter" indicates that he has deduced that Polonius has ordered Ophelia to shun him; thus Hamlet also knows that Ophelia cannot be trusted, since she must obey her father.

This sets up the Nunnery scene: He still loves Ophelia, but knows he cannot share the truth with her, so being near her is painful for him. His first "Get thee to a nunnery" speech can grow out of a real desire for Ophelia to go away to safety, for both their sakes. When Ophelia lies about the whereabouts of her father, however, Hamlet suspects they are being spied upon and he becomes truly angry and hurt; he lashes out at her with the second "Get thee to a nunnery" in the sense of a brothel, and hurls the love letters in her face.

We discuss his decision to use the Players to create the mousetrap, and his choice to postpone killing Claudius. Next we examine the Closet scene: After his impulsive choice to kill what he thinks is the lurking Claudius (as he said he would in the Praying scene), Hamlet faces another choice. The Ghost instructs him to try to continue with his efforts for revenge, but also to save Gertrude from herself; this he does with love and concern. Mark has added some light kisses of Gertrude during his repeated goodnights which are quite touching.

The events which follow are beyond his control; he finds himself about to board the ship, and just when things look most hopeless, he makes his crucial choice. Perhaps the Buddhists are right: We don't find enlightenment until we give up.

Now ready, he takes advantage of his opportunities on the ship and in each thing "is Heaven ordinant." As he tells Horatio about these events (in scene 52), he also asserts his resolve to kill Claudius:

> —is't not perfect conscience
> To quit him with this arm? And is't not to be damned
> To let this canker of our nature come
> In further evil?

He has only two choices remaining: to fight Laertes despite a clear premonition of death, and to kill Claudius, which he does, ironically, after he knows that he is dying himself.

This rehearsal should help Mark experience the through-line of the role; it will only be from this perception of the whole that he will be able to refine each individual moment.

FIRST RUN-THROUGH ON SET: JANUARY 15

The composer, sound designer, and lighting designer sit with me through today's run-through. As we watch, we talk through each light and sound cue, and time each; it is an unusual opportunity to do this three weeks before the technical rehearsal, and far better than the usual "paper tech."

Jeannie and her costume crew sit through the run-through as well, checking the progression of clothing for everyone from scene to scene. The time available for each costume change is also checked (only one minor costume change will have to be eliminated).

The shape of each of our Parts is emerging. We run Part One in one hour and eighteen minutes; I hope it will eventually play at eight minutes less. Part Two runs fifty-nine minutes today, and should be about fifty-three minutes when we open; Part Three should run fifty-five minutes when the fight is finished. This means a total running time of three hours and thirty-five minutes, more than I had hoped; I look through the text again for cuts, but I find none.

We can have our set for three more rehearsals; I decide to devote one to each Part to begin working on some of the details I've noted today, and to give the actors a chance to begin strengthening the connections within the scenes.

Mark is becoming stronger with each rehearsal. The longer arcs of the part are beginning to emerge for him; I think our strategy of roughing out the entire play has been useful to him.

What mixed feelings! A difficult phase of the work completed, but so much left to do! I come away from today's run-through with several pages of notes: some concern form—blocking to correct, logistics of soldier and crowd movements to adjust, prop and costume questions—but most relate to the work we have not yet done to specify the underlying structure of the action in each beat. We have much to do in the remaining three weeks.

FOURTEEN
SHAPING, PACING, AND FOCUSING

Assuming that you have been using a traditional rehearsal strategy, you have now roughed in the broad outlines of the production and have explored the general direction in which the natural energies of the production are moving; you are now ready to begin making firm choices and to establish details.

During the exploratory phase of rehearsals you have been deeply involved in the inner workings of the production; you may have become so fascinated with the evolving work of the actors and designers that you may have lost your perspective. Now you must reassert your position as an ideal audience of one. As Robert Brustein puts it,

> There comes a time after the building blocks have been created when the director must reimagine himself as a spectator, and try to experience the production the way the audience will. At the same time, he must maintain a critical distance in order to push the production forward to its final realization.

This next phase of the work, then, requires a special frame of mind which involves the dual consciousness of being an observer and a participant, a leader and a follower at the same time. This dual consciousness was mentioned by several of the directors who answered my questionnaire: Gerald Freedman says,

I have a split personality—both operating at the same time. Empathy with the actor and character *and* a neutral audience position, waiting to be interested, moved, impressed and surprised.

Nagle Jackson puts it this way:

There are two "me's" at rehearsal, one observing the other. One is immersed in the play as a sort of innocent John Doe who has never seen the action before and responds or does not respond. The other "me" watches that John Doe, figures out why things work for him or do not. It's a weird kind of schizophrenia, but always interesting.

This kind of "schizophrenia" assists you in bringing the production into sharper and sharper focus, each detail becoming more definite in its relationship to the whole. This process involves three simultaneous editing procedures: the *shaping* of the action through the actors' sense of the beats and crises, the *pacing* of the action through the strength of the action/reaction connections and the selection of the proper tempo and rhythm for each action-phrase, and the *focusing* of the production through the elimination of all unnecessary detail. In this chapter we will examine each of these processes in turn.

SHAPING THE SCORE
OF THE PRODUCTION

Your study of the play's structure has prepared you to recognize the proportion of rising and falling action in each beat, in each scene, and in the play as a whole; this rhythmic shape has begun to emerge from the specific interactions of the actors beat by beat, scene by scene. You will now assist the actors in developing their specific sense of the sequence of stimulus and response through which the action may flow in a basically consistent, repeatable way. The sense of this specific sequence serves the actor as a kind of map by which he or she can retrace the journey of the role anew at each performance. Stanislavski called this the *score* of the role, a sort of skeletal outline of the action which the actor internalized until it became second nature. In *Creating a Role* he described the operation of this inner model:

With time and frequent repetition, in rehearsal and performance, this score becomes habitual. An actor becomes so accustomed to all his objectives and their sequence that he cannot conceive of approaching his role otherwise than along the line of the steps fixed in the score. Habit plays a great part in creativeness: It establishes in a firm way the accomplishments of creativeness. In the familiar words of Volkonski, it makes what is difficult habitual, what is habitual easy, and what is easy beautiful. Habit creates second nature, which is second reality. The score automatically stirs the actor to physical action.[19]

It is your primary task during this phase of the rehearsal process to assist the actors in making the final selections of the sequence of objectives which form their scores, and to provide the frequent repetitions in rehearsal which allow the score to become second nature.

In doing this, however, you must not misunderstand the role of habit as it is described by Stanislavski above: What becomes habitual is not the specific physical actions of line delivery, gesture, or movements, but rather, the underlying sequence of objectives which stirs the actor to physical action. This sequence provides the actor with the sense of the through-line of his or her character's action. In creating the map of the role, the score is the path which is proven, through trial and error, to be the best route through the chain of stimulus/response which carries the action of the scene; you must make sure, however, that the journey itself is taken anew each time. The danger is that the physical actions will become habitual, rather than the score which generates them. When this happens, the reality of stimulus/response and the making of choices which give life to the action suffer, and the experience of the actors becomes mechanical. When this happens, the transformational process by which character is generated out of the action ceases as well.

You can help prevent this by maintaining a spirit of exploration throughout the rehearsal process; this later phase in which details are set and polished must not become mindless drill, but rather the finer and more subtle examination of the action. Remember Zelda Fichandler's metaphor of the theatre as a laboratory for the study of life: your specimen is the particular action of your play, and under the microscope of your rehearsal process you are examining it under increasingly stronger magnifications.

THE TEMPO-RHYTHM OF THE PRODUCTION

As each actor's score develops, you will guide the specific choices so that the connections made with the scores of the other actors serve to move the action with the desired tempo (speed) and rhythm (rise and fall of dynamic energy) so as to produce the larger patterns of the play's architecture.

These larger rhythmic patterns come into focus as the action begins to flow in longer and longer arcs. In *Hamlet*, for instance, we have a sense throughout the first two acts that tension is building in the basic situation as Hamlet maneuvers to establish Claudius's guilt. In the third act, the mousetrap is successful in catching "the conscience of the king," and Hamlet has an opportunity to act; but he hesitates, postponing the execution of Claudius to "a fitter time." As a result, the fourth act sweeps Hamlet helplessly into Claudius's plan for a fatal voyage to England; it looks like our hero is done for. At the opening of the last act, a period of uncertainty passes during which Ophelia goes mad and her brother returns to avenge the death of his father. Word comes that Hamlet is safe, but Claudius persuades Laertes to join in a plot to kill Hamlet. Word comes that Ophelia has drowned herself, further motivating Laertes: Everything is in place for a showdown!

At this moment of greatest tension, Shakespeare takes us to the graveyard and the slowest, most reflective, and least eventful scene of the play ensues. This gives enormous weight to Hamlet's philosophical reflections and further builds suspense. When the funeral of Ophelia enters, it is inevitable that violence erupt between Hamlet and Laertes, but Claudius (like Hamlet earlier) awaits a better time, and this momentary outburst serves only to whet our appetite for what must come.

At last we enter the final scene—but again nothing happens, while Hamlet banters with that notorious fop, Osric. Then in the last seven pages, and most intensely in a two-minute eruption of violence, the four remaining principals are killed and the kingdom changes hands.

The way in which this action ebbs and flows, rises and falls, and at last explodes, heightens the meaning of the play as an event. Think of rhythm as the *punctuation* of the action, just as commas, semicolons, colons, and periods punctuate this book. If you imagine trying to read this without punctuation without knowing where a phrase starts or stops even where sentences end you can see that rhythm is a reflection of the way we shape information and experience into meaningful patterns what you are doing as you read this is to insert the punctuation that I have omitted without clear rhythmic shaping the meaning of an experience will suffer.

Add to this sense of rhythmic shaping the way tempo affects the meaning of an event: An action performed quickly is a different action than the same action performed slowly. It is this combination of the proper sequence of tempi with the proper rhythmic shaping that Stanislavski meant by the term *tempo-rhythm*. Many directors feel that the establishment of the tempo-rhythms of the performance is one of the most important directorial functions. Several of the directors who answered my questionnaire mentioned the importance of rhythm; most emphatic was Richard Foreman, who says that the essence of directing is

> uncovering and fixing in place the *rhythms* that will allow the idiosyncratic quality of each performer to serve properly the text. Rhythmic organization is 98 per cent of directing.

It may require some experimentation to discover the correct tempo-rhythm for each scene. If you have been working according to the principles we have been discussing, you will actually have been attending to rhythm all along, so the basic shape of the performance should already be emerging; now it is a matter of focusing and specifying that shape, finding where it needs to move more slowly, and where its momentum needs to sweep in unbroken arcs to moments of crystallized meaning. All this is done through the actors' sense of the stimulus/response chain which builds from crisis to crisis; it is in the adjustment of these moment-to-moment transactions that tempo-rhythm is shaped. Through your side-coaching and notes, you are guiding each actor's choices so they best contribute to these larger patterns of tempo-rhythm.

Stanislavski placed enormous emphasis on the power of tempo-rhythm to give each actor the experience of his or her character's inner world, and you will find that this phase of the work will pay great dividends in the development of character and the emotional life of the play. Again, however, allow these developments to occur naturally from the flow of the action; acknowledge them, but keep them in their proper place as the results of action, not the cause.

The play had certain unique and specific rhythms written into it, since the playwright wrote against the background of the particular rhythmic sense of his or her time and place. It may be that the rhythmic quality of an older play, or one from another culture, is difficult for your actors to fulfill. If necessary, you can use special rehearsal techniques to heighten the rhythmic qualities of the show: Some directors use extensive musical side-coaching, such as clapping their hands or beating a dance drum, to help the actors feel the shape of the action. When appropriate to the material, overtly musical rehearsals with the actors singing and dancing may help to extend their sense of the rhythm; playing recordings of selected pieces of music at rehearsals may also be useful.

Whatever techniques you may use, your aim is to assist the actors in internalizing the rhythms of the show so that they become part of their very being during performance; this is what completes and unifies the score of each actor's role and provides the solid base on which the entire performance will rest.

SHAPING THE PERFORMANCE
FOR THE AUDIENCE

The rhythms of the action are primarily reflections of the architecture of the play, but at this stage of rehearsal you will also become aware of how the rhythms of the play will relate to the rhythmic sense of your particular audience. The playwright has made certain assumptions about the rhythmic response of an audience and, like good music, the flow of the play will resonate in the audience's muscular responses: A rhythmic congruence will be created between stage and audience, and the natural bodily rhythms of the spectators will actually become an indistinguishable part of the performance.

This is most obvious in comedy, with the special rhythm of setup, payoff, and laugh; when this shape is properly realized, the natural spasmodic rhythm of the audience's laughter becomes the basis for the performance. You can experience this by listening to a good comedian; pay no attention to what is said, but feel the rhythm of setup, payoff, and laugh; feel how the tremors of the after-laughs are utilized, and how the natural period of relaxation is modulated to build up to the next wave of laughter. The great comedians get the most out of their material through their rhythmic skill; Neil Simon packs laughter into his scripts as much by the rhythmic shape of his scenes as by the intrinsic funniness of the material.

This is not to say that comedy is shaped primarily to produce laughter, but rather that the rhythm of laughter is a natural aspect of good comic writing. You and your cast needn't *make* anything funny; you simply fulfill its natural rhythmic qualities and *let* it be as funny as it is; there is no excuse for the embarrassing pause when a laugh was expected but fails to materialize. There is a wonderful story about Alfred Lunt and Lynne Fontane doing a long Broadway run of a comedy: Lunt had been getting a good laugh by asking for a cup of tea at a particularly incongruous moment of a scene, but one night the laugh died; he struggled for weeks to recapture it, experimenting with different timing, inflections, and business, all to no avail. One night in the dressing room Fontane solved the problem: "Why," she asked him, "don't you try asking for a cup of tea instead of a laugh?"

The special rhythmic concerns of comedy require the presence of an audience: Since your repeated viewings make an accurate comedic response impossible, you cannot be this ideal audience. It is more effective to provide a rehearsal audience, at least for the final run-throughs before opening.

Tragedy also has its own way of feeding off the natural bodily rhythms of the audience through the natural progression of grief: Claudius is describing the rhythmic effect of most tragedies when he says "When sorrows come, they come not single spies, but in battalions," and Gertrude points out their cumulative impact when she observes that "One woe doth tread upon another's heel, so fast they follow." Most tragedies are based on a sense of inevitability and of a rushing of events toward calamity. It is important that the momentum of these events be so powerful as to sweep both the characters and the audience before them.

PACING THE PRODUCTION

As we have said, tempo refers to speed, while pace refers to the momentum of the through-line of action regardless of its speed. Momentum is maintained by the completeness of each individual connection in the chain of stimulus/response through which the action flows. When the actors are distracted or superficial in their reactions and choices, the pace suffers; this is why telling the actors to go faster may actually harm the pace of the show!

The connections are most complete when each actor is fully in action, fully absorbed in the process of stimulus, choice, and objective. For this reason, a well-paced scene will feel shorter in subjective time even though it may actually be longer in objective time. On those wonderful occasions when the action of the scene takes over and there are no faulty connections to impede its flow, the scene moves under its own power. The actors are so swept along by the natural momentum of the action that they need exert very little effort: they no longer need to *make* the scene happen, they can simply *let* it happen; they are more moved than moving. When this happens, the actors are often amazed at how short the performance has seemed.

When the actors experience the flow of the action in this way, that same flow will usually sweep the audience along as well. Not only will the show seem shorter, but it will also be unified into a single experience. The greatest accomplishment, rhythmically speaking, is for the entire play to feel like one prolonged gesture, each moment and scene being clearly articulated aspects of that gesture, fully integrated into the flow of the whole: As Stanislavski put it, they should be like "vertebrae in the spine of the play."

In order for this to happen, the actors must themselves experience the long arcs of the action, and there are several rehearsal strategies which can help in this. The most common one is to work longer and longer segments of action during the latter stages of rehearsal, culminating in the run-throughs prior to the technical and dress rehearsals. Another (which I prefer) is to do run-throughs at regular intervals throughout the rehearsal process, so that each part is developed in constant reference to the experience of the whole. In certain cases I have worked exclusively in large patterns (usually act by act), allowing the details to fill themselves in through frequent repetitions of the whole.

One extremely useful device to help actors experience the larger patterns of the action is the *high-speed run-through*, a rehearsal in which the show is done at twice or three times normal tempo, but with each stimulus/response transaction being fully experienced. If the actors are allowed to blur the details, this device can be counterproductive; your aim is to enhance the actors' experience of the relationship of part to whole by feeling the flow of the action through each part and sensing the larger patterns of action they form. For this reason, this type of rehearsal is most useful near the end of a rehearsal process, after the individual connections are strong and their relationship to the whole has been clearly experienced.

The high-speed run-through can also help to test the choice of tempo in each section of the play. During exploratory rehearsals you have probably been moving slowly, and the high-speed rehearsal offers an opportunity to see if a faster tempo is right for a given section. I sometimes do a high-speed run of each scene when the scene is first assembled.

FOCUSING THE PRODUCTION

Stanislavski sometimes encouraged his actors to cut eighty percent of what they were doing in an effort to distill the performance to its essence. Just as the lens of a spotlight condenses the light from the filament into a powerful beam, so the focusing of a production condenses the power of the action into a single stream, eliminating extraneous elements and impediments.

This is the result of a rigorous evaluation of the usefulness of every choice, every movement, every detail: Does it carry its own weight? Does it advance the action? The underlying assumption here is that less is more: If one thing can do the job of two or three things, that one thing is more powerful and meaningful. This applies to physical details—movements and gestures, but also to psychological details like choices and emotional transitions. Whereas your early rehearsal exploration for choices and objectives went through the play with a fine-tooth comb, your aim now is to make each detail justify itself and to winnow the wheat from the chaff.

The most severe scrutiny will naturally be directed toward the pauses in the show: Does each enhance the action? Is something significant happening during each pause? Pay special attention to the thinking of the actors: Many actors tend to think *between* lines instead of *during* lines, and it may be that pace and focus can be improved by encouraging them to incorporate more of their thought processes into the dialogue. This is especially useful in Shakespeare and other classical writers, who reserved only a very few major choices to be made without the support of dialogue; modern plays, on the other hand, often encourage more thinking between the lines.

In general, extraordinary pauses, such as significant moments of crucial choice, should be used sparingly: Think of such moments as the jewels which must be properly set against a contrasting background in order to reveal their full beauty. These special moments must be identified and developed, and the flow of action by which each is set up must be economized.

Perhaps the best way to winnow the production is through frequent repetition of the whole: Once a healthy amount of boredom has set in, and the newness of each detail has worn off, there is a natural economizing, a kind of survival of the fittest amongst all the details of the production. Try to schedule your rehearsals with this in mind.

Again, the high-speed run-through can be a useful winnowing mechanism, since details of minimal power tend to fall away during such rehearsals.

SPECIAL REHEARSALS

Now that the action is basically established and the score of the production is somewhat stable, you can adjust the conditions of rehearsal in order to heighten various aspects of the production. You might choose, for instance, to do a run-through in some real location which will help the actors to develop the proper sense of atmosphere. I recently did a production of *The Time of Your Life* which benefitted enormously from a rehearsal in an actual working-class bar; and a *Midsummer Night's Dream* which was helped in the same way by a run-through in the woods by lantern light. I also recall doing the *King Lear* storm scenes in a real storm, and a splendid production of *Oedipus Rex* in which the lead actor was prepared for his "blind" entrance by walking blind-folded and barefoot over a floor strewn with thumbtacks for a half-hour each day in the last week of rehearsal.

The aim of such devices is to provide a real sense memory of a particular place or condition, one that is designed especially for the needs for show. Besides such physical conditions, certain psychological or social conditions may be useful rehearsal mechanisms: I remember a student director who achieved extraordinary results in a production of *Woyzeck* by forbidding anyone in the cast from speaking to the actor playing Woyzeck during the last three weeks of rehearsal; his sense of alienation and victimization was palpable by the time the play opened.

Needless to say, any such extreme device should be used in response to a specific need, with great care, and with the full cooperation of the actors involved.

Even when radical devices are unnecessary, simple things can be done in the rehearsal hall to keep concentration fresh and the show growing in these later stages of rehearsal. My friend, Lou Florimonte, sometimes uses the device of reversing the ground plan for one rehearsal, so that the actors are forced to think their way through the physical aspects of the show anew.

This is the phase of rehearsal during which you must also turn a critical eye on the physical design of the show and ensure that the use of the stage space, the flow of the action within the ground plan, and that the auditory aspects of the production are effective. Avoid if you can, however, blocking rehearsals per se; ongoing and gradual editing of the staging can guarantee good staging without ever distracting the actors from the action itself.

This is also the time when you and your stage manager are taking care to establish the technical cueing of the show in preparation for technical rehearsal. I like to have the stage manager call all sound and light cues aloud during the last weeks of rehearsal, both to test their timing and to prepare the actors for what can otherwise be the traumatic intrusion of technical elements in the last weeks. A full complement of rehearsal props and costumes is also essential in this regard.

HAMLET LOG, PART 11: WORKING THROUGH FOR CONNECTIONS— JANUARY 16

When I arrive a half-hour early for rehearsal, I find Ophelia alone on the set, working through her scenes by worklight; many members of the cast have been putting in this kind of extra time. When the rest arrive, we begin working through Part One. I encourage the actors to stop to work out problems; our main interest is in fleshing out the specific connections within the outline of the action we have established.

When we reach the first crowd scene (12) we go through moment-by-moment to set the specific crowd reactions; these are always a problem because most actors don't take them seriously (luckily there is usually someone in the group who serves as a kind of "spark plug"; ours is Bill Keeler, who doubles as the Player King). I mark each reaction in my script, and later will type them up and post them on the callboard with the specific nature of each response. I will even suggest some appropriate lines for each, though I encourage people to invent their own as well. The important thing is to get each of the actors thinking in terms of personal and specific reactions instead of doing a group reaction (which always ends up sounding like "rhubarb, rhubarb").

The rest of Part One is worked in detail. After rehearsal, Megan and I talk; she is afraid our sympathetic treatment of Gertrude is a product of her natural tendency to want to be liked by the audience, but I assure her that it works well in our network of relationships. Although I had originally thought of the relationship between Hamlet and Claudius as the main plot source, I now see a triangle at the center of the play involving the ambivalent feelings among Hamlet, Claudius, and Gertrude, with Hamlet's feelings toward Ophelia also being altered by this central conflict.

Composer Todd Barton delivers a tape of the mousetrap music, the funeral chant, and some entrance calls for approval; we are moving away from our original "primitive" idea toward a Renaissance sound, since the statement made by the set and costumes is so strong.

Chris Villa gives me a diagram of the areas of the stage that will be used in various phases of the fight; he wants to move the fight up the stairs and onto the catwalk during the final section, and this will require moving the onlookers. We will have to work this through carefully as we lose the set in three days.

WORK-THROUGH PART TWO: JANUARY 18

We continue working through to establish specific connections. In the Nunnery scene (31) we have been struggling for some time with the blocking of Hamlet's frequent "farewells" to Ophelia; we have been treating them as false exits, as if he is torn between wanting to leave and wanting to stay and vent his anger. As we work on it tonight, though, I realize that our blocking problem springs from a basic misunderstanding of the action: Hamlet is not trying to get away from Ophelia, he is trying to drive her away from him; the "farewells" are said by him to her, at first because she is in danger (with the subtext "save yourself"), then in anger (with the subtext "go to a brothel"). This realization immediately solves the staging problem.

In instance after instance we find that blocking problems are actually moments when the scenic action is unclear or incorrect.

We work through the Mousetrap scene, developing the crowd's participation in it and giving special focus to Hamlet's relationship to Claudius as his trick nears its climax. We have decided precisely which lines of the play-within-the-play Hamlet has written (it is the speech by the murderer, Lucianus); this is the speech to which Hamlet refers when he earlier says "Speak the speech, I pray, as I pronounced it to you." His advice to the Players, then, was specifically aimed at the actor who plays Lucianus, whose performance must be good enough to disarm Claudius. Now the peformance begins and this same actor enters; evidently Hamlet sees that his advice has not been heeded, because he says "Leave thy damnable faces and begin."

The Closet scene receives more attention; it is serving as the emotional center of the play for Hamlet. There is usually one such scene for each character (for instance, Claudius's is his Prayer, and Ophelia's is the Nunnery scene.) These scenes serve as an emotional home base, giving a sense of direction to the scenes which precede them as well as to those which follow; such scenes need to receive special rehearsal consideration, since growth in these scenes will usually create growth in the entire performance.

Tonight we concentrate on the ending of this scene to develop a sense of urgency. Hamlet has three false exits after he starts to dispose of Polonius; each is a loose end which he must tie up before leaving, since it is likely he will not be able to see Gertrude privately again until everything is over. The momentum will come from making all three items part of one beat, that beat being "to say goodbye to mother so as to prepare her for what will soon happen."

The remaining scenes go very well; in all, a very valuable rehearsal. Afterward, Chris Villa and I walk through the fight ground plan to prepare the blocking of the crowd prior to tomorrow night's work-through of Part Three.

WORK-THROUGH PART THREE: JANUARY 19

At this afternoon's fight rehearsal, Chris shows me the blocking he has developed. This is not merely choreography, but is based on a moment-by-moment scenario of the dramatic action which underlies the fight; as a result, the fight has a story of its own. It moves in larger and larger areas of the stage until it finally moves up the stairs onto the catwalk above, where Laertes receives his fatal hit; Hamlet then drops to the stage as Laertes leaps after him from the stairs. The onlookers will have to move as the fight flows through each area, and we plan this. We also rough through the banner and torch movements in the entire play, which Chris will choreograph during the next few days.

At the evening call we work through Part Three, and I am paying special attention to pace since this Part needs to run a bit more tautly than it has so far. The attack by the Rabble is worked again; each of the eight members of the crowd has written lines for the group outcries, and we check these; we also pay some attention to their interaction with Laertes so that something like a real scene, with conflicting objectives, results.

After Laertes breaks in (scene 45), his reaction to seeing his sister's insanity requires a difficult shift in emotion from the anger of his entrance. Since Ophelia is on the catwalk above, I encourage him to call out to her gently, as one might call to a sleepwalker in danger of falling, and this action provides the required shift in tone.

Likewise, when Gertrude later brings the news of Ophelia's death, we experiment with a simple and almost numbed tone; this is much more touching and clearer than the hysterical entrance we have been using, and Laertes is able to respond to the news in a deeper, more heartbroken way. Again, I am looking for the loving, gentle side of Laertes to balance his angry outbursts in these final scenes.

The Graveyard scene presents the problem of achieving a reflective respite from the rush of the action, but without losing tension. I suggest to Hamlet that his curiosity about the Gravemaker is not idle; someone who works daily with death (and is able to sing while he digs) may have answers to his questions about that dark country he knows he must soon enter. With this playable objective, the scene immediately takes on a good pace. What really happens in this scene is that Hamlet comes to terms with his own mortality; by the time the funeral procession enters, he is ready to die whenever he must.

The funeral is beginning to run very well; the mechanics of it are turning into action. The Osric scene is likewise taking shape; Osric suggests that he is not such a fool as to miss the fact that Hamlet is making fun of him, and he does his best to defend himself and to give tit for tat; this helps the pace of the scene considerably.

At last we come to the fight and stop to walk it through by the numbers. The crowd adjustments are easily made; as the fight expands and the onlookers scatter we get much more visual excitement; as Hamlet and Laertes move up the stairs, those below move downstage in order to see, and so by the end the whole stage is alive with movement. We run the scene three times and it all works better than I had hoped. Chris and the actors will now begin drilling the specific details of the fight in earnest.

I ask Peter to record everyone's position at the end of the play in order to begin planning the curtain call. Since this is our last rehearsal on the set until technical rehearsal in two weeks, we have a final safety discussion about the catwalk railings, and the cast agrees that they are not needed after all.

I am satisfied that we have utilized our time on the set to very good advantage; it has been very hard work but worth it.

WORK-THROUGH WHOLE SHOW: JANUARY 20

We've reserved eight hours for a working through of the entire play today, stopping whenever needed, but the work progresses so well that we are able to complete the rehearsal in four hours. Even so, we find numerous new values, and go back to work a few details.

The first meeting between Hamlet and Rosencrantz and Guildenstern gets special attention: In previous rehearsals, this encounter was contaminated by the knowledge of what was to come, and Hamlet had treated them warily from the outset; today, he is genuinely glad to see them and only gradually discovers that they are not to be trusted.

The question of Hamlet's madness continues to haunt us: How real is it? It may be that Hamlet, like a Pirandello hero, begins by feigning madness, only to be drawn into some degree of genuine madness. I have examined the later soliloquies again, however, and remain convinced that Hamlet is never really mad. I suggest that his antic disposition is entirely a ploy to try to prove the Ghost's allegation; therefore, his aim is *not* to seem dangerous, but the reverse, to seem *harmless*. This is more than mere common sense; one of the scholarly articles brought into the auditions pointed out that *antic* has a meaning far different from *crazy* and implies more a spirit of silliness or playfulness. We work the Polonius/Hamlet scene, when we first see Hamlet in his antic disposition, in this way. Mark finds a very child-like, regressive tone that works well, lightening the scene considerably; this is a more active, purposeful, playable view of things. I have urged Mark to become gradually more and more silly at each rehearsal; I hope he will go much further, and I offer every encouragement.

There is a wonderful discovery in Act IV: Laertes has rushed in and has threatened Claudius at sword point. When his sister enters mad, he forgets his anger and kneels beside her; he rises and goes with her to her exit, leaving his sword lying on the ground. The crafty Claudius picks it up and gives it back to Laertes as he disavows any responsibility for Polonius's death, saying, "And where the offence is, let the great axe fall." Laertes, who moments ago was threatening death and revolution, is beginning already to move toward a partnership with Claudius, and the deal will be concluded in the Chapel scene to follow.

I am especially pleased that Hamlet's soliloquies are becoming completely integrated into the flow of the action and not seeming like reflective pauses. Each of them involves a choice that furthers the main action, and it is this active line that must be pursued in each.

In the evening slot, we have a brief recording session to do the cheers, army sounds, party noises, and angry Rabble sound effects. Our plans for the technical aspects of the show seem complete but if anything doesn't work, I will simply cut it; the acting values are strong enough that none of the technical elements is essential.

Concern over the running time is again expressed by the production manager. If the 2:00 P.M. matinee performances of *Hamlet* don't end by 5:00 P.M. sharp, the 8:00 P.M. performances of *The Matchmaker* (in which Mark also plays the lead!) won't be able to start on time. Today I cut the speeches about the boy actors in the Rosencrantz and Guildenstern scene, but I can find no other cuts that will not leave an incomplete connection in the fabric of the main action. I offer to eliminate the second intermission on matinee days only, a savings of twelve minutes. This would produce a seventy minute Part One, and a one-hundred minute Part Two; not a very attractive idea, but better than an incomplete production.

We have now completed eighty-two hours of rehearsal; the rotation schedule has been adjusted to give us extra time on our set during these first weeks; now we must pay back the other shows and will have a five-day layoff. As I leave for a visit with my family, I feel good about all that has been accomplished and confident that a new phase of work will be ready to start when we return.

HAMLET LOG, PART 12: PACING— *JANUARY 26-FEBRUARY 3*

We return to the show after the five-day layoff. This and the next two rehearsals will be spent reworking each Part; I will be looking for pace, noting any section which seems at all slack.

As we rehearse each scene, we begin by thinking about the main things that happen which move the story forward: What is different in the world of the play when the scene is over? Has something new happened? Has a relationship changed? Has a new facet of character or attitude been revealed? We discuss each scene in these terms before working it. As the scene is then run, I watch and record exactly what I see happening; this produces an item-by-item scene breakdown, which I compare with the breakdown I did of the play during my preparation; I am glad to see that it is more complete and insightful. I type it up and have it distributed to the cast.

Examining the action in this way tests the strength of the connections we have developed so far; in the sections which seem slack, I try to find new values which will give the actors stronger objectives to play, thus giving the scenes better pace; below are a few examples.

In the first scene, the importance of the Ghost as a sign that "something is rotten in the state of Denmark" is stressed, and the need of the soldiers to speak with it in order to discover what is wrong drives the decision to summon Hamlet.

In the large scene (12) which follows, the attempt by Gertrude and Claudius to talk Hamlet out of his funk is supported by all present, who are eager to end the period of mourning and to begin a celebration of Claudius's coronation. This makes Hamlet seem all the more alienated from the court, driving his bitterness.

In the Polonius/Ophelia scene (13), we notice that Polonius's admonitions grow in severity, from his urging that she be cautious of Hamlet, to ordering her to "be scanter" of her presence, to "Do not believe" him, finally to shun him altogether. I suggest that he is driven to this severity by Ophelia's continued resistance to his milder admonitions and we work on it to heighten this sense of obstacle, giving Ophelia a more active role in the scene, and giving Polonius more reason to play into her reactions.

The section of scene 22 among Polonius, Claudius, and Gertrude which follows the arrival of Rosencrantz and Guildenstern still feels slack; Polonius has many flowery speeches in which he proposes his plan to deal with Hamlet's madness. I suggest that he feels responsible for Hamlet's condition (by having ordered Ophelia to spurn him) so that he needs to sell his plan to the King and Queen in order to compensate; his flowery rhetoric is part of this salesmanship.

In order to drive the ending of the Part, I suggest that Hamlet begins to formulate his idea for the mousetrap as soon as the Players arrive; he auditions them, then sends everyone away in order to work out the details of his fledgling plan alone. This launches Hamlet into the act-ending soliloquy with a strong objective—to perfect his plan.

During our five-day layoff, fight rehearsals have continued; it is now completely blocked. We run through it several times and it looks very good indeed; Chris will have ample time in the three weeks that remain before preview to perfect it.

Peter Allen (stage manager) and I discuss briefly technical problems concerning smoke for the Ghost's appearance and the use of blood packs during the fight; a meeting is scheduled with the prop master to settle things.

WORK-THROUGH PART TWO:
JANUARY 28

We continue working through for pace, focusing on the new developments in each scene; we are regaining the momentum lost during the layoff, and this rehearsal is even more productive than the last.

In the Nunnery scene (31), we clarify Hamlet's shift in attitude toward Ophelia, with the first section of the scene driven by the self-hatred he has just expressed in "To be or not to be," as he tells her "why would thou be a breeder of sinners," "we are arrant knaves all, believe none of us." His first "get thee to a nunnery," then, means not only "go away to safety" but also "take vows of celibacy and don't help to perpetuate this awful world."

Hamlet's advice to the Players (32) is worked again to give it the specific urgency of the plot to unmask Claudius; there is a tremendous tendency to hear these famous lines in a general way and we must do all we can to tie them into the main line of the plot.

In the Mousetrap scene, we work again to keep the flow of Hamlet's plot moving up to the unmasking of Claudius; on Claudius's exit, his eyes naturally meet those of Hamlet before he calls out "Give me some light. Away!" and I urge them both to explore this moment of eye contact. I believe that this is the moment when Claudius decides that Hamlet must, at all cost, be killed; I will wait to see what Denis and Mark find in it for themselves.

Throughout, I am trying to consolidate the flow of scenes into larger units; several transitions are eliminated in favor of playing through a given sequence as one thought. We also pay particular attention to those scenes in which the given circumstances provide a sense of urgency: For instance, the advice to the Players and the subsequent instructions to Horatio must be completed before the court enters for the play. If the through-line of the action is strong wherever possible, the reflective passages will be highlighted by contrast.

WORK-THROUGH PART THREE:
JANUARY 30

We continue to consolidate the action into larger units, looking for the drive in each section. This Third Part is quite cohesive already, since the action (except for the Gravedigger scene) is very compact. This demonstrates how Shakespeare has varied the tempo and internal dynamic of the play: The general pattern is one of steady condensing of the action toward the climax (the last four pages are incredibly dense), but with occasional pauses for thematic development (as in the Gravedigger and Osric scenes). I am glad our production seems to accurately reflect these changes in tone and pace.

The cast continues to work out the detailed causal connections within the scenes; it is a pleasure to work with people who have an appetite for this.

After the main rehearsal, Peter, Chris, Mark, and Bruce experiment with blood packs. One pack taped to Hamlet's arm produces the small wound inflicted by Laertes's sword; a sponge full of "blood" hidden on the catwalk above produces a huge gash on Laertes's neck; the effects are quite good.

We have only two rehearsals before first tech next Saturday; they will both be run-throughs. These two-day layoffs between rehearsals are preventing the show from fulfilling its natural momentum; we will just barely pull it all together. The Tech rehearsals here are usually just cue-to-cue for the lights and sound, but for the actors' sake, I am insisting on full run-throughs with technical adjustments on the fly or by notes afterward. I also encourage Peter to drill the backstage crews before our tech for things like the operation of the trap and tapestry; it will be important that our tech run smoothly so as to be a useful rehearsal for the actors.

RUN-THROUGH ENTIRE SHOW: FEBRUARY 2

This is one of the two rehearsals before first tech; enough of the specific moment-to-moment connections have been established that the show should start to move entirely under its own power as the momentum of the through-line takes hold, but we've had a three-day break, and it's been a week since we last worked Part One, so I am apprehensive.

To help guarantee that our Technical rehearsal goes well, the lighting designer, Bob Peterson, is sitting with the stage manager and me tonight, and will be checking on specific cues. Earlier in the week we talked through the show cue-by-cue in a paper tech, but this live viewing is the best way to be sure we are prepared. Dick Hay and Todd Barton are also with us to double-check set and sound cues. It is wonderful when designers are this conscientious (and genuinely interested) about watching rehearsals.

A fight warm-up done, I call the entire cast together to outline the remaining rehearsals and encourage everyone to begin planning their offstage activities (prop movements and costume changes) so as to minimize the disruptions at the tech rehearsal; my hope is that both techs can be useful rehearsals for bringing the show together by giving the actors a chance to experience the through-line of the action.

This is made especially important by the repertory schedule, which causes a full week gap between our second tech and our first dress, while the other shows begin their techs. We do have one three-hour slot between tech and dress and will use this for a high-speed run-through, but we will depend heavily on everyone's personal discipline to overcome this erratic schedule; the momentum of our work in the last three weeks has suffered badly.

I begin tonight's rehearsal by reminding everyone of the time-line of the play: Shakespeare has skillfully compacted the action into three periods of about two days each; this quality of real time gives a natural momentum to the action. I also remind everyone about the deadlines and urgencies Shakespeare has built into the given circumstances of most scenes, and we go over the list distributed earlier (see Appendix Five).

We then begin. I am glad to see that very little prompting is required, and that the action is moving well. During the run-through, I write individual notes on separate sheets for Hamlet, Claudius, Gertrude, and Polonius; giving them these notes individually will save precious time. The main thrust of these notes is to strengthen their through-lines: For example, at the moment in the Mousetrap when Claudius realizes how much Hamlet knows, he decides that Hamlet must be dispatched as quickly as possible (the prayer which follows immediately can be by motivated not only by the reminder of what Claudius has done, but also as preparation for Hamlet's murder). Once Claudius decides he must kill Hamlet, every other choice he makes in the play is driven by this necessity.

Of most interest to me tonight, however, is Hamlet's through-line. I have two full pages of notes for Mark alone (see Appendix 4). The outline of his entire performance is now clear; most of my notes simply confirm what I see in him. For instance, I realize for the first time tonight that when he gets caught up in the Pyrrhus speech (which he shares with the Player King in scene 22), it is because he identifies with Pyrrhus, "whose sable arms, Black as his purpose" seeks the King Priam in order to kill him; how wonderful it is when we then learn from the Player that Pyrrhus, finding Priam, begins to strike but

> . . . his sword,
> Which was declining on the milky head
> Of reverend Priam, seemed i' th' air to stick.
> So as a painted tyrant Pyrrhus stood,
> And like a neutral to his will and matter
> Did nothing.

The Player King is taking a specific position as he says this; in the soliloquy which follows, Hamlet will take up the prop sword and mimic this pose as he cries "Oh, Vengeance!" This will be his position in the Chapel scene as he pauses with his dagger over the head of Claudius. This repetition of poses has occurred accidentally, but now that it is recognized, I will sharpen it. Thus do patterns of meaning emerge from the work.

In case after case, what is happening is that the pieces are falling into place, in the sense that the relationship of each moment to the main action of the play is beginning to assert itself. This natural and beneficial process is usually irreversible once it begins, and I am sure that in the case of this complex and mysterious play, it will continue for the next seven months of performance as well.

The running time of tonight's run-through is bothersome: Part One is seventy-seven minutes, Part Two is fifty-eight, and Part Three is sixty-two. This means that each of the first two Parts is about five minutes longer than I had hoped, while Part Three is fully ten minutes longer! This puts the whole show at three hours and seventeen minutes, plus two intermissions, for a total of three hours forty minutes—twenty minutes longer than my last estimate. The individual connections are strong; now we must increase the underlying tempo; the high-speed run-through next week may help.

FINAL RUN-THROUGH: FEBRUARY 3

Pat Patton, the production manager, and Jerry Turner, the artistic director, are attending tonight's rehearsal: some decision must soon be made about the length of the show and the changeover problem for the matinee performances.

The stage manager also introduces a number of members of the running crew who are visiting rehearsal tonight: the lighting board operator, the running prop master, the sound operator, and the house manager, all preparing the specifics of their contribution to the performance. I continue to be amazed at the conscientiousness of the staff of this theatre. They do things right!

The presence of so many guests makes some of the cast nervous at first, and the first scene is tight, but we soon settle down. I am glad we are having these visitors and hope there will be guests at the dress rehearsals, so as to allow Hamlet to begin making contact with people during his soliloquies, and to bring out the humor in the show (comedy, especially, never really comes into focus until there is an audience).

I am alert for any slack moments, much in the way that a weaver would look for loose threads before taking a rug off the loom. I find only a very few.

There are a few discoveries tonight: For instance, Hamlet accidentally leaves his jester's cap on the floor in the chapel, and Claudius finds it as he exits; he realizes that Hamlet has been there, and rushes to find him in Gertrude's room, carrying the cap with him. I suggest a final payoff to the prop by having him give it to Rosencrantz and Guildenstern when he sends them off after Hamlet, like a hunter giving the scent to his dogs.

We are finding more opportunities for the love in the play to be manifested; Hamlet and the Ghost reach out to try to touch one another's hands, though both know they can't; in the final scene, we work out a way for Gertrude to die in Hamlet's arms as she warns him about the poison with her last breath. Mark's loving nature makes these moments special, and his Hamlet will be special for this capacity for love.

The final fight continues to solidify, and as Mark and Bruce become more technically confident, it is becoming a breathtaking event.

The overall running times are identical to last night's, and I can't imagine it losing more than five or six minutes through further improvement in pace and tempo. As far as the matinee scheduling problem goes, the management of the theatre decides that the show is tight and that cutting would harm it. The possibility of dropping the second intermission on matinee days will be discussed, but otherwise the show should go as is; the evening performances may have to be delayed a half hour.

After rehearsal I go home and read through the play again; I "shake" the play very hard to see if anything "falls out" because it's not an integral part of the whole: I find only three small cuts.

FIFTEEN
FINAL SYNTHESIS

These last few rehearsals are a tremendously challenging time for the director. The work of the actors is coming to fruition and they may be in a vulnerable and unstable frame of mind; at the same time, the show is moving from the rehearsal hall into the actual performance space, and there are enormous pressures and disruptions as the technical elements of the production are introduced and the opening approaches.

This is a time of great activity for the director: You are being called upon to make decisions on the spot about many important details, without time for much experiment or adjustment. At the same time, you are essentially helpless to change the main thrust of the production and are at the mercy of the planning, experimentation, and rehearsal you have done so far. A production develops tremendous momentum, and as it begins to move under its own power it requires greater and greater effort to steer it in a new direction. If the basic conception of your production is amiss, the changes you make now may tend to be of a cosmetic nature only, though productions sometimes, through herculean effort, find their proper direction at the eleventh hour.

On the other hand, if your basic approach has been correct, you will probably be on the verge of tremendous discoveries as the work comes to fruition; it is not unusual for major problems to clear up only in this last, hectic phase of rehearsal.

This is also your last chance to adopt that distanced, naive attitude of the ideal audience of one and to make sure the first-time viewer is going to get what he or she needs in order to experience the play; at the same time, you don't want to fall prey to the "Kleenex mentality," which strives to make the play so easily accessible that there would be no value in repeated viewings. The ideal is to direct in such a way that a spectator would be encouraged to return, both because of the satisfaction of the initial experience and because of the recognition that the production possesses depths and detail which would reward subsequent viewings.

AUDIBILITY

No matter how careful your planning, nor how accurate your rehearsal set has been, moving onto the actual set and experiencing the show in the actual performing space will necessitate numerous adjustments in your staging, and perhaps in the shaping and dynamics of the production as well. One thing that you will check as soon as the actual set is available is the *audibility* of the production, since the rehearsal space has probably not prepared the actors for the vocal demands of the performance space.

Checking the audibility of the show can be tricky: By now you have practically memorized the entire script, and it will be difficult for you to know whether a first-time audience might have trouble understanding what is said. Consider having someone with "fresh ears" come in to check projection as soon as you move into your performing space.

Remember that it is one thing to *hear* and another to *understand*; you will find that audibility is more a function of clarity than of volume. Poor projection is most often an acting problem which cannot be solved by simply telling the actors to speak louder: it is usually due to a lack either of confidence or of understanding, and must be treated accordingly.

There are times, of course, when poor projection is merely technical and it may be enough in such cases for you to provide the actors with immediate feedback on audibility so they can adjust their sense of vocal energy to the acoustics of the space. Again, it may be advisable with some actors to help them find an adjustment in the inner phase of action which will justify an increase in vocal energy.

Notice also the relationship between visual and auditory focus: It is often difficult to understand an actor who's face you cannot see (actors in masks, for instance, must compensate in volume and clarity more than the merely acoustic obstruction of the mask requires). Paradoxically, you will find that the correct blocking of a scene will often give the visual focus to the listener, since it is the reaction to what is being said which is often the main dramatic interest. But for some mysterious reason, good visual focus on the listener actually improves the audibility of the speaker!

EDITING THE BLOCKING

Seeing the production in the actual performance space inevitably changes your perception of the way the action occupies the stage space, and you will find yourself editing the blocking in these first rehearsals on the set. If you are fortunate, the basic patterns of blocking which have emerged as a spatial expression of the action will still work; what usually needs adjustment is the sense of scale and the proportional relationships within the blocking pattern.

For instance, it is common to find that the actors may not be taking enough space and will be standing too close to each other; the sense of psychological distance established in the rehearsal hall is often too intimate for the stage: the actors look like they are climbing on top of one another, and blocking one another in the process. The increase in dynamic energy required by the larger performance space necessitates not only a higher vocal energy, but also a larger "envelope of space" around each actor.

I have also noticed that if people are standing too close to one another, their relationship has nowhere to go; there is greater dramatic potential in the relationship when they stand a bit further apart and express closeness by reaching toward one another than there is by merely being close. This kind of enlargement of the actor's "envelope" is the spatial equivalent of "louder," and the adjustment must be made with the same concern for the integrity of the show's reality.

We have so far stressed blocking as the spatial manifestation of the action, but you must also consider the blocking as a pure design element. In the last weeks of rehearsal, and especially since moving the show into the actual space, when you have the opportunity to see the blocking from the true audience perspective, you may want to make some specific adjustments in the patterns of the blocking itself. Here are the sorts of questions you will be asking yourself as you watch these rehearsals:

1. Is the flow of the show through the space pleasing? Do the exits and entrances follow one another with spatial logic?
2. Is one area over-used or another avoided unnecessarily?
3. Are the significant moments properly placed on the stage? Is my attention drawn to the person making the crucial choice? Am I seeing the important reactions?
4. Are some adjustments of position needed to heighten the spatial design of the blocking for balance and composition?
5. Are the visual images created by the blocking vivid and and meaningful?

VISUAL METAPHORS

It may be that some of the stage pictures which have emerged from your work with the actors, or which have suggested themselves through visual associations, could be sharpened and extended into explicit metaphors which express meaning, relationship, and theme. In his questionnaire, Robert Brustein said that, for him, the essence of directing was "finding the appropriate visual and histrionic metaphors for exposing" the heart of the text.

Such visual metaphors, whether they are consciously recognized or not, may relate to some specific imagery with which the audience has an association: For example, in my first production of *King Lear*, we found a very touching moment when Lear and his Fool were about to be parted for the last time: As the exhausted Lear fell asleep, he and the Fool reached their hands toward one another but were not quite able to touch, their fingertips reaching out. This moment had a special visual impact, and it was only during a photo call weeks later that its source was clarified when the photographer asked that we do "the Sistine Chapel bit."

This particular visual metaphor had come up accidentally in the flow of our work, and this is perhaps the best way for such things to happen. It is possible, however, that specific images may suggest themselves a priori and be built into the blocking. I remember a powerful moment in Grotowski's *The Constant Prince*, for example, in which the actors formed Michelangelo's *Pieta*. Unless such premeditated imagery is totally justified by its placement in the flow of the blocking, however, it may call attention to itself in a distracting way. Your aim in such cases is to create transparent images through which we can see the action of the play: If the stage imagery becomes opaque and we begin to see it for its own sake, in a way which obscures the action, then you have done the play a disservice. The best blocking is the blocking you don't notice.

Visual metaphors may also be of a more abstract nature. In my production of *King Lear*, Lear and Gloucester came together on the heath, the one mad and the other blind: As they recognized each other, Gloucester knelt at Lear's feet and Lear bowed down over him, comforting him in an embrace, so that the two interwoven bodies formed one pattern (similar to the yin/yang circle). This image, though not overtly recognizable as an ideograph, expressed directly the combination of the spiritual and physical modes of human torment which Lear and Gloucester represent.

TECHNICAL AND DRESS REHEARSALS

These final rehearsals are the time when lighting, sound, costumes, and shifting of scenery are incorporated as dynamic elements in the production. Though this is the specific business of the technical rehearsals, you should begin to prepare for these rehearsals as soon as run-throughs begin. The rhythmic aspect of your production concept and the work you have already done to shape, pace, and focus the show has determined at least the rough outline of the cueing for the show; now your stage manager will be watching with an eye to the exact placement and timing of cues and shifts. If possible, the designers also should be brought into a rehearsal at this stage to check these things for themselves.

The coordination of the technical elements is facilitated by a "paper tech," a session in which you, the designers, and the stage manager talk through the show, cue by cue. Through discussion, you come to initial agreement on the placement, duration, and content of each cue. Though not all theatres hold paper techs as a matter of course, I encourage you to insist upon one. Be sure also that the designers have actually watched a run-through of the show before the session; one very good format for a paper tech, in fact, is for those concerned to sit together at the back of the hall during a run-through and talk through the cues as they occur.

In most theatres, the paper tech is followed by what is variously called a "dry tech," "level session," or "cue-to-cue" rehearsal in which each light, sound, and scenery cue is set in sequence. Such rehearsals are usually held without the actors, with someone walking the stage as a guinea pig for the light levels. If for any reason it is suggested that you set the light and sound cues with the actors present, I urge you to resist the suggestion with all possible force; it is not only inconsiderate to the actors to subject them to a stop-and-start cueing session, but it also plays havoc with the pacing and shaping of the production. Your rehearsals thus far should have established the timing of the transitions and other cues well enough that initial cueing can be established without the actors; these initial timings and levels will undoubtedly be adjusted in subsequent rehearsals anyway. (An exception to this is the type of show in which there are long scenes between cues during which light levels can be adjusted on the fly.)

When setting light levels, the most important thing to remember is that visibility is a function of being able to see the actors' eyes. This is a function not only of brightness, but of angle and color as well; make sure your designers understand this early on. When setting sound levels, you will have to compensate for the change in the auditorium acoustics when empty; in my experience, the tendency is to overcompensate, so remember that most of the time it is better to be too soft than too loud.

Following the dry tech, the first technical rehearsal is held. This is the rehearsal at which all technical elements should be present in the flesh (no rehearsal substitutes, though some items may not yet be detailed or painted), and all scene shifts, lighting cues, sound cues, and effects should be run. If the show is particularly complex, it may be wise to stagger the introduction of technical elements rather than try to deal with everything at once. If this is done, insist that those elements which most effect the actors be added first, such as props, furniture, motivating or environmental sound effects.

Insist also that any costume pieces which must be handled by the actors (for dressing or undressing on stage, for instance) be present at the technical rehearsal; in fact, strive to have props, furniture or set pieces, and costume pieces involved in the business of the actors introduced well before the technical rehearsal. You might suggest that these pieces come into an early run-through, then be taken back into the shop for finishing while the actors continue with their rehearsal substitutes. The value to the actors in having worked with the real thing is enormous.

In most theatres, one or two technical rehearsals are followed by a tech-dress or preliminary dress rehearsal when the costumes, though not necessarily complete in every detail, are worn. The addition of the costumes will sometimes require adjustments in the lighting levels, which can be made on the run or through notes. Be sure that all costume changes, which have been approximated in earlier rehearsals, are now attempted a tempo.

Finally you are ready for dress rehearsal. Most theatres schedule two dresses, but this must not be an excuse for the first to be incomplete in any way. The first dress is an opportunity to see the show under performance conditions, while the second allows any adjustments discovered in the first to be made and assimilated by the actors. Too often the first dress becomes merely another tech; do all you can to prevent this.

At many theatres, the dress rehearsals are extensively photographed. Request that photographs be taken during the first, but not the second dress rehearsal, or that a separate photo session be placed in the schedule for which you select a number of photogenic moments. In any case, insist that the final dress be under total performance conditions.

What has been said so far about the technical and dress rehearsals is consistent with tradition, but may not represent the best possible sequence of events for your particular production. Consider the best strategy for these last rehearsals; do you need props or sound effects early? Is there a particular element that needs to finished for earlier rehearsals? Consult with your management, design, and technical staffs as soon as possible to arrange for such things. Even if the traditional sequence is to be followed, insist on getting specific agreement on all deadlines: Exactly when will the finished props be introduced? How complete will costumes be at the first dress? When will make-up first be used? Insist also on agreement about the procedures for these final rehearsals: Which will be uninterrupted run-throughs and which (if any) will stop and start? Who will have the authority to stop a rehearsal and for what reasons? How will you communicate with the designers and stage manager during the rehearsal? Can you have an intercom headset of your own during the rehearsal? (Insist on this.) Don't leave things to be determined on the night!

PREVIEWS, OPENING AND AFTER

The birth trauma of most productions is severe, but if the preparation has been good the show will be needing an audience. If the preparation has been correct, the audience's response will actually complete the the show. In fact, think of the opening as the beginning of another phase of the process in the growth of the production. There are many things which happen when an audience's presence is felt.

For this reason, it is wise (as we have said) to introduce an audience before the official opening (that is, before reviewers are invited), and this is the purpose of previews, at which the audience is usually admitted free or at a reduced price. If there are no previews, the final dress rehearsal is a good time to invite a sample audience, though an actual preview is better, and a number of previews even better yet.

Two things are necessary to make previews valuable, however: First, that there be rehearsals following the previews at which notes from the preview experience can be assimilated; and second, that the preview audience be a representative one, not a group of friends or people with a vested interest in the production (this is why opening nights are often misleading; second nights usually seem "off" by comparison).

The opening itself is often a period of disruption, and judgements must be passed with care: The actors are receiving a tremendous adrenalin surge and many qualities of the show, both good and bad, may be accentuated; this is the moment when the right note can give enormous benefit, and the wrong note can do great harm. After a few performances, however, things will settle down and the new phase of growth will begin; as Alan Schneider says, productions are never finished, only abandoned. If the initial rehearsal process has laid the groundwork properly, there will be a whole new realm of discoveries to be made in actual performance. For this reason, I greatly enjoy returning to a good play for subsequent productions after a time, not to repeat the work but to *continue* it.

Unfortunately, the tradition of professional theatre in this country, even in resident repertory, makes it difficult if not impossible for a director to pursue this phase of the work: On the opening night, control of the production is often transferred to the stage manager, whose charge (by contract) is to maintain the production in the condition it was left by the director; the natural process of evolution is frozen and subsequent growth in the show may actually be resisted. Even if changes in cast are subsequently necessary, they are made by the stage manager, who rehearses an actor to take over the role as if one were changing a spark plug in a car.

All this is the logical extension of the consumerist mentality of American culture: We regard plays not as living entities which change and grow in meaningful relationship to their environments, but as products packaged for sale. Do what you can to overcome this attitude in the way you rehearse: One good way is to bring your stage manager into your process, discussing important choices with him or her, even turning over some aspects of rehearsal if possible; train your SM to recognize and to nurture the symptoms of legitimate growth in the show after opening.

Another inescapable consideration about the opening is the impact of reviews; unless you are fortunate in having a prolonged period of previews, the reviews will appear just as the production is in its most vulnerable state, and their impact can be enormous. Again, the resilience of the show under the manifold pressures of opening is dependent on whether or not your rehearsal preparation has dealt with the essential action and relationships; if all that is holding the show together is a mechanical outer form, the chances are that it will crack under strain like the veneer it is.

In all, the challenge of this hectic time is to keep the show's sense of purpose alive. We so easily forget that we have a more important reason for our work than the plaudits of the press, the applause of the audience, or even the good opinions of our colleagues. Remember Stanislavksi's advice to a group of young actors:

> Yes, you must be excited about your profession. You must love it devotedly and passionately, but not for itself, not for its laurels, not for the pleasure and delight it brings to you as artists. You must love your chosen profession because it gives you the opportunity to communicate ideas that are important and necessary to your audience . . . You must keep the idea of the play alive and be inspired by it at each performance.[20]

It is tremendously difficult to do this in the last days, as the excitement and terror of the impending opening mount; the danger is great that the performance will become an end unto itself and lose its sense of purpose. Only you can keep that sense of purpose alive—in yourself. If you are able to do this, you may find that you and your cast approach the opening not with apprehension but with the commitment of those who have an important job to do, a valuable gift to bestow.

WEANING THE PRODUCTION

It is a truism that the one thing most needed by actors at the crucial time of an opening is confidence, and directors do many things to help build confidence, including outpourings of camaraderie (parties and flowers) and pep talks that would put Knute Rockne to shame. While such displays of concern and affection are nice, I doubt seriously whether confidence can be built in such ways. You must first consider the true source of confidence for your actors.

I recently spoke with a group of Australian directors about the approach to directing being developed in this book. After a time, one fellow asked, "at what point do you stop fooling around and tell the actors what to do?" I explained that I tried hard not to tell actors what to do, but to help them find it for themselves. He was shocked: "But how," he asked, "will they have any confidence if you don't tell them what to do?"

This is the key: confidence comes only from within, from knowing for yourself what you are doing. The confident actor is one who has both a clear sense of overall purpose (superobjective) and a well-developed score (sequence of objectives) through which the superobjective may be pursued. Pep talks and enthusiasm from you can never substitute for these two essentials.

In fact, most actors need to be forced to find their own sources of confidence through the gradual withdrawal of input and support from you. Too much input in the final stages of rehearsal can keep an actor dependent; better to allow some details to go untreated than to distract or dishearten your actors with a flurry of last-minute notes. This is part of the whole process of weaning the production.

As the form of the production evolves and completes itself and comes to stand on its own, you are more and more like the parent watching the child getting ready to move out of the house: Have the wisdom and strength at this time to release your grasp. You may find it difficult; most directors have withdrawal symptoms which are exacerbated by the feelings of helplessness which accompany final rehearsals and opening.

There may even be moments when, out of your own anxiety, you are tempted to betray the work you have done so far: I remember watching one production in which weeks were spent doing movement improvisations and other experiments designed to generate the form of the production. Things were going fairly well when, two weeks before opening, the director lost heart, discarded everything, and blocked the show in a mechanical way; the results were understandably poor as the actors lost all confidence in the work they had done. While it is sometimes necessary to change an unproductive methodology, don't do so merely because you lose your nerve at the eleventh hour; have the guts to stick to your game plan.

Once the opening is past and you have left the show, you can expect a depression of some intensity to follow. You have for weeks been fully involved in a complex task which has involved intense social contact; something very much like love will have sprung up between you and at least some members of the cast. It is heartbreaking to leave the party when it is, in a sense, just starting. Try to rest and to assimilate the experience for a time, then get to work again. One thing you can always do is to read more plays! There's always that next time when someone may ask, "What show would you like to do?"

THE HAMLET LOG, PART 13: FINAL SYNTHESIS—FEBRUARY 4-20

The tech weekend begins with the preliminary setting of light and sound levels, meaning the setting of the individual cues themselves. This morning the set was moved back onstage and the lighting crew spent all day doing the fine focusing. The instruments themselves were hung and rough-focused weeks ago when the rep plot—the composite lighting system that handles all four of the shows in this theatre—was installed.

Tonight, Bob Peterson, the lighting designer, begins to build the look of each scene. After three hours, only half the show is finished and I go through it with him, cue by cue, making sure the most important acting positions are well lit, checking the mood and sense of time in each scene, and working the transitions between scenes.

During our paper tech I gave Bob my priority for the lighting: It should distinguish one time and place from another, but without interrupting the flow from scene to scene. This I translated into three specific conditions:

1. We should be aware of changes in the light only between scenes;
2. Cues within scenes should be restricted to those motivated by specific changes in time, such as the sunrise, or the entrance of large numbers of people with torches;
3. There should be no blackouts, only cross-fades.

Despite our advance planning, however, the cues are written very slowly. By the time we lose our crews at 1:00 A.M., we have set only the first two parts. The stage manager, designer, and I discuss strategy and agree that we will restrict our first technical rehearsal (tomorrow night) to running this much of the show; we will then stay on after first tech and write the rest of the show from midnight to 2:00 A.M. tomorrow night, resuming the tech at Part Three on Sunday afternoon, with a complete tech run-through Sunday night (Sunday is the "ten-hour day" allowed us by the rules of the League of Resident Theatres.) I am inwardly furious at this delay, but there is nothing to be done.

The next afternoon, Peter and I meet with Douglas Faerber (sound) and Todd Barton (composer) to set the sound cues. We have had many of these cues played in rehearsal on a cassette machine over the past week, so the placement and timing of cues is established; our main concerns now are volume and directionality. There are eight speakers surrounding the auditorium, and the highly flexible sound system allows us to feed any combination of sound from the three tape decks to speakers in any combination; Douglas and Todd have done a splendid job of pre-planning which sounds should be on which tapes so as to be mixable and to allow smooth transitions from one sound to another. This technical freedom allows us to create many splendid effects, such as bringing Fortinbras's drums closer and closer while cannons fire in the distance. We also check the wireless microphone for the Ghost and add a slight digital reverberation; this almost imperceptibly extends his voice all around the theatre.

We spend two and a half hours at this, and it is an exciting session indeed. I am exuberant when the sound session ends; it is one of the few times that the actuality of the effects have equalled and even surpassed the hope of their conception.

FIRST TECHNICAL REHEARSAL—
FEBRUARY 5

Tonight we run Parts One and Two as planned: there aren't as many stoppages as I had feared, since the scenes are long enough for the lighting and sound adjustments to be made as we run. The actors are able to get some meaningful rehearsal, and morale is good.

As it turns out, it was probably a good thing that we had to run only half the show tonight; this helped to lessen the inevitable pressure of technical rehearsal. The sound and lighting operators are doing an excellent job; they have the advantage of having watched the show, and Peter is calling the cues perfectly. The backstage preparation has also been excellent. Peter has created a computer program which produces up-to-the-minute prop running lists, so the presetting of props and weapons goes without a hitch.

The scenes are overlapping very well; in fact, the eye and ear are overwhelmed by the simultaneous light and sound changes and the shifts in visual focus, so we lengthen these transitions to allow each new environment to establish itself before the scene proceeds.

The actors are dismissed a half-hour early, and Bob, Peter, and the board operator stay behind, as planned, to complete the cues for the show. After two hours' work, we are finishing the Graveyard scene when the lighting board, an early computerized model, "crashes." All on its own, it does a slow fade to black, then snaps on every light in the theatre. We fear that the memory of all our work has been lost. The system is shut down and reset, then a hard copy of the disc memory is printed out; we are thankful to find that our cues are still there. With only twenty minutes of work time left, we rough in the last two scenes by borrowing the memories of similar earlier scenes.

SECOND TECHNICAL AND DISASTER:
FEBRUARY 6

Sunday afternoon begins with an hour of fight rehearsal: While negotiating one difficult move, Bruce Gooch (Laertes) falls off the edge of the stage and dislocates his left shoulder; we tie his arm to his chest and rush him to the hospital; the severity of his injury may make it impossible for him to open the show, and there is no understudy. We are able to continue the technical rehearsal with a stand-in.

A few hours later, Bruce returns from the hospital, his shoulder having been reset and braced immobile against his body. He wants to continue rehearsal, but he ought to rest and is sent home. We are still not sure whether he will be able to open; the doctor has suggested three weeks of rest and there are less than two weeks before opening.

The incident, and the days of long hours, are putting everyone on edge; the afternoon rehearsal is a tense affair. Still, we are able to set the cues for the remainder of the show.

After the actors are gone, we use the time to clean up some lighting questions and notes. Given the tension and the complexity of the show, I am apprehensive about tonight's tech run-through; it is our last rehearsal on stage before our dress rehearsal one week from tonight! Oh, the joys of repertory!

Partly to keep myself busy, I spend my dinner break in the sound booth experimenting with different combinations of drums, bells, cannon, and music for the final exit of Hamlet's body; I decide to blend the music from the play-within-the play (which is also Ophelia's mad song) into the exit, with good effect.

The evening rehearsal begins with a meeting in which Peter reports that Bruce is resting, and that Robert Sicular (Rosencrantz) will continue to read his part. We will have to wait for further news from the doctors before we can decide what else to do.

This is my third fourteen-hour day and I am groggy before rehearsal begins, but once underway I am alert again and on the lookout for trouble—but none occurs! In fact, we have to stop only once. The show runs three hours and fifteen minutes, excluding intermissions; more important, the show has real dramatic power and some moments are the best they've ever been. Mark feels that Hamlet is for the first time riding the emotional wave of the action from start to finish; his death is particularly touching, and the lighting and sound cues support the final exit well. I am relieved to know that we have a dependable finish.

We are done a bit early and I take the opportunity to block the curtain call; I've spent several hours planning it in detail. I've had to consider three main things: safety in the blackout, flow, and the politics of the sequence and groupings of the calls. I am using a seven-phase call: the first four have seven people each; then a threesome of Ophelia, Laertes, and Polonius; then Claudius and Gertrude by themselves; and finally Hamlet. In this way the entire call takes only thirty-five seconds. We are able to block and rehearse the call in fifteen minutes and it looks quite good at once.

An effective method of stabbing Polonius has finally occured to me, and I take a moment after rehearsal to work it out: When Gertrude cries for help, Polonius yells and flails at the curtain as he tries to get out from behind it; Hamlet grabs the struggling figure around the waist, trapping it in the folds of the arras, and stabbing it repeatedly with his dagger; as Polonius slumps downward, Hamlet holds him until they are both on their knees, clutched in an embrace with the tapestry still between them, Polonius in his death agony, the blade still in him. After the brief dialogue with Gertrude, Hamlet pulls his dagger out and Polonius falls forward and out of the curtain, his body preset with blood. This method is safe, believable, and horrifying.

I am glad we have been able to run our final technical rehearsal without stopping, and the fifty-odd cues and backstage operations have gone quite well; this is a tribute to the months of preparation and the skill of the stage managers and technical staffs. Still, the unresolved situation of Laertes and the long break before our dress rehearsal seven days from now leave us all nervous.

EMERGENCY PLANS: FEBRUARY 9

Bruce may not heal as fast as we had hoped: The doctor wants him to keep his shoulder immobilized for eleven days, which takes us precisely to the day of the preview performance. Since it is Bruce's dagger arm which is injured, Chris Villa has worked out a version of the fight with swords only; still, it is not certain that Bruce will be well enough to do even this.

We decide that Dan Mayes, who plays Marcellus, will understudy Laertes in case Bruce cannot perform; Marcellus would then be played by Cornelius, whose lines would in turn be incorporated into the role of Voltemand. Dan has five days to learn Laertes's lines, and rehearsals are scheduled to teach him the fight. We will use the one-handed sword fight regardless of which actor plays Laertes so that Hamlet need learn only one altered fight; later in the season, when Bruce is fully mended, we will restore the fight to its original form.

In the hope that Bruce will perform, however, he will attend the fight rehearsals in a few days in order to learn the simplified fight. I regret the temporary adjustment in our breathtaking climactic fight, but there is no choice.

HIGH-SPEED RUN-THROUGH:
FEBRUARY 11

We have been away from the show for five days, during which the cast has been busy with technical rehearsals for four other plays; I will be satisfied if today's three-hour rehearsal merely revives the cast's recollection of the lines of *Hamlet*. This is a perfect time for a high-speed run-through.

A high-speed run-through can serve to crystallize the larger patterns of action, and improve pace by revealing those spots where unnecessary time is being taken. To avoid the actors' becoming mechanical in their delivery, however, I stress that we will do the show quickly and lightly, but retaining all the causal connections of action/reaction which tie the moments together. As we go, I will be noting any values that are lost; this will indicate that they are either tenuous or unnecessary; I will also watch for any vague or unrealized connections of action/reaction.

I am amazed at the smoothness of the run-through; despite the five day layoff, only three or four lines are missed, the blocking is perfect, all the notes given in the last technical rehearsal have been solidly incorporated, and the shaping of the show is vivid and precise. Not one important point is missed, and the connections of cause and effect from moment to moment are real. Bruce, his arm taped to his body, has his best rehearsal to date; we skip the fight.

I am much heartened by this rehearsal, but we are not out of the woods yet.

FIGHT REHEARSAL: FEBRUARY 11

Dan Mayes (Laertes's understudy), Bruce, and Mark work with Chris on the details of the simplified fight. Because of Bruce's injury, we have eliminated the daggers, leaps, and tussles, so that the ferocity of the fight is lessened; but it is still a good fight. My greatest concern is that Mark relearn the fight without being distracted from the rest of his performance; to make matters worse, Mark and I have both gotten the flu, which has been making the rounds of the company.

FIRST DRESS REHEARSAL:
FEBRUARY 13

Dress rehearsals are difficult for me; I feel useless and impotent. As the full weight of physical production descends upon the show, there is simply too much to deal with. This is when the months of preparation and communication with the designers and technical staff pay off.

I find myself again pondering our traditional rehearsal process: Eight weeks spent rehearsing the acting, and then only four technical and dress rehearsals in which to put all the production elements together—so much for the actors to assimilate at the last moment! It's bound to make us all feel impotent.

The entire design/technical staff is in the house taking notes: technical director, master electrician, production manager, and each designer and their staffs—there must be ten people from costumes and wigs alone. This, plus the photographer shooting from the first rows, creates a continuous distraction. The actors are handling it well, however, and I do the best I can to concentrate.

I am sitting at the rear of the house to check audibility and sightlines. I force myself to reduce my awareness of the design and technical elements and concentrate as much as I can on the actors; for the past four rehearsals I have had to give them only partial attention.

The show begins on time at 8:00 P.M., but soon we have to stop to solve

Ghost problems: The batteries that drive his self-contained lighting are not working properly, and the wireless microphone has problems. Murphy's law is at work. After the initial problems, however, the show begins to move with greater authority.

The costumes, though pinned and unfinished here and there, look splendid and are completing the visual image of the characters. Makeup, which has more or less been left up to each actor, seems fine; the lighting levels are being adjusted in response to the costumes as we go; sound is also running very well and levels are being fine tuned.

I end the evening with four pages of notes and no time to give them; luckily there is one session before the final dress in which I can rework some things. I want to make a few minor changes in staging: We will give up on the Ghost's magical appearance through the tapestry; instead, the Ghost will loom out of the darkness at the end of the catwalk above left; I will reblock the Norwegian Army scene to simplify it; two of the large-group processions are so slowed by the women's trains that they need to be retimed and have sound cues lengthened.

Most important, I have a number of notes for Mark about "drive" through the longer arcs of the role; he is still quite ill, and with the distractions of a first dress rehearsal he has lost the momentum of some sections. But in all, the show has gone quite well indeed; the ending, even with the fight only walked through, has worked. We will be entirely ready for a complete final dress.

We finish just in time and the actors are dismissed; the designers meet with me to set priorities, while Mark is held for an hour of program pictures. It is almost 2:00 A.M. when we get home.

Unable to sleep, I go through agonies of doubt. Mostly, I fear that the show is over-produced: For years I avoided this scale of technical embellishment as a matter of principle, choosing to rely on acting alone as much as possible; perhaps I should have maintained this principle for this production as well. But now is not the time for such second thoughts; the die is cast.

NOTE SESSION: FEBRUARY 17

We meet in the rehearsal hall and talk through the show scene by scene; I invite the actors to search their memories and to bring up any concerns they had at the first dress rehearsal. My notes fall into three categories: blocking, pacing, and interpretation.

For the first, there are some slight blocking changes in large-group scenes to adjust for the look of the costumes or for the lighting, and some changes in intimate scenes where people are standing too close together given the bulk of their costumes.

In terms of pace, I have some notes on sections where the momentum of the action seemed to lag. This was sometimes due to poor cueing due to distraction, but more often because people are not pursuing their objectives, nor remembering the sense of urgency provided by the given circumstances.

The costumes and props suggest some new business and meanings; for instance, Claudius's prayer is enhanced by Denis's use of his crown: He removes it on his reference to "those effects for which I did the murder," clutches it to his chest on "May one be pardoned and retain th' offense?" and finally, as he kneels, lays it on the floor before him as an offering to heaven. I have encouraged the cast to pursue inspirations of this kind, even in these final rehearsals: I will evaluate them as they occur.

After walking through a few of the changes, most of the cast is dismissed; Bruce is now certain that he will be able to perform, so another fight rehearsal is held to solidify the redesigned fight.

FINAL DRESS REHEARSAL:
FEBRUARY 18

Before rehearsal we spend forty-five minutes doing last-minute onstage checks: the Ghost is walked with temporary self-contained lights (his batteries have not been delivered so he will not be lit during the rehearsal); we walk through the reblocked Army scene and the trouble spots for the long gowns; we work the opening and closing of the tapestry (which we have in completed form for the first time tonight); there is a last fight rehearsal. The house is then opened.

Tonight's rehearsal is attended by some 150 staff, company members, and friends. Though I am glad for the exposure to a trial audience, this adds to the normal nervousness of a final dress; to make matters worse, the rehearsal will not be under performance conditions as I had hoped: the lighting and sound designers are making last-minute adjustments in levels, and the technical director is communicating with crews, so three headsets are active in the house. The costume and props staffs are also in the house taking notes. I am unpleasantly surprised to see that the photographer is back, shooting from the first rows throughout the rehearsal! All this produces considerable disruption; Peter is having difficulty calling the show because the headset channels are in constant use and the board operators are having to listen to several persons at once.

This situation, though maddening, is really no one's fault; in repertory, the crush of opening many shows at once is enormous. In our case, six large productions will open within a three-day period; there are only two or three other theatres in North America which could even attempt such a schedule.

Despite the distractions, the show runs without stopping; I do my best to put the technical matters out of my mind and concentrate on the acting, but it isn't easy.

I am not very happy with what I see. The actors are distracted, and as a result, much of the show has gone on automatic pilot; they are rushing, skipping over crucial choices, and jumping to results without living through the process of reaction and choice. The reality and intrinsic drama of the event have vanished and have been replaced by a mere image, a sort of "report on what we have rehearsed." It is interesing that while tonight's show is six minutes faster than we've ever done it, it seemed infinitely longer.

There is a real scare when the Player King, momentarily blinded by the lights, turns to exit and falls off the stage; luckily he doesn't hurt himself and we go on without stopping.

There are a few new elements that create problems: The Dumb Show robes are difficult to use in the small area defined as the Player's stage; the two soldiers who help carry Hamlet's body are wearing their cloaks for the first time and are stepping on them, so the procession grinds to a snail's pace and the ending is ruined.

I have some five pages of notes: Those for the technical end are passed on through Peter; those for the actors will be given at our note session in two days. The cast is held for a brief photo call, and refreshments are served in the Green Room after.

Although nothing is said, it is clear that the cast understands that the momentum of the show's growth has been interrupted at a crucial time; just when everything should be coming together and developing even greater richness, we are struggling just to maintain what we have already established. I go home filled with doubts: My advance planning, which seemed so thorough in expectation of such problems, has not prevented them, and may even have contributed to them.

NOTE SESSION: FEBRUARY 20

On a rainy Sunday afternoon, after an hour's fight rehearsal, the entire cast meets for notes on the final dress. To save time, I have written out the individual notes for the principals.

We think through the show as a group, scene by scene. Most trouble spots in the staging are fixed immediately by the actors, who volunteer to make adjustments for one another; we make note of some sections that we will walk through after notes for adjustments.

After the specific notes I give a general note: I thank everyone for maintaining their concentration through the many distractions they have endured, but caution them about keeping their thinking fresh; the show is becoming mechanical and rushed.

This is partly due, I'm sure, to concern over the length of the show, but I stress that three hours twelve minutes playing time is not long as productions of *Hamlet* go; if we rush without living through each choice, without genuinely hearing and seeing our stimuli, then the chain of cause and effect which makes the show happen suffers. This note is well understood and supported by the cast.

After everyone else is gone, Mark and I go over his notes. He is concerned at having been distracted during the dress rehearsal, but I assure him that the longer arcs of the role are becoming clearer and clearer; as one moment after another has begun to fall into place, I have been able to give him more specific notes. I feel that if I could stay with the show during the first weeks of performance we could really get down to work!

Our first preview is day after tomorrow, with opening night three days later.

HAMLET LOG, PART 14: OPENING AND AFTER: FEBRUARY 22

In preparation for the preview, I have spent a day forgetting about the show; I want to approach it in the frame of mind of an ordinary audience member.

The house is nearly full; there are a surprising number of children in the audience. We start just a few minutes late, and the technical aspects of the show go very smoothly; Peter, the stage crew, and the operators do a splendid job. There are only a few technical notes: We are seeing the Ghost with the Ghost's self-contained lights for the first time, and the effect is not what I had hoped; I decide to cut them and to adjust the front lighting to compensate. Also, the acoustics in the house are different with an audience, and the environmental sound levels turn out to be much too high; we will start adjusting them downward.

Except for these few items, I am free to focus entirely on the acting, and I am basically pleased by what I see.

The First Part, which is largely expository, hasn't the drive I hope it will eventually develop; the answer may be in taking the Ghost more seriously. We also need to realize the threat of war more fully; I will consider redefining the entrance of the court in 12 as less of a celebration and more the desperate hope of a threatened society in its new leader: Will he save us?

The Second and Third Parts are much better and the audience responds well. It is amazing how much your perception of a show changes when an audience is present! There are obvious things, like the laughs which weren't expected or have been forgotten about through over-familiarity. Hamlet especially is getting some real belly laughs in his capture scene with Claudius; his jokes about the dead Polonius are much appreciated; and his kissing Claudius surprises and amuses the audience. There are other strong moments, as when Gertrude picks up the poisoned cup and announces that she will drink: It felt

Figure 15-1. A *Hamlet* Portfolio. *Oregon Shakespearean Festival, Ashland, Oregon. 1983. Photos by Hank Kranzler.*

a. Scene 11: Allen Nause (Horatio) and Daniel Mayes (Marcellus). "This bodes some strange eruption to our state." *Hank Kranzler.*

b. Scene 12: Denis Arndt (Claudius) and Bruce Gooch (Laertes) at center. "What wouldst thou have, Laertes?" *Hank Kranzler.*

Figure 15-1. continued

Scene 12: Denis Arndt (Claudius) and Megan Cole (Gertrude). ''Good Hamlet, cast thy nighted color off...'' *Hank Kranzler.*

d. Scene 13: Gayle Bellows (Ophelia) and Bruce Gooch (Laertes). ''Fear it, Ophelia, fear it, my dear sister...'' *Hank Kranzler.*

Figure 15-1. continued

e. Scene 15: (Left to right) Allen Nause (Horatio), Mark Murphey (Hamlet), Charles Noland (Barnardo), and Daniel Mayes (Marcellus). "Come on. You hear this fellow in the cellarage." *Hank Kranzler.*

f. Scene 21: Richard El-more (Polonius) and Gayle Bellows (Ophelia). "He took me by the wrist and held me hard." *Hank Kranzler.*

Figure 15-1. continued

g. Scene 31: Richard Elmore (Polonius) and Gayle Bellows (Ophelia), with Denis Arndt (Claudius) looking on. "Ophelia, walk you here." *Hank Kranzler.*

h. Scene 31: Mark Murphey (Hamlet). "To be, or not to be—that is the question." *Hank Kranzler.*

Figure 15-1. continued

i. Scene 34: Megan Cole (Gertrude), and Mark Murphey (Hamlet). ''O Hamlet, thou hast cleft my heart in twain.'' *Hank Kranzler.*

j. Scene 43: (Left to right) Denis Arndt (Claudius), Paul Vincent O'Connor (Osric), Robert Sicular (Rosencrantz), Craig Rovere (Guildenstern), Mark Murphey (Hamlet). ''Now, Hamlet, where's Polonius?'' *Hank Kranzler.*

Figure 15-1. continued

k. Scene 45: Gayle Bellows (Ophelia). "I would give you some violets, but they withered all when my father died." *Hank Kranzler*

l. Scene 52: Mark Murphey (Hamlet). "It will be short; the interim is mine." *Hank Kranzler*

Figure 15-1. continued

m. **Scene 52: Mark Murphey (Hamlet), Allen Nause (Horatio). "The rest is silence."** *Hank Kranzler.*

as if some people were ready to cry out for her to stop, though a preview audience tends to be unusually demonstrative.

I am especially pleased that the crisis of the play is completely clear to me for the first time tonight: As Hamlet leaves for England, his back is finally up against the wall; up to this time he has had the choice of whether to act or not since Claudius had not yet taken any direct action against him, but at last Claudius has acted, and Hamlet has no more room for evasion; it looks very much like he has indeed lost. He has no choice but to throw his fate to the winds, which is the quality of his last soliloquy.

Then, in the storm, he finds the letter, and is able to forge it. When, the next day, the pirates attack and he is able to escape with them, he can no longer doubt that heaven is on his side! The tangible proof is overwhelming. He returns with the certain conviction that heaven is with him; he is beatified, in a state of grace. He is one with his world.

These perceptions come from what I see emerging in the production and in Mark's performance. The next day I share them with him and they fit with his emerging experience; I feel that we have at last had that magical touch with the heart of the play. The frustration and doubt of the dress rehearsal have somewhat abated, and I look forward to Friday's opening.

OPENING NIGHT: FEBRUARY 25

This is the opening not only of *Hamlet* but of the entire Festival. There are a great many events surrounding the performance, and many members of the audience have attended this afternoon's preview performance of *The Entertainer* in which Denis (Claudius) has played a brilliant Archie Rice, and Bruce (Laertes), his son.

Before the house opens, we work through a new lighting cue for the Ghost's disappearance, and reduce the sound levels for the environmental cues. All prop and costume work has been done and the show should be entirely complete tonight.

The house is full, and it is an oddly mixed audience, many of whom have obviously been drinking a bit at various events. I decide to sit in the midst of the house to check the sound levels with a full house, though it is nerve-wracking to do so.

The First Part is again edgy and lacking in momentum; it plays two or three minutes longer than at preview. The Second and Third Parts catch fire, however, and the ending pays off very well indeed and Mark receives a standing ovation. Still, tonight's show was a bit ragged; the momentum of the action wasn't as strong as it should have been, and the whole ran six minutes longer than the preview. Some of the extra time is due to the laughs earned by Polonius, the Gravedigger, and again for Hamlet in his capture scene.

I have six pages of notes; since there is no further rehearsal opportunity (and the show is too long for a note session before or after a performance) I retire to write them out.

Technically, the show has gone very well indeed, though I decide to reduce the environmental sound levels drastically.

The notes for the actors are mostly details of projection and timing; there are, however, some new discoveries. The most exciting is the love Hamlet is expressing in his dying farewells to Laertes, Gertrude, and Horatio; in each case I suggest specific ways to extend them physically. I also want Horatio to kiss Hamlet's dead eyes after "flights of angels sing thee to thy rest."

I feel just now ready to embark on a whole new phase of the show's development; I wish I could stay with it for a few weeks of performance. I hope the way in which we have worked will permit the cast to follow the intrinsic energies of the production as it develops in performance over the next eight months. I speak with Peter and encourage him to use his own judgment in permitting this growth to occur, and to keep it on track. He already has a sense of where it may go and which actors may need guidance or even restraint.

REVIEWS: MAY 1

Two months have passed. My "post-partum depression" was headed off by a production of the musical *Happy End*, by Brecht and Weill, which began rehearsal two days after *Hamlet* opened. After the long weeks of the intense, detailed work on *Hamlet*, I found it a relief to work on this exuberant, broadly theatrical play; the production was an outpouring of irreverant joy, like the satyr play after a tragic trilogy.

In fact, I have realized in retrospect how much my theatrical energies were weighed down by the work on *Hamlet*, and I began a long process of puzzling out what happened and how I feel about it. Today I gave Peter a call to see how things are going: He reports that audiences are responding well and that the show is growing; however, the opening of the three outdoor summer plays has necessitated some changes in cast, and Fortinbras, Voltemand, and some other characters have been replaced. I have an odd, disassociative reaction to this news.

I receive a packet of reviews from Ashland. Festival productions are widely reviewed, and *Hamlet* always excites special critical attention, so the packet is thick. Almost all of these reviews are based on the opening night, but they differ radically in their response: Some are enthusiastic, some are negative, and many are mixed; most liked certain scenes enormously and disliked others, but not the same scenes!

The best of the reviews is by Wayne Johnson in *The Seattle Times*, who says,

> Any theatre that can mount a production of *Hamlet* as good as the one that opened here Friday night is a treasure to be cherished, a resource to be nurtured. And any theatre whose season includes a distinguished *Hamlet* will find the principal public and critical focus on that play which, as Anthony Burgess wrote, "of all plays, the world could least do without.". . . In Ashland, director Robert Benedetti had the refreshing idea of presenting *Hamlet* as clearly and directly as possible, with the emphasis not on conceptual frills or explication but on intelligent, straightforward presentation of the play—and let its mysteries take care of themselves . . . Its running time on the stage of the Angus Bowmer Theatre may seem daunting: three hours and forty-five minutes. But that could be the quickest three hours and forty-five minutes you'll ever spend in the theatre. Mark Murphey does extraordinarily vivid, focused work as Hamlet . . .

The worst review is by Robert Hurwitt in *California* magazine. He says,

> *Hamlet* may well be, as Anthony Burgess has noted, "the play which, of all plays ever written, the world could least do without," but one could easily do without this production. With a few exceptions the performances are ably executed, but the acting and direction are terribly, tediously timid—as though director Robert Benedetti and his cast aspire to give us no more than the average of each character as established through more than 350 years of performance tradition . . . it all scarcely matters because there's so little life onstage . . . On opening night, solil-

oquy followed soliloquy like set, self-contained audition pieces as the play dragged on for three hours and forty-five minutes.

It is hard to remember that they are describing the same performance! Depressing, though, that Johnson's review will be read by a few thousand people in Seattle, while Hurwitt's will go to millions all over the West Coast, and his capsule comment in the magazine's cultural listings ("a timid and desultory *Hamlet*") will run every month for seven months! Why should this one review have more power to reflect on our work than does the production itself? At least some 75,000 people will see the show and be able to judge for themselves . . .

LOOKING BACK: APRIL 5, 1984

More than a year has past, and it has been a busy time. The experience of *Hamlet* is coming into some perspective, and I am gradually resolving my anger over the review in *California* magazine; I am heartened at having received numerous letters from absolute strangers praising the production, and knowing that the theatre has received letters from people expressing their disagreement with the review.

I've spoken to Mark, and he considers the experience to have been of great importance to him as an actor. Throughout the nearly one-hundred performances, he continued to discover and grow. Over the nine months, a great many actors were replaced, including Claudius and Gertrude, and with each of these changes Mark discovered new values in the script.

I have been sorting out my feelings about my work on *Hamlet*, however, and I now see both negative and positive aspects. On the positive side, I can list the following:

1. My preparation, and the handling of the complex technical aspects of the production, was basically good;
2. The process overall was well-handled, especially given the special problems of a long and diffuse rehearsal schedule;
3. My work with the designers and actors enabled them to make strong personal contributions to the show;
4. The detail and the overall shape of the production pleased me, especially since my natural energies lean more toward broad and exuberant material than *Hamlet*; I feel the experience improved me as a director, and I have been doing better work since.

This last is the main reason I feel that *Hamlet* was a beneficial experience for me. Even more important to my growth, however, was the recognition of those things I felt negative about:

1. I allowed the situation to control me and the production too much; I underestimated the negative impact of the prolonged and erratic rehearsal schedule on

the emotional growth of the production, and failed to pursue and drive it more to compensate;

2. I unwittingly invited the show to be over-produced and gave too much of my attention to technical matters at the expense of the acting;

3. I did not have a sufficiently specific reason to do this play: The idea of mid-life crisis was valid, but too general; what was needed was a specific translation of this idea into a theatrical vision that could have motivated the stage life of the entire play, rather than only those specific scenes for which I had special feelings (the Mousetrap, the Praying scene, the Queen's Closet, the Chase and Capture).

4. I was too in awe of the play, not willing enough to treat it in the kind of exuberantly theatrical manner I enjoy most;

5. Most important, I did not penetrate the heart of this play in other than intellectual terms; as it has for many directors before me, *Hamlet* remains a "dark country" which I must enter again some day.

I must also consider whether the advantages of being a "director for hire" with established companies are sufficient compensation for the drawbacks; perhaps it is time to rededicate myself to creating a theatre of my own.

AFTERWORD
A CAREER IN DIRECTING

I have tried to perceive some pattern in the various ways in which people become directors, but none seems to exist: The only common thread seems to be that most directors have emerged from other areas of theatre, from stage management, design, writing, and often, acting. Perhaps this is because many persons discover their interest or need to direct only after working in other areas; or it may be that it is so difficult for a young person to be hired as a director that they have to work in other areas first. Whatever the reason, it is probably a good thing for a director to experience the theatre in a variety of ways before directing, since there is almost nothing about the theatre which a director may not need to know.

This was also the unanimous opinion of the directors to whom I sent my questionnaire. Their advice to a young person seriously considering a career in directing was exemplified by W. Duncan Ross:

Try acting for a number of years, then get a job as assistant to a first-class director.

There were some other ideas as well; here is a sampling.
Jack O'Brien:

Do everything else first. A director "becomes . . ." He or she should act, stage manage, try writing, a little design, and primarily "hang out" with as many different first-class persons as is humanly possible. Because the director is the conduit through which so many kinds of information are passed, he or she has to feel comfortable with all of those different processes. Directing is the last thing you think about or, often, even do.

Mark Lamos:

I would suggest that a young person who is seriously considering a career in directing should assist, or at least be able to watch, an older, more experienced director over a period of time. I was fortunate to spend three years as an actor at the Guthrie Theatre during Michael Langham's tenure as artistic director. Though I wasn't planning a career in directing at the time, I now realize that Michael was my mentor . . . Too many directors do not understand literary structure. They want to conceptualize a play before they understand what it means; this does not allow the play to speak for itself . . . Barring financial necessities, a director must make a personal connection with each play he directs or the experience will be empty, meaningless . . . The director must incorporate all of the arts into his work . . . He must be intuitive and remain vulnerable while leading a production team and cast. I think a good director realizes that his job is basically collaborative.

Nagle Jackson:

Learn how to act. When you get tired of performing, gather some of your actor-friends around you and see if you can create anything. See if they like you as a director. If not, forget it . . .

Joseph Chaikin:

Apprentice with gifted and experienced people.

Gerald Freedman:

My advice to prospective directors is to get as broad an education as possible. Read the great works and study art history. Do some acting, and experience concerts, ballets, and sporting events. Apprentice yourself to a working director.

David Chambers:

Advice to a young person considering a career in directing:
> -Reconsider
> -Read EVERYTHING, from the stock report to the Tibetan Book of the Dead . . .
> -Keep in mind that there is no way to reflect life unless you have one. In short, live.
> -Ambition is probably 75 percent of talent. 20 percent is knowing the difference between ambition and greed. The last 5 percent has something to do with imagination, intellect, and music.
> -Reconsider again. If you still must direct, then do. There are ways.

Richard Foreman:

Direct, even in your apartment. Keep directing, under any available circumstances (bad actors, no money, whatever), and learn from other, nontheatrical arts. Use some of *their* strategies, structural principals, and energies.

Tom Markus:

Get the broadest possible liberal arts education with a focus on the sister arts, NOT on the theatre. Then, apprentice yourself to someone whose work you admire and with whom you have a symbiotic working relationship. Then marry someone rich!

I would add one specific piece of advice to all this: Arm yourself with those entrepreneurial skills you might need to produce your own theatre. Why wait for someone else to give you a chance when you can create your own opportunity? This is the one great advantage which beginning directors have over any other kind of theatre artists; take advantage of it!

This idea was also expressed by John Dillon, and it is with his advice that we close:

I've never found two directors who have the same story of how they began their theatre careers. I find this fact of a director's life to be exhilarating: It means each director has to invent his own life and his own career, to find his own unique way of scaling the castle walls. This process is made bearable by the fact that directors probably have more control over their careers than anyone else in the theatre. With perseverance and the ability to fast-talk some actors and designers, the young director can usually get a production started . . . Getting a start for the young director thus requires tenacity and imagination more than anything else.

APPENDIX 1
MASTER
SCENE/PLACE/TIME/
CHARACTER CHART

ACT I	11	12	13	14/15	21	22 MATIN BELLS
LIGHT & SOUND NOTES → WINTER	MIDNIGHT ON BATTLEMENTS WIND & FOG TOLLING BELL	WEDDING RECEPTION- VERY FESTIVE •MORN PEALING BELLS & CANNON SHOTS	LATE AFTERNOON ON THE WHARF WIND, WATER, GULLS, SHIPS	MIDNIGHT ON BATTLEMENTS AS IN 11, 15 IS IN GRAVEYARD	5 AM ON THE WHARF FOG, SHIP'S BELLS, WATER	6 AM IN THE OUTER LOBBY COLD, CRISP- COCKCROW, ANIMAL SOUNDS, ETC.
HAMLET		•IN BLACK		STILL IN •BLACK W/CAPE		MORNING CLOTHES •NO LONGER BLACK
CLAUDIUS		•WEDDING DRESS				MORNING GOWN- •JUST GOT UP
POLONIUS		•SUNDAY BEST	•W/CAPE		W/CAPE & •TORCH	•SAME-NO TORCH
LAERTES		•SUNDAY BEST	•W/ CAPE			SOLDIER OPENS •TAPESTRY
HORATIO	•HAT & CAPE	•SAME		•SAME		
PL. KING		•A LORD				TRAVELLING PLAYER •CAPE, ETC.
GHOST	•ARMOR			•SAME		
ROSENCRANTZ		SOLDIER W/ •BANNER				TRAVELLING CAPE, •THEN WITHOUT
GUILDENSTERN		•A LORD				TRAVELLING CAPE, •THEN WITHOUT
MARCELLUS	•W/ TORCH	•SAME		W/ DARK •LANTERN		
VOLTEMAND		•MILITARY LOOK				•W/ TRAVELLING CAPE
CORNELIUS		•MILITARY LOOK				•W/ TRAVELLING CAPE
FRAN/OSRIC	FRANCISCO •W/TORCH	•OSRIC-IN CROWD (IF TIME TO CHANGE)				
BARN/FORTIN	•W/ PIKE	•SAME		•W/ PIKE		
REYNALDO		•REYNALDO	•W/TRUNK		W/ CAPE & •DUFFEL	
PL. QUEEN		PAGE TO CLAUDIUS •W/CROWN ON PILLOW				•W/ TRAVELLING CAPE
PRIEST		•MONSIGNOR RANK				•SAME
SOLDIER 1		•W/ BANNER	•W/ TRUNK			TRAVELLING PLAYER •W/ TRUNK
SOLDIER 2		•W/ BANNER	•W/ TRUNK			SOLDIER, •NO BANNER
SOLDIER 3 DRUM		•W/ DRUM				AS TRAVELLING PLAYER •W/ DRUM
SOLDIER 4 RECORDER		•W/ BANNER				AS TRAVELLING PLAYER W/ RECORDER & BELLS
GRAVEDIGGER		•SOLDIER ABOVE				SOLDIER •OPENS TAPESTRY
GERTRUDE		•WEDDING GOWN				MORNING DRESS - •JUST GOT UP
OPHELIA		SUNDAY BEST •BRIDESMAID?	•W/ CAPE		NIGHTGOWN •W/ CAPE & TORCH	
LADY 1		W/ CORNELIUS				
LADY 2		W/ VOLTEMAND				
SERVING WOMAN		IN WAITING •TO GERTRUDE				IN WAITING ON GERTRUDE- MORNING DRESS
NOTES:	•A MONTH SINCE THE DEATH OF OLD HAMLET	•CLAUDIUS LETTERS TO NORWAY •STREAMERS OR RICE OR SOMETHING THROWN ON ENTRANCE	•WE WANT TO IMPLY THE WHOLE HARBOR IN THE HOUSE	•WE HEAR THE PARTY GOING ON BELOW~ •GHOST'S VOICE UNDER STAGE	•POLONIUS MONEY & LETTERS •SIX WEEKS PASS BETWEEN 15 AND 21	•A VERY INFORMAL LOOK-PEOPLE ARRIVING, MUDDY, ETC. MORNING CHORES BEING DONE:
TIME →	•FROM START TO 15 IS ONE 24-HOUR PERIOD →				•BUT FROM HERE TO 44 IS ALL ONE DAY →	CONSIDER CROSSOVERS BY COOK, GROOMS, ETC. (PROPS ONLY) •PLAYERS BRING TRUNKS & ETC. IN, USE SOME PROPS FOR SCENES.

ACT II / WINTER STILL	BELLS 31 — 1 PM THE NEXT DAY, SAME PLACE MUSIC?	32 — 9 PM SAME DAY, COURT-YARD. PARTY IS A MASQUERADE	33 — 10 PM IN CLAUDIUS' CHAPEL BELLS?	34/41 — 10:10 PM IN GERTRUDES DRESSING ROOM	42 — 10:20 IN CHAPEL VERY DARK	43 — 10:30 IN ANOTHER HALL VERY DARK	44 — 2 AM THAT NIGHT ON THE WHARF. AN ARMY IS DISEMBARKING. FOG
HAMLET	• NOW FULLY DRESSED	• SAME · JESTER'S COSTUME?	• SAME	• SAME	• SAME	• SAME	• SAME W/ CAPE
CLAUDIUS	• DRESSED FOR THE PARTY	• SAME W/ MASK	• SAME	• SAME		• SAME	
POLONIUS	• DRESSED FOR THE PARTY	• SAME W/ MASK	• SAME	• SAME			
LAERTES		• SOLDIER W/ BANNER			• SOLDIER W/ TORCH	• SOLDIER W/ TORCH	• SOLDIER W/ HAM'S GEAR
HORATIO		• AS BEFORE NO MASK					
PL. KING		• IN COSTUME					
GHOST				• GHOST			
ROSENCRANTZ	• DRESSED FOR THE PARTY	• SAME W/ MASK	• SAME	• SAME	• SAME	• SAME	• W/ TORCH & CAPE
GUILDENSTERN	• DRESSED FOR THE PARTY	• SAME W/ MASK & TORCH	• SAME W/ TORCH	• SAME W/ TORCH	• SAME W/ TORCH	• SAME W/ TORCH	• W/ TORCH & CAPE
MARCELLUS		• AS BEFORE W/ TORCH					
VOLTEMAND		• W/ MASK FANCY DRESS				• SAME W/ TORCH	• SAME W/ TORCH
CORNELIUS		• W/ MASK FANCY DRESS				• SAME	• SAME W/ TORCH
FRAN/OSRIC		• OSRIC W/ MASK				• OSRIC NO HAT	
BARN/FORTIN		• BARN. W/ TORCH					• FORTINBRAS
REYNALDO		• STEWARD W/ WINE					
PL.QUEEN		• IN COSTUME					
PRIEST		• W/ DEVIL MASK	• PRIEST			• PRIEST	
SOLDIER 1		• IN COSTUME AS LUCIANUS					• NORW. CAPT. W/ WEAPONS
SOLDIER 2		• SOLDIER W/ TORCH					• NORW. SOLD. W/ WAR GEAR
SOLDIER 3 DRUM		• AS PLAYER W/ DRUM					• NORW. SOLD. W/ BANNER
SOLDIER 4 RECORDER		• AS PLAYER W/ RECORDER			• W/ TORCH	• SAME	• ENG. SOLD. W/ WEAPONS
GRAVEDIGGER					• W/ TORCH	• SAME	
GERTRUDE	• DRESSED FOR THE PARTY	• SAME W/ MASK		• DRESSING GOWN			
OPHELIA	• DRESSED FOR THE PARTY	• SAME W/ MASK					
LADY 1		• W/ MASK					
LADY 2		• W/ MASK					
SERVING WOMAN		• SERVING WINE		• OPENS TAPESTRY			
NOTES: THIS ACT ALL ONE 12-HOUR PERIOD	• ONE CRITIC SUGGESTS THAT HAMLET IS WEARING MOTLEY FROM NOW TILL TRIP TO ENGLAND. ? • IN ANY CASE, THIS IS THE PERIOD OF FEIGNED MADNESS. • THIS ACT IS ALL ONE DAY →	PLAYERS & SERVS. ARE SETTING UP FOR THE SHOW. • 2 CHAIRS ARE IN FOR C&G; RUG FOR THE STAGE. • THE PROLOGUE IS DONE WITH MASKS. THE PLAYER COSTUMES ARE VERY STYLIZED, EVEN DREAMLIKE.	• POSSIBLE GOBO TO ESTABLISH CHAPEL, FOR CLAUDIUS TO PRAY IN?	GERT HAS JUST DRESSED FOR BED—A SMALL ROOM	A "HOLLOW," SOUND IN VOLT & CORN. HELP R&G TO CORNER HAMLET. A CHASE SCENE BY TORCH LIGHT	ECHO-TYPE SOUND IN BOTH OF THESE SCENES IF POSSIBLE	• SOUNDS OF THE ARMY IN VOMS, CREAKING SHIPS, BELLS, WATCH CRIES, ETC.

ACT III	45 THE OUTER LOBBY, EARLY MORNING HUNTING CALLS	46 THE WHARF, MORNING	47 CLAUDIUS' CHAPEL, A FEW MOMENTS LATER... BELL✓	51 GRAVEYARD, TWILIGHT (SAME AS 15) SLIGHT FOG FORMING	MUSIC — 52 GREAT HALL, SUNSET BELLS AT END AS IN BEGINNING	COSTUME SUMMARY
EARLY SPRING						
HAMLET				SEA CLOAK- "A NEW MAN"	•SAME	MOURNING/MADNESS/SEA CLOTHES
CLAUDIUS	•HUNTING OUTFIT		•SAME	•BLACK CAPE	PARTY DRESS AGAIN	WEDDING/MORNING/HUNTING/PARTY
POLONIUS	•RABBLE				OTHER •AMBASSADOR W/ TORCH	POLONIUS/RABBLE/AMBASSADOR
LAERTES	•TRAVELLING DRESS		•SAME	•BLACK CAPE	FIGHTING •DRESS	LAERTES/FIGHTING/SOLDIER
HORATIO	•AS BEFORE	•SAME		•SAME	•SAME	NO CHANGES
PL.KING	•RABBLE			•PALL BEARER	ENGLISH •AMBASSADOR	A LORD/TRAVELLING PLAYER/COSTUME/RABBLE/AMBASSAD.
GHOST						GHOST
ROSENCRANTZ	•RABBLE				•SOLDIER W/ BANNER	SOLDIER/ROSENCRANTZ/RABBLE
GUILDENSTERN	•RABBLE				•A LORD AS IN 12	A LORD/GUILDENSTERN/RABBLE
MARCELLUS	•AS BEFORE	•SAME		•PALL BEARER	•W/ TORCH	NO CHANGES
VOLTEMAND	•W/ WEAPON		•SAME	•PALL BEARER	•AS BEFORE	MILITARY LOOK/FANCY DRESS
CORNELIUS	•W/ WEAPON			•PALL BEARER	•AS BEFORE	MILITARY LOOK/FANCY DRESS
OSRIC	•SAME			•PALL BEARER	BIG HAT W/ WEAPONS, •FANCY DRESS	FRANCISCO/OSRIC HUNTING STUFF
FORTINBRAS					•TRAVELLING CAPE	BARNARDO/FORTINBRAS
REYNALDO	•RABBLE				•STEWARD W/ WINE	REYNALDO/STEWARD/RABBLE
PL.QUEEN	RABBLE KID (SAME AS 51)			YOUNG GRAVEDIGGER	PAGE •AS IN 12	PAGE/TRAVEL. PLAYER/QUEEN/RABBLE·DIGGER
PRIEST		•SAILOR		PRIEST (DOCTOR)	•SAME	PRIEST/SAILOR/RABBLE
SOLDIER 1				•SOLDIER W/ TORCH	•SAME	SOLDIER/TRAVEL. PLAYER/LUCIANUS/NORW. SOLDIER
SOLDIER 2				•SOLDIER W/ TORCH	NORW. SOLD. •W/ BANNER	SOLDIER/NORW. SOLDIER
SOLDIER 3 DRUM	•RABBLE				SOLDIER W/ DRUM	SOLDIER/TRAVEL. PLAYER NORW. SOLDIER/RABBLE
SOLDIER 4 RECORDER	•RABBLE			SOLDIER •W/ TORCH	•SAME	SOLDIER/TRAVEL. PLAYER NORW. SOLDIER/RABBLE
GRAVEDIGGER				•GRAVEDIGGER		
GERTRUDE	•MORNING DRESS AS IN 22		•SAME	•BLACK CAPE	PARTY DRESS •AGAIN	WEDDING/MORNING/PARTY/DRESSING GOWN
OPHELIA	MAD W/ •FLOWERS			•IN COFFIN		BRIDESMAID/NIGHTGOWN PARTY/MAD/DEAD
LADY 1					•W/ CORNELIUS	NO CHANGES
LADY 2					•W/ VOLTEMAND	NO CHANGES
SERVING WOMAN	•RABBLE				•SERVING WINE	WAITING/MORNING (?)/RABBLE
NOTES	A WEEK OR SO LATER... •GERT IS IN BAD SHAPE- CLAUDIUS HAS BEEN OUT HUNTING W/OSRIC •RABBLE IS SEEN IN VOM ONLY •SWITZERS COULD BE ORDINARY SOLDIERS... •RABBLE CARRY PITCHFORKS, ETC...			•TWO DAYS LATER... •PALLBEARERS NEEDONLY WEAR CAPES W/ HOODS •YOUNG CLOWN IS EATING A BAG LUNCH, W/ STOUP •COFFIN LOWERS W/ ROPES -	•NEXT DAY... •TWO CHAIRS BROUGHT OUT FOR K & Q.	(73-77 COSTUMES)

APPENDIX 2
PROMPT SCRIPT
FOR SCENE 14

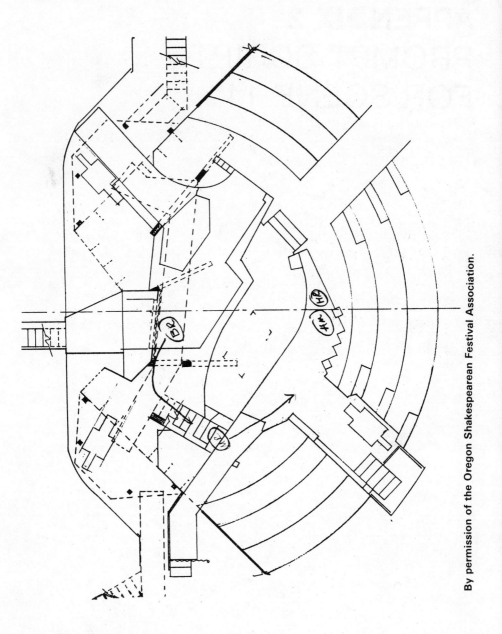

By permission of the Oregon Shakespearean Festival Association.

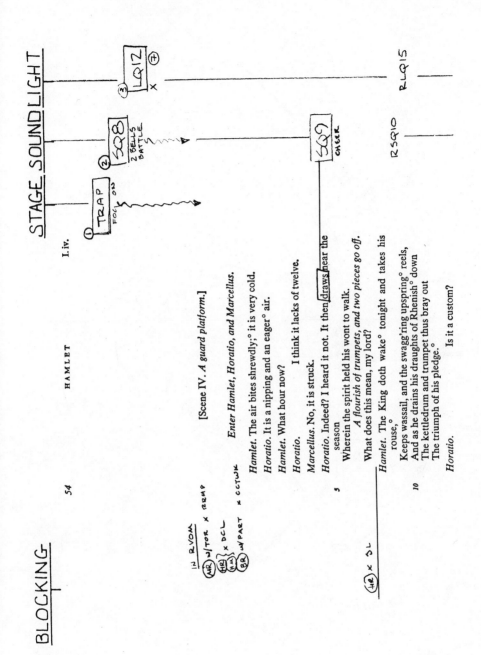

BLOCKING

54

HAMLET

I.iv.

[Scene IV. *A guard platform.*]

Enter Hamlet, Horatio, and Marcellus.

Hamlet. The air bites shrewdly;° it is very cold.

Horatio. It is a nipping and an eager° air.

Hamlet. What hour now?

Horatio.   I think it lacks of twelve.

Marcellus. No, it is struck.

Horatio. Indeed? I heard it not. It then draws near the season

5   Wherein the spirit held his wont to walk.

A flourish of trumpets, and two pieces go off.

What does this mean, my lord?

Hamlet. The King doth wake° tonight and takes his rouse,°

Keeps wassail, and the swagg'ring upspring° reels,

And as he drains his draughts of Rhenish° down

The kettledrum and trumpet thus bray out

The triumph of his pledge.°

10   *Horatio.*   Is it a custom?

TRAP
FOLL ON

SQ8
2 BELLS
BATTLE

LQ12
X

SQ9
CHEER

IN R.VOM
MR w/TOR X TRAP
HO
HA X DCL
BR W/PART
X CCTWN

HE X DL

R SQ10

R LQ15

221

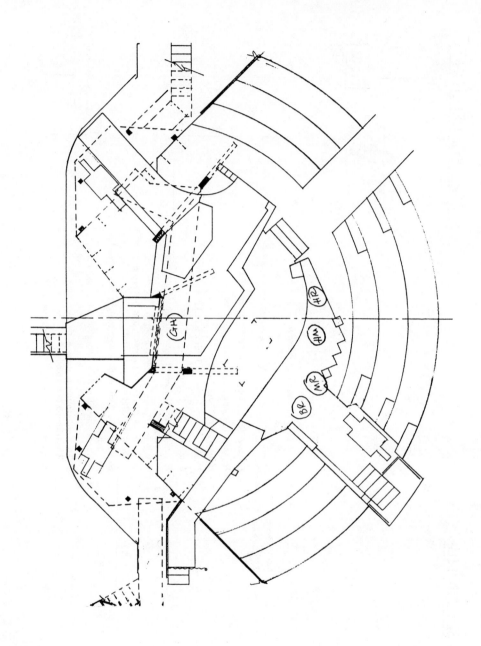

QUICK

SQ10
GHOST ↑

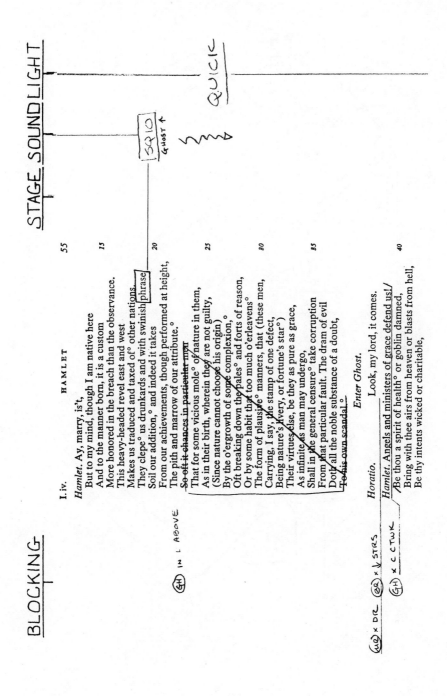

I.iv. HAMLET

55

Hamlet. Ay, marry, is't,
But to my mind, though I am native here
And to the manner born, it is a custom
More honored in the breach than the observance.
This heavy-headed revel east and west
Makes us traduced and taxed of° other nations.

15

They clepe° us drunkards, and with swinish phrase
Soil our addition,° and indeed it takes
From our achievements, though performed at height,
The pith and marrow of our attribute.°

20

So oft it chances in particular men
That for some vicious mole° of nature in them,
As in their birth, wherein they are not guilty,
(Since nature cannot choose his origin)
By the o'ergrowth of some complexion,°

25

Oft breaking down the pales° and forts of reason,
Or by some habit that too much o'erleavens°
The form of plausive° manners, that (these men,
Carrying, I say, the stamp of one defect,
Being nature's livery, or fortune's star°)

30

Their virtues else, be they as pure as grace,
As infinite as man may undergo,
Shall in the general censure° take corruption
From that particular fault. The dram of evil
Doth all the noble substance of a doubt,

35

To his own scandal.°

Enter Ghost.

Horatio.   Look, my lord, it comes.

Hamlet. Angels and ministers of grace defend us!
Be thou a spirit of health° or goblin damned,
Bring with thee airs from heaven or blasts from hell,
Be thy intents wicked or charitable,

40

(GH) IN L ABOVE

(HO) x DR (HO) x ↓ STRS

(GH) x C CTWK

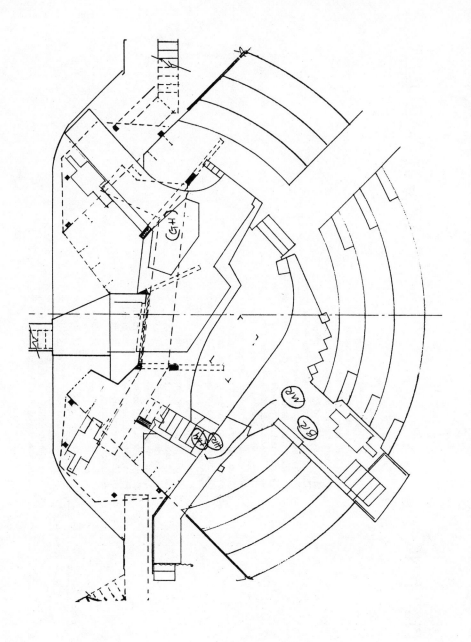

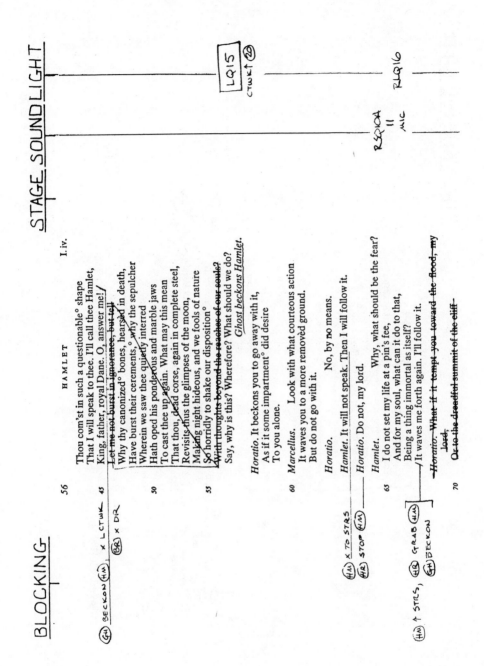

BLOCKING

STAGE SOUND LIGHT

HAMLET   I.iv.

56

Thou com'st in such a questionable° shape
That I will speak to thee. I'll call thee Hamlet,

45   King, father, royal Dane. O, answer me!/
Let me not burst in ignorance, but tell
Why thy canonized° bones, hearsed in death,
Have burst their cerements,° why the sepulcher
Wherein we saw thee quietly interred

50   Hath oped his ponderous and marble jaws
To cast thee up again. What may this mean
That thou, dead corse, again in complete steel,
Revisits thus the glimpses of the moon,
Making night hideous, and we fools of nature

55   So horridly to shake our disposition°
With thoughts beyond the reaches of our souls?
Say, why is this? Wherefore? What should we do?
                              Ghost beckons Hamlet.

Horatio. It beckons you to go away with it,
As if it some impartment° did desire
To you alone.

60   Marcellus.   Look with what courteous action
It waves you to a more removed ground.
But do not go with it.

Horatio.   No, by no means.

Hamlet. It will not speak. Then I will follow it.

Horatio. Do not, my lord.

Hamlet.   Why, what should be the fear?

65   I do not set my life at a pin's fee,
And for my soul, what can it do to that,
Being a thing immortal as itself?
It waves me forth again. I'll follow it.

Horatio. What if it tempt you toward the flood, my
lord,
Or to the dreadful summit of the cliff

70

225

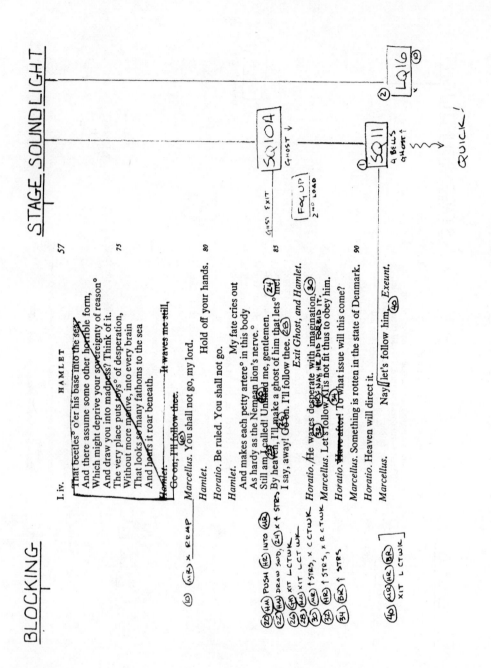

HAMLET

I.iv.

That beetles° o'er his base into the sea,   57
And there assume some other horrible form,
Which might deprive your sovereignty of reason°
And draw you into madness? Think of it.
The very place puts toys° of desperation,   75
Without more motive, into every brain
That looks so many fathoms to the sea
And hears it roar beneath.

Hamlet. ————— It waves me still.
Go on, I'll follow thee.

Marcellus. You shall not go, my lord.

Hamlet. ————— Hold off your hands.   80

Horatio. Be ruled. You shall not go.

Hamlet. ————— My fate cries out
And makes each petty artere° in this body
As hardy as the Nemean lion's nerve.°
Still am I called! Unhand me, gentlemen.   85
By heaven, I'll make a ghost of him that lets° me!
I say, away! Go on. I'll follow thee.

Exit Ghost, and Hamlet.

Horatio. He waxes desperate with imagination.

Marcellus. Let's follow. 'Tis not fit thus to obey him.

Horatio. Have after! To what issue will this come?

Marcellus. Something is rotten in the state of Denmark.   90

Horatio. Heaven will direct it.

Marcellus. ————— Nay, let's follow him. *Exeunt.*

Handwritten blocking notes:

(6) (MAR) x REAP

(20) (HAM) PUSH (HR) INTO (MAR)
(22) (HAM) DRAW SWD, (24) x ↑ STPS
(26) (HR) XIT LCTWK
(28) (HAM) XIT LCT WK
(30) (MAR) ↑STPS, x CCTWK
(32) (HR) ↑STPS, x CCTWK
(34) (BK) ↑STPS

(40) (HR) (MAR) (BR) XIT L CTWK

Stage/sound/light notes:

LQ 16   (2) (9)

SQ 10A
GHOST ↓
GHOST EXIT
FQ UP 2ND LOAD

SQ 11   (1)
4 BELLS GHOST ↑

QUICK!

226

APPENDIX 3
OPENING REMARKS
TO THE CAST
OF HAMLET

Shakespeare was about thirty-six when he wrote *Hamlet*; I think it is not mere projection to see in it many of the concerns we associate with the mid-life crisis, particularly the overwhelmingly tangible encounter with our own mortality and the resultant reassessment of the values according to which we live. Hamlet's crisis of values is accelerated and intensified by the injunction of his dead father for vengeance; he must find the meaning of his life in ethical action under the most urgent and trying of circumstances.

The Elizabethan view of the good man reflected the Renaissance preoccupation with the principle of balance: balance in the very elements of our physical being (Earth, Water, Air, and Fire) and balance in their corresponding humors (Melancholy, Phlegm, Blood, and Choler), which produces good health. This physical balance had its spiritual counterpart, and it is this spiritual balance with which *Hamlet* is most concerned.

In the great Chain of Being which the Elizabethans saw as connecting the highest and the lowest planes of existence, man stood at the nodal point. As E. M. W. Tillyard quotes Pythagorean doctrine:

> Man is called a little world not because he is composed of the four elements (for so are all the beasts), but because he possesses all the faculties of the universe . . . the godlike faculty of reason, and the nature of the elements which consists in growth and reproduction. In each of these faculties he is deficient;

just as the competitor in the pentathalon, while possessing the faculty to exercise each part of it, is yet inferior to the athlete who specializes in one part only . . . For we possess the faculty of reason less eminently than the gods . . . our energies and desires are weaker than the beasts'; our powers of growth are less than the plants'. Whence, being an amalgam of many and varied elements, we find our life difficult to order. For every other creature is guided by one principle; but we are pulled in different directions by our different faculties . . . we are drawn toward the better by the god-like element, and at another time toward the worse by the bestial element within us.[21]

The great task, then, was to order one's life by achieving balance. For the Elizabethans the crucial balance was that of the godlike faculty, Reason, and the bestial quality, Appetite. This balance was in turn achieved by a balance of the two highest faculties of the mind, Understanding and Will. The faculty of reason produces Understanding, and the appetite is controlled by the Will. The two must work in tandem, the Will being thoroughly enlightened by Understanding, in order for man to "be victorious in the eternal battle between passion and reason."

As Tillyard points out, "It may not be an accident that of the heroes in Shakespeare's four tragic masterpieces two, Othello and Lear, are defective in Understanding and two, Hamlet and Macbeth, in Will." The progress of each play is the unfolding of the consequences of the imbalance and its painful correction.

How is this balance achieved? For the Elizabethans, the remedy lay in man's angelic capacity to learn to know himself. Once achieved, however, this self-knowledge would lie useless unless it was put to work in the world through the action of the Will; it is the capacity of the Will to act upon the Understanding achieved by Reason that was the fulfillment of Elizabethan ethics. Will in the absence of Understanding will be at the service of mere appetite—as were Gertrude's physical appetite, Polonius's ambition, Laertes's desire for vengeance at all cost, Ophelia's for love, and Claudius's for all these things. But Understanding without the action of Will is—as Hamlet's was— itself a kind of immorality (of which we are all, like the good burghers of Nazi Germany, nowadays guilty).

For the Elizabethans, man was the microcosm not only of the order of the physical world, but of the sociopolitical world as well. In all the plays we see upheaval within reflected by upheaval without: in *King Lear* the rule of monsters as well as the storm itself; in *Othello* "when I love her not, chaos is come again"; in *Macbeth*, the civil war needed to kill the snake, not merely "scotch it." In each of these plays, the upheaval flows outward from an unbalanced leader into an unbalancing of society; *Hamlet* however, *begins* at this point.

Here, an upheaval of social and moral law has already been created by the imbalance in Claudius—and, in part, in everyone else in the play: Gertrude refuses to know herself, Polonius is an eager ally, Ophelia follows her orders, Laertes sinks to ignoble treachery, and Osric is representative of a whole herd of beasts who have "come to feed at the King's mess." Indeed, Claudius reminds everyone in his first speech that they "have freely gone/ With this affair along." The civil war threatened by the unsettled masses is not yet come, but it is inevitable.

Into this condition of moral and social upheaval comes Hamlet, who finds himself "born to set it right." How like Orestes he is in this: torn between the dictates of Apollo to mend the social fabric, and the dictates of the Furies who oppose the act. No wonder the Ghost is careful to exempt Gertrude from his cry for vengeance; Hamlet must not, like Orestes, commit matricide. But even the execution of Claudius is difficult enough for Hamlet; it is the work of a lifetime merely to order our own lives, much less to find ourselves responsible for the reordering of the world.

But it is this very responsibility to reorder the world—to bring an end to war, to injustice, to hunger and deprivation—which we now see that we share with Hamlet; we are each of us "born to set it right."

Specifically, then, the underlying dramatic action of the play is the search for the balance of Understanding and Will which will bring inner balance; this individual balance will in turn permit the right action, which will restore worldly balance. The crisis, the moment between the Aristotelian ravelling and unravelling, is the moment when Hamlet finds this balance within himself and thereby becomes ready for right action—for, as he says, "the readiness is all."

Working backward from the end of the play, I find this moment in his last soliloquy, watching the army of Fortinbras (his eventual successor) doing what he has so far failed to do: He will leave for England a changed man, ready to reject any thought which does not enhance his capacity for right action, willing at last to "quarter" his thoughts and to reject those which are not true Understanding at all but merely "coward," but without in any way rejecting the primacy of Understanding itself.

Up to this moment he has responded inappropriately to every opportunity which has arisen because he has not yet achieved that balance of emotion and reason. He has woven the prolonged deceit of his feigned madness and of the play-within-the-play in search of evidence sufficiently damning to overcome his reticence; when at last Claudius's reaction to the mousetrap gives him this proof, and fortune offers him the perfect opportunity to kill a solitary and defenseless Claudius, he again delays, providing an elaborate (and reasonable) rationalization; then, some fifteen minutes later, he kills the wrong man in an unbridled fit of outrage (and perhaps Oedipal jealousy as well).

Once in balance, however, Hamlet gives up his scheming and rationalizing and allows the flow of events to carry him, making the effective response in each situation that arises. As he does, he discovers that Fortune, which has heretofore been his enemy (due to his own resistance to her) now becomes his ally; he finds himself in a storm and rightly decides to go above deck; he happens in the dark and tempestuous night to lay his hand directly upon the letter carried by Rosencrantz and Guildenstern, he discovers its contents and happens to have the penmanship necessary to forge a new message, finally ("even in that was heaven ordinant") he has his father's signet wherewith to reseal the letter. Truly is he allowing divinity to shape his end, and will continue to do so despite a clear premonition of death.

In this we see the particular sense of balance which Hamlet achieves—not through the scheming and rough-hewing of a Claudius or a Polonius—but through a profound acceptance of what is and the making of right responses. Hamlet is enlightened; he is ready to act in the world as it is because he has come to know himself as he is. He is ready at each moment to live because he is ready at each moment to die, and the quality of his readiness is a quiet, almost humorous acceptance:

> If it be now, 'tis not to come; if it be not to come, it will be now; if it be not now, yet it will come. The readiness is all. Since no man of aught he leaves knows, what is't to leave betimes? Let be.

Explore the ways in which your character fits into this scheme, specifically in what way you contribute to Hamlet's eventual enlightenment. Consider also the ways in which your character is out of balance so as to contribute to the imbalance of the world; think about the imbalance in your physical being (elements and humors) and in your spiritual being, especially in the relationship of Appetite and Reason, or Understanding and Will. Merely allow this information to guide you as you work; this is not so much information to be conveyed to an audience as it is a context of perception and experience for you as your character develops.

APPENDIX 4
SAMPLE NOTES
TO HAMLET

(These notes were taken during the preview performance and given to Mark in writing.)

Scene 12: Start your first soliloquy by turning and making eye contact with the audience *before* speaking; establish your relationship with them at this first opportunity.

"My father, I think I see my father . . ." move up onto the vom ramp as if he were out there—this will lead Horatio and the others to think you actually see him there (as they have); then, when Horatio in alarm says "Where, my lord?" your puzzled reaction on "In my mind's eye" should get a laugh.

Scene 22: When you say to Polonius that you "would he were so honest a man" (as a fishmonger) let the sarcastic subtext surface just a bit more.

Your humming as you entered reading was an excellent touch; explore humming and muttering throughout this scene. Continue to let the antic disposition carry you further; I'll tell you if you go too far. The use of the cape as a security blanket is excellent; I especially like using it as a woman's shawl, as a king's robe, as the maternity smock on "conceive," as a picnic blanket (so that you can walk on it with Rosencrantz and Guildenstern), etc. I'm getting his love and *need* for "performing" in the guise of madness as a way of not "holding his tongue." *Enjoy* the traditional freedom of the jester.

Do the last of the three "Except my life's" differently every night until it refuses to change, if ever. Throwing down the book on "tedious old *fool*" is good.

Let the real emotion of the Priam speech, as you identify with his situation, carry you even further; you are surprised by how perfectly the speech expresses your condition.

Keep "insert a speech of some sixteen lines" more secret from Rosencrantz and Guildenstern. I am seeing that the idea for the mousetrap is really taking hold; *drive* through "About my brains, Hum" as you rush to develop the details of the plan; this is producing a good act ending.

Scene 31: "To be or not to be" began well; take your time with it; save the cross down for later in the speech, on "For who would whips . . ." as the idea of suicide becomes tangible. Draw your dagger and press its point into your chest on "His quietus make with a bare bodkin," and take a moment to imagine what it would feel like to drive it home.

When Ophelia says "At home, my lord," be looking away from her, so the shock that she has lied can register on the turn; then look around upstage for those you think may be lurking there, and give *them* "Let him play the fool in's own house." Likewise threaten the unseen Claudius with your dagger on "All but one shall live . . ."

Your impulse to kiss Ophelia in the midst of calling her a whore is excellent; follow it fully. By this time there's not a lot of difference in his mind between sex and murder.

Scene 32: The advice to the Players went well; focus specifically on the one who will play the murderer as you caution against grimacing. Hopefully we will forget that this is a famous speech and take it as the plot element it is. Then excellent urgency in the instructions to Horatio; you must fill him in before the court arrives. The entire Mousetrap scene went beautifully.

You have now proven the Ghost's charge and you know what you must do; you also know that what the Ghost told you about Gertrude must also be true. When Rosencrantz and Guildenstern, and then Polonius, summon you to your mother's room, your feelings about her rise, and you must be alone for a moment to gain control over them or you may harm her; so from "Bye and bye is easily said" on, *drive* them all away in order to have that time alone. Horatio will be the last, and I've asked him to approach you, knowing what must be in your mind, asking with his eyes if you are all right; let him know with your eyes that you are, and he will leave also.

Scene 33: The decision to give Claudius a temporary reprieve is now tied emotionally to the feelings you are having about Gertrude; you want to get them when they're together, in their "enseamed bed." Then, when Polonius calls out from the arras and you "take him for his better," everything you say you want to do to Claudius so that he will "kick at heaven" comes true, and all the pent-up fury you have suppressed here in the chapel can break out in the stabbing of Polonius.

Scene 34:   While you have the knife in his guts, let the fury flow through the lines to Gertrude, then one last thrust as you withdraw it on "Aye, 'twas my *word*." When Polonius is revealed to you, take all the time you need to realize what has happened before "Alas, poor wretch . . ."

Cut the last "Goodnight, mother" as you are dragging the body out; it gets a snicker from the audience.

Scenes 41-44:   This sequence is going very well; your "little boy act" with Claudius in 43 is especially fine, and the goodbye kiss you give him has the residue of what you wish you had done in the chapel. The final soliloquy had better drive; take the time to assess your whole situation against the new context of Fortinbras's army. The full recognition of what it is "to be truly great" is a shift in your whole value system. You then feel a release when you give yourself permission to "henceforth be bloody."

Pull up your hood as the rain starts to fall on your exit.

Scene 51:   In the graveyard scene, you were "making friends" with death, actually preparing to die; the humor here is crucial to this.

When you tell Yorick's skull to "go to my lady's chamber and tell her to paint an inch thick . . ." remember that your "lady" is Ophelia, whom you have, when you last saw her, likened to a whore in makeup; you tell Yorick to let her know that "she must come to this . . ." Then, when you recognize that it is indeed Ophelia's grave you have lingered over . . .

Scene 52:   Yes! I saw for the first time that you now feel that GOD IS WITH YOU. Your excitement in telling Horatio the story of the sea voyage is because you have finally realized that heaven (destiny) is truly on your side, that heaven "is ordinant" in your affairs; you are more deeply joyful now than ever in your life, you are *beatified*. Of course "the interim" is yours, and you can enjoy the hell out of making fun of Osric; then, when the challenge to fight is delivered, your heart once again drops into your stomach, as it did when the Ghost first delivered *his* challenge; but this time you rise immediately above this intimation of mortality; you "let be" because your life, in the scheme of all things, is now a trifle to you.

In the same spirit, you love the bout itself; "I'll do this bout first. Come!" You are not merely accepting whatever fate has in store here, you are rushing eagerly to meet it.

When Gertrude looks in your eyes as she says "Pardon me" and drinks the wine, let her know through your eyes that you pardon her.

Take the time to caress Gertrude's dead cheek, and let all the love you feel for her flow through your fingers.

As you are preventing Horatio from drinking the poison, keep your face level with his or you are badly upstaged.

You die *before* you say "The rest is silence"; it's as if your last line is a report to us of what lies beyond, in that "country from which no traveller returns." It is all perfect stillness; feel the perfect stillness within yourself; then release into it *everything*. Allan will take care of your body . . .

APPENDIX 5
DEADLINES
AND URGENCIES
IN HAMLET

PART ONE

11: The army is on alert; the Ghost may appear at any moment.

12: The new King has a war crisis to deal with; the court is eager to release its pent-up fears after the month of uncertainty since old Hamlet's death. In the second part of the scene, the news of the Ghost must be *secretly* imparted to Hamlet and arouse his fears that "All is not well."

13: The tide and wind are right, the ship *must* leave; then the unpleasantness between Polonius and Ophelia must be attended to.

14: The Ghost must be made to speak in order to discover what ill it bodes.

15: The Ghost's "hour is almost come"; then the oath of secrecy must be sworn and all return to their posts before sunrise.

21: Again, the ship is leaving; then the terrified Ophelia must be comforted and the King told what has happened.

22: The arriving travellers must be taken in; then Polonius must sell his theory and plan before Claudius and Gertrude lose patience with him. Polonius is then eager to set his plan up, and Rosencrantz and Guildenstern must be tested; finally the Players must be welcomed and, as Hamlet's idea develops, "auditioned" for their part in the mousetrap scheme.

PART TWO

31: Polonius's plan is about to be set in motion; since Rosencrantz and Guildenstern have failed, it is the only hope of discovering the cause of Hamlet's behavior.

32:   The build here is entirely up to the moment of the poisoning in the play; the advice to the Players is to guarantee an effective performance, and Hamlet's jesting builds to it also. Once the King has "blenched," Hamlet knows that he must act soon since the gauntlet is down; Claudius knows that Hamlet knows, and Hamlet knows that Claudius knows that he knows.

33 to 44:   Occur in real time as Claudius acts to dispatch Hamlet with all haste; he prepares by attempting to assuage his heavy conscience with prayer, since it will soon be burdened with another death. Hamlet gets "cocky" and wants to have the perfect revenge, only to kill the wrong man at the right time; the death of Polonius gives Claudius exactly the opportunity he needs to dispatch Hamlet openly and with the support of the Court.

PART THREE

45 to 47:   Also in real time; the populace is upset, Ophelia is mad, and Laertes is returned and is raising a horde; further, the news of Hamlet's demise in England should arrive at any moment.   Once Hamlet's return is known, however, the need to kill him is even more immediate, since he may know of the English plot. Momentarily thrown off stride, Claudius immediately recognizes Laertes as the perfect tool (unexpected necessity brings the best out of any good improviser).   Once the plot for the fight is laid, everything drives toward its fulfillment; even the death of Ophelia serves to whet Laertes' determination for it.

51:   Hamlet returns knowing that he is in imminent danger; the graveyard gives the chance to make his peace with death.   The confrontation with Laertes heightens the drive toward the fight, as Claudius has to restrain Laertes to wait until that night.

52:   Hamlet and Claudius both have premonitions of death (Claudius earlier in 45), and each knows they are nearing the end; there is no turning back for either of them, nor for Laertes.

FOOTNOTES

[1] Rollo May, *The Courage to Create,* New York: W. W. Norton & Co., Inc., 1975, p. 93.

[2] Nikolai M. Gorchakov, *Stanislavski Directs,* trans. Miriam Goldina, New York: Harper & Row, Publishers, Inc., 1954, p. 121. By permission of the publisher.

[3] Michel Saint-Denis, *Theatre: The Rediscovery of Style,* New York, 1960, pp. 76-77. This and the following excerpts from this work are used by permission of the publishers, Theatre Arts Books, 153 Waverly Place, New York, N.Y. 10014. Copyright (c) 1960 by Michel Saint-Denis.

[4] Gorchakov, *op. cit.,* pp. 16-17.

[5] Saint-Denis, *op. cit.,* pp. 76-77.

[6] Henrik Ibsen in a letter to the Norwegian Theatre, July 2, 1859.

[7] Rene Wellek and Austin Warren, *Theory of Literature,* New York: Harcourt Brace Jovanovich, 1956, p. 142.

[8] *ibid.,* p. 138.

[9] *ibid.,* p. 142.

[10] *ibid.,* p. 145.

[11] Saint-Denis, *op. cit.,* p. 79.

[12] *ibid.,* p. 78.

[13] *ibid.,* p. 77.

[14] Gorchakov, *op. cit.,* p. 63.

[15] Eugen Herrigel, *Zen in the Art of Archery,* New York, 1971, p. 58. Copyright 1953 by Pantheon Books, Inc., a Division of Random House, Inc.

[16] Gorchakov, *op. cit.,* p. 119.

[17] *ibid.,* p. 77.

[18] *ibid.,* pp. 95-96.

[19] Constantin Stanislavski, *Creating a Role,* New York, 1961, p. 121. Used with permission of the publisher, Theatre Arts Books, 153 Waverly Place, New York, N.Y. 10014. Copyright (c) 1961 by Elizabeth Reynolds Hapgood.

[20] Gorchakov, *op. cit.,* pp. 40-41.

[21] E. M. W. Tillyard, *The Elizabethan World Picture*, New York, 1944, pp. 67-68.

INDEX

Action
  arc, 166ff., 170
  blocking and, 145–48
  character and, 37–38, 52–53
  choice and, 52–53
  defined, 36–37, 125ff.
  environment and, 62, 68–70
  flow, 166
  physical and psychological, 130, 165
  reaction, 126–27
  relationship and, 54ff.
  scenic, 135
  score, 135, 146, 165–66, 191
  shape, 44–47, 166ff., 170ff.
  theme and, 47–49
Adjustments, 129–30
Alignment of effort, 23, 72, 76, 111, 112
Antagonist. *See* Protagonist
Anxiety, 6–7
Aristotle, 36, 40, 44, 53
Artaud, Antonin, 41

Bacchae, The, 37, 40
Bald Soprano, The, 41
Basic Training of Pavlo Hummel, The, 41
Beat, 42, 46, 126
Blocking, 68, 145ff., 185

Breakdown
  Hamlet, 42–43
  plot, 41
  scene/character/time/place, 64–65, 215
Brecht, Bertolt, 84
Breuer, Lee, 16, 112
Brustein, Robert, 14, 164, 186

Camera game, 134
Casting
  attitude toward, 88
  character relationships, 87, 91
  control, 87–88
  preparation, 57
  techniques, 88ff., 92
  time and, 88
Cause and effect, 52–53
Chaikin, Joseph, 9, 213
Chambers, David, 4, 213
Character
  action and, 37–38
  choice and, 52–53
  function, 56–58
  language, 58–59
  qualities, 59
  relationships, 54–56

tempo-rhythm, 168
in text, 57
Choice, 52–54
Ciulei, Liviu, 77
Climax, 37, 44–47
Coaching, 57
Collaboration, 5–6
Comedy, 168–69
Confidence of actors, 190–91
Conflict, 40–41, 44, 46, 53, 54
Connections, 125ff.
Cooke, Alan, 6
Corrective mechanism, 133–34
Costumes in rehearsal, 187–88
Creative state, 110ff.
Crisis, 37, 42, 44–47, 127, 167
Cues, technical, 149
Cutting, 63–64

Deadlines and urgencies, 133–34
Death of a Salesman, A, 37, 40, 92, 155
Dennis, Gil, 29
Denouement. *See* Resolution
Dillon, John, 86, 214
Director
and actor, 57
attitude in later rehearsals, 164–65
as audience of one, 9–10
as creator, 15
ethics, 13
as executive, 23
as gardener, 21–22, 109
mind of, 7
skills, 10
as storyteller, 10
and superobjective, 54
and text, 11–16
Discovery, process of, 10–11
Dramatic function, 55
Dramaturg, 29
Dress rehearsal, 188
Dumbwaiter, The, 45

Emmes, David, 72, 128
Emotion, 127
Endgame, 55
Everyman, 78
Exposition, 47

Fichandler, Zelda, 4–5, 5–6, 10, 66, 166
Florimonte, Lou, 172
Foreman, Richard, 15, 115, 167, 214
Freedman, Gerald, 4, 164–65, 213
Function, dramatic, 55

Ghost Sonata, The, 41
Given circumstances, 38–39, 129
Glass Menagerie, The, 68–69
Gorchakov, Nikolai, 61–62, 148–49

Grotowski, Jerzy, 15, 84, 111, 129, 186
Ground plan, 68–70, 77, 145–47, 172
Guthrie, Tyrone, 9

Haas, Tom, 110–11
Habit and actors, 165–66
Hamlet. See individual topics
Henry IV (Pirandello), 80
Henry IV, i (Shakespeare), 55
Houseman, John, 6, 29

Ibsen, Henrik, 13
Improvisation, 114
Inciting incident, 40, 46–47, 53
Inner monologue, 134
Intention, 129
Ionesco, Eugene, 41

Jackson, Nagle, 6, 9, 165, 213

King Lear, 51, 55, 92, 148, 186

Lamos, Mark, 4, 86, 115, 128, 213
Landscape of a play, 66–67
Langham, Michael, 18
Leibert, Michael, 6, 111, 115, 134
Lighting
function, 149–50
levels, 187
Linklater, Kristin, 114

Macbeth, 37
Mack, Maynard, 34
Markus, Tom, 214
Marley, Donovan, 6
Marowitz, Charles, 4, 15, 111
May, Rollo, 7
Metaphor, central, 14–15, 77–79
Midsummer Night's Dream, A, 128
Ming Cho Lee, 77
Momentum, 183. *See also* Pace
Mother Courage, 40–41

Norms, system of, 20ff., 47, 109, 111, 112
Nunn, Trevor, 16

Objective, 126ff.
O'Brien, Jack, 10, 12, 53, 72, 77, 86, 110, 212–13
Olivier, Laurence, 29
Othello, 40, 54, 91

Pace, 133–34, 165, 169ff.
Paper tech, 187
Paraphrase, 58, 114
Pauses, 171
Phaedre, 69
Pictures, stage, 148ff.
Platt, Martin, 148

Play, life, of, 18–20
Plot
  and action, 36–37
  breakdown, 41
  and choice, 52–53
  defined, 40
  organization, 41
  subplots, 54–55
Preparation of script, 62–64
Production concept, 61–62
Projection, 184
Protagonist, 40, 54
Purpose, sense of, 190

Ravelling, 127
Reaction, 52–54, 126ff.
Rehearsal
  atmosphere, 110–11
  costumes in, 187–88
  dress, 188
  first remarks, 112
  as a journey, 112–13
  literary versus theatrical mode, 114
  paper tech, 187
  process, 109–10
  in real locales, 171–72
  social aspects, 111
  technical, 186–87
Relationship, 54ff., 145
Research, 29–33
Resolution, 37, 44–47
Response. See Stimulus/response
Rhythm, 46, 145, 165ff.
Romeo and Juliet, 40, 45, 47
Ross, W. Duncan, 9, 212
Run-through, high speed, 170–71

Saint-Denis, Michel, 11, 22–23, 27, 28, 40
Scene, 45–46
Schneider, Alan, 5, 189

Score of a role, 135, 146, 165–66, 191
Script, preparation of, 62–64
Sense-memory, 172
Set, geography of, 147. See also Ground plan
Sound, 149–50
Spine of play, 126, 170
Stage pictures, 148ff.
Stanislavski, Constantin, 10, 12, 37, 56, 62, 66,
    114, 125, 126, 130, 135, 148–49, 165–66,
    167, 168, 170, 190
Stimulus/response, 125–26, 129, 166, 169ff.
Storyboard, 77
Streetcar Named Desire, A, 92
Style, 22
Sullivan, Dan, 11, 24, 115, 134
Superobjective, 37, 53–54, 56, 125, 191
Sympathaeia, 37

Tempest, The, 47
Tempo-rhythm, 167–68
Theme, 47–49, 54
Theory of Literature, The, 20–21
Through-line, 125ff., 166
Tillyard, E. M. W., 32, 51, 84, 227–28
Time of Your Life, The, 128
Timon of Athens, 18
Tragedy, 169
Transformation, 127
Trial, The, 79

Ulysses in Nighttown, 147
Unity, 36, 38, 49, 52, 65

Waiting for Godot, 37, 40, 45, 54
Warren, Austin, 20–21
Watkins, Ronald, 14
Wellek, Rene, 20–21
Wooden, John, 131

Zen in the Art of Archery, 32, 115, 133